MW01034572

"Richard Wickliffe has succee[...] and informative book with c[...] stories. Despite spending 30 years in the belly of the beast myself, I actually learned a lot. A must-read for any consumer. A most enjoyable read."

—Director John Askins,
Division of Insurance Fraud,
State of Florida (Ret.)

"Mr. Wickliffe does an excellent job chronicling schemes in a way that's entertaining and educational. A must read for anyone interested in these fascinating true-crimes that exist around us every day. Having spent 33 years leading insurance organizations, including my time as President of one of the largest carriers in the U.S., I saw the incredible impact fraud has on consumers. The title is spot on because we all pay for it."

—Glenn Shapiro,
President of Allstate Insurance Company (Ret.)

"A fantastic read. The book has insurance knowledge, wonderful stories, humor and the realization that insurance fraud has a serious economic and social impact on our society. As the Supervisory Special Agent for the Medical Fraud Task Force in South Florida, one of our major cases was Operation Sledgehammer which was worked tirelessly for many years with SIU teams and Law Enforcement.

—Fred Burkhardt,
Supervisory Special Agent,
National Insurance Crime Bureau (Ret.)

- *Insurance crimes steal over $308.6 billion annually from consumers in the U.S. alone.**

- *If insurance fraud were a corporation, it would be in the Global Fortune 500. It could purchase twice the gold in Fort Knox.*

- *The world of insurance fraud investigation is invisible to most, yet involves crimes that ultimately affect us all.*

* Fraud Stats, Coalition Against Insurance Fraud. https://insurancefraud.org/fraud-stats/

YOU PAID FOR THIS

My Twenty-Five Years
Investigating Insurance Crimes

Written and Illustrated By
Richard Wickliffe

Milwaukee Wisconsin USA

Published By:
Genius Book Publishing
PO Box 250380
Milwaukee Wisconsin 53225 USA
GeniusBookPublishing.com

ISBN: 978-1-958727-24-9

240423 Trade

Contents

Dedicated to my amazing wife Anthea and our three children for their unwavering support throughout my professional odyssey. After challenging days, I always returned to a true home.

PART ONE –
THE FRAUD TAX

Chapter One
The SIU

Imagine you're at a neighborhood party. Stan, the nondescript neighbor you never talk to, approaches. Unsure what to say, you attempt, "Hi… Stan. How's work?"

"My work?" Stan beams. "I got a great insurance story!" He moves into your space to drone on about his days navigating the rigors of risk management.

At that point, you either plan to fake a phone call or pray your significant other shouts, "It's time to heat your casserole." Anything but being cornered with insurance stories. Is anything more boring than an insurance person talking about their job? After all, it's a product that's only used when you've experienced a terrible loss—perhaps a car crash, fire, theft, injury, or death. Who wants to dwell on that?

I'm hoping to change that perception. My decades of combating insurance crimes have revealed a fascinating investigative niche unknown to most of the public. Our cases were filled with creativity, amusement, and sometimes pure evil. And even more significant, the cases financially impacted every one of our lives.

For a quarter century, I investigated insurance fraud, based out of Miami—which, as you may or may not know, has had a small fraud problem.

Former Governor Rick Scott described "Florida's embarrassing problems" with its insurance system. While describing a $910 million scheme, he coined the term "fraud tax" to describe the financial burden these crimes place on all consumers.[1]

For the first five years, I investigated a broad range of fraudulent property and injury cases. For the following twenty, I managed diverse teams of insurance investigators for the largest property/casualty insurer in the United States, representing over 9 percent of the market, and a global top-ten carrier based on revenue.

Not for one moment was the job boring or routine. What other career could possibly lead to dealing with organized crime rings, art and jewelry theft, staged accidents, human trafficking, and faked deaths? We had to investigate without having a badge, a gun, or any real authority. Law enforcement had no duty to help us, though many times our cases intersected. We were the unsung heroes of the company's SIU (Special Investigation Unit).

I must pause the swelling orchestra to issue a disclaimer that none of the following statements, narratives, or opinions reflect those of my former company. I will not disclose any confidential or proprietary information or trade secrets or name any specific carrier unless notated, and I have changed the names of parties and companies unless otherwise cited. The described scenarios are all true, and I will discuss how to avoid being a victim of the same crimes in our personal lives.

So, what is an SIU? It is a division within an insurance company that investigates potentially fraudulent insurance cases. SIUs are at the forefront of the ongoing fight against insurance crimes. Their job is to detect, deter, and pursue actions against fraudulent activities. SIU professionals who investigate insurance crimes are also employed by federal, state, or local law enforcement and anti-fraud organizations such as the NICB (National Insurance Crime Bureau).

Insurance fraud is probably as old as the carpenters who inflated repair costs after Noah's flood, but the first formal SIU was established in Massachusetts by Kemper Insurance in 1976.[2] The primary concern at the time was auto-related fraud. Next, with larger property losses, arson became the focus of most SIU teams. Then came the shift into injury, medical, healthcare, and even organized crime.

Today, virtually all insurance companies worldwide have established SIU teams to help protect the financial integrity of their businesses. Most states have passed legislation mandating that insurance companies establish SIUs, as well as requiring anti-fraud training, essentially asking the carriers, "So, what are you doing about it?"

For the state in which I was housed, Florida Statute 626.9891, also known as the Fraudulent Insurance Act, mandated every insurer admitted to the state shall create anti-fraud units to investigate and report fraudulent insurance acts, or contract with a third party to investigate possible fraudulent acts.[3]

With the creation of SIU teams, carriers needed to staff them with experienced people trained to investigate, take statements, and knock on doors, sometimes in unsavory areas. Therefore, employees couldn't be easily intimidated and would have to work professionally with attorneys and law enforcement.

SIU teams also serve as liaisons to law enforcement including local and state police, FBI, fire marshals, Coast Guard, and ATF, as well as attorneys, surveillance experts, forensic analysts, and private investigators. Their relationships with experts in those fields are their greatest assets.

SIU representatives are not any sort of law enforcement. There are no badges, and they can't make arrests. They are employees with specialized investigative training who represent the carriers. Many times, fraud is committed by people who aren't the policyholders, such as medical clinics, unscrupulous attorneys, organized crime rings, body shops, dishonest agents, or our newest class of perpetrator: cybercriminals.

Regrettably, there's job security in the field of fraud investigation—and it's on the rise. According to 2022 data from the Insurance Information Institute, about 75 percent of insurers stated fraud has increased significantly, with an 11-point increase since 2014.[4]

To keep up, a cottage industry of fraud detection firms has grown at a similar pace. The insurance fraud detection market, an entire industry of fraud analytics, is estimated to be a $912.3 million market in the U.S. alone, expected to grow 13.7 percent from 2019 to 2025.[5]

Here are some facts to enlighten you on the crisis:

- Right now, you and every one of your family members are paying over $932 per year in increased premiums just to fund insurance fraud. That's nearly $3,800 for a family of four.[6]
- Fraud occurs in about 10 percent of all property/casualty losses.[7]
- Non-medical insurance fraud is estimated at $45 billion per year. [8]

In the following chapters, I'll describe various cases, categorized by type and escalating in severity. Most are cases that our SIU teams or I investigated; others are from our colleagues in the industry.

I'll begin with routine burglaries, including "art theft on the high seas." It'll escalate into arson for profit, the monstrous acts of some arsonists, and even ritual sacrifices gone wrong. Then we'll move on to organized crime, including the Russian mob's varied enterprises. I'll illustrate boat theft schemes and their use in human trafficking. We'll shift to the rise of illicit medical clinics. Then we'll recover sunken cars that contain haunting secrets. I'll explain how not to fake your death, and I'll conclude with my team's role in the terrifying Pain & Gain double murder case (complete with robbery, extortion, and torture). I told you there was never a boring day.

Bottom line: Greed and opportunity continue to increase insurance crimes. Laws and corporate responsibility have hardened the need for SIU investigators as the schemes grow more creative, complex, brazen, and sometimes deadly.

Chapter Two
The Giant Slot Machine

When questioning our insureds after a loss, one response was common: "Do you know how many years I've paid my premiums and never made one claim?"

In other words, now it's their turn. "The Johnsons had an accident and now travel the world like royalty…" "My cousin had a shack and now owns a mansion…" With that mindset, the insurance company is like an enormous slot machine. After years of diligently paying their premiums, it should be their turn for that overdue windfall.

Public acceptance of insurance crimes is a driver behind their growth. According to the Insurance Information Institute, studies of public attitude suggest a portion of insurance fraud is motivated by revenge or retaliation for a business exchange they believe was unfair.[9] Some people retaliate in order to "get payback" or finally "get their money's worth." Someone might speak to a friend or neighbor who had an insurance claim and boasted about how easy it was. Perhaps the carrier paid with little investigation or never asked for any documentation.

I recall people saying, "My friend reported a claim, and they didn't have to show you anything," or, "My neighbor didn't have to give you a recorded statement, so why me?"

Before I launch into any stories or cautionary tales, explaining a few principles or definitions will make reading easier as I strive to avoid dreary insurance jargon.

How a Claim Works

Any new insurance claim is received with the presumption of being valid. Insurance policies are unilateral contracts where the carrier promises to pay covered losses. In turn, the policyholder promises to be honest and forthright, and to pay their premiums.

In a theoretical decent world, it works like this: The unfortunate policyholder suffers a loss—hopefully something small like a fender bender, but it could be a serious accident, fire, medical emergency, burglary, theft, or death.

The insured reports the loss to their insurance company or agent. Within a reasonable amount of time, a representative contacts the policyholder to obtain the facts. Based on the complexity, they may ask for supporting documents or photographs, or schedule a specialist to examine the affected property. When all documents are collected and verified, the company should make a settlement offer. Payment could be based on estimates, replacement cost, or the policy limits. The customer may need to negotiate based on any factors the carrier overlooked. The two parties come to an agreement, and the company then pays the claim and closes it. The consumer is content they were compensated, and the carrier is pleased to have a satisfied customer.

But notice the phrase "… documents are collected and *verified*." If the company can't confirm certain facts, it can't yet make a payment. Perhaps the facts don't add up, the damage appears exaggerated, or the parties have given conflicting accounts of what happened. It would seem reasonable that the company can't make a payment until any discrepancies are explained.

Regrettably, in the business world, use of the "honor system" wouldn't sustain commerce for long.

What is Fraud?

Fraud occurs when someone knowingly lies to gain a benefit to which they would not otherwise be entitled. In the case of insurance fraud, it means deliberately deceiving an insurance company for the purpose of financial gain. Typically, it's being untruthful to obtain money or replacement of an item (a home, art, a vehicle, jewelry, etc.).

Common frauds include submitting claims for injuries or damage that never occurred, "padding" or inflating claims, misrepresenting facts on an application, and staging accidents. Parties that commit insurance crimes include:

- Organized criminals who steal (or launder) large sums through fraudulent activities
- Professionals who inflate service costs or charge for services that were never rendered
- A policyholder who wants to use the claims process for financial gain

So how does a claim get assigned to an SIU team for further investigation? First-line adjusters handle the vast majority of claims. But when a claim requires an investigation beyond the scope of their training, they should refer the claim to a Special Investigation Unit.

The claim should contain "suspicious loss indicators" to warrant an assignment to SIU. It makes for a cleaner referral if the claim meets prescribed criteria, so many carriers use a list of fraud indicators published by the National Insurance Crime Bureau (NICB).

In my twenty-five years, the NICB was an invaluable partner in our fight against fraud. It is the nation's leading nonprofit organization dedicated to preventing and detecting insurance fraud, and it receives support from over 1,000 carriers. Its special agents worked with us and law enforcement to assist with the identification and prosecution of insurance criminals. Most of their agents are former law enforcement, coming from diverse specialties, offering a wealth of knowledge.

Here are examples of suspicious loss indicators by type:

Death claims
- Someone dies while overseas, especially in less developed countries
- Someone has a significant amount of life insurance, especially if they acquired it soon before the death
- The death certificate is suspicious

Disability
- The disability coincides with the date of a layoff, a plant closing, or job termination
- The claimant is making subjective complaints such as back pain, headache, or soft tissue injuries
- The claimant refuses to give a physical address or uses a P.O. box

Auto damage and injuries
- A phantom hit-and-run crash: the at-fault vehicle vanished from the scene
- A vague accident with multiple passenger—imagine eight grown men stuffed in a Corolla
- A claimant has had low-impact or repeated accidents with excessive medical bills

Theft of jewelry or valuables
- The appraisals are suspicious or the claimant purchased the items from a merchant that's no longer in business
- Jewelry "mysteriously disappears" while someone is traveling or in a hotel (with no report)
- Alarms or security cameras were inactive or broken at the time of the alleged theft

Vehicle theft (auto or boats)
- The vehicle loan is delinquent, or repossession is imminent
- The vehicle has had recent mechanical work or problems

- The vehicle has an anti-theft transponder but was stolen without keys

Injuries

- The allegedly injured parties threaten to hire an attorney if the insurance company doesn't pay the claim quickly
- Multiple parties are using the same medical clinic or attorney
- The claimant has a history of similar claims, slip and falls, etc.

In the past two decades, software has been developed to identify fraud more rapidly. Online tools include Verisk's ISO, the world's largest database of property/casualty claims.[10] The adjuster can enter a claim into its database, which then compares it to over 1 billion existing claims. If there's a match, the company is alerted. Examples of positive hits might include a person who has had prior losses, multiple policies for the same property, or use of the same photographs in other claims.

The goal is to identify fraud faster. More SIU operations rely on analytics that can search records that would have taken a person days or weeks to interpret. Still, there is value in hands-on field investigation, as the following chapters will illustrate.

There are a few terms we frequently use in our investigations. Since I may refer to them, I've attempted to define them here, and they are by no means legal definitions.

- Statements – This refers to a recorded statement. Most investigators will agree a recorded statement is more valuable than a non-recorded conversation. It helps document the person's version of the loss.
- Examination Under Oath (EUO) – An EUO is a more formal statement. Unlike a recorded statement, the person swears to answer truthfully under oath. An attorney, along with a court reporter, usually administers an EUO. The person does not need to have their own attorney, but some choose to bring one. Unlike

a deposition, the attorney typically cannot participate, interject, or object.

- Open-Source Investigation – This refers to using the internet for background searches. An "open source" is anything publicly available to the masses such as property and corporate records, or even criminal records. Social media is vital, where people boldly announce to the world their social habits, relationships, or (fantasized) economic status.

Warning: Open-source investigation is also used by bad actors as a method to learn more about *you* so they can tailor their schemes to specifically target you. More on that in Chapter 34 about cybercrimes.

The following chapters are categorized by type, with details about some of my favorite cases and noteworthy investigations handled by my peers, including some close calls with organized crime, smuggling, human trafficking, arsonists, and cybercrimes.

A caution: None of this content should serve as a how-to guide for aspiring criminals. All described narratives have one thing in common: the perpetrators were caught. And today, insurance carriers have technology and procedures light-years beyond what we had in our investigative arsenals. There are now cameras on almost every corner, databases with millions of records, electronic verification of documents, and photos with trackable metadata.

As mentioned in my published articles and lectures nationwide, understanding these schemes is the first step toward identifying and preventing them in the future, as well as safeguarding us from becoming targets in our personal lives.

PART TWO –
THE PHANTOM THIEF

Chapter Three
The First Lie: Theft

Don't let the truth get in the way of a good story.
—Mark Twain

My career in the world of SIU began in 1993. I had worked for four years handling property damage, theft, and injury cases for one of the largest insurers in the U.S. "Routine" claim handling had gotten a little tedious. I was only twenty-seven years old, engaged to be married, with my whole career before me.

In the golden age of wearing dress clothes and ties, I recall standing in our office with my Styrofoam cup of coffee reading job opportunities on a bulletin board.

I read a posting for a role in SIU. The job described investigating potential fraud in South Florida. I was hesitant at first, envisioning the people who might commit fraud: large, daunting, perhaps armed criminals. But while working Hurricane Andrew cases, I had met Luis, an SIU investigator, who explained the work wasn't intimidating. SIU reps weren't cops, didn't make arrests, and only investigated the validity of cases. He said I'd be a great fit within their team.

I had nothing to lose. I interviewed and got the job. I later learned there were few applicants because working in Miami's SIU seemed unnerving to some. In fact, at that time, the company offered a bonus to entice people to apply. In addition to having the right investigative skills, it was just as important to have an outgoing team that could collaborate.

I had to hit the ground running. At first, I rode around with Luis, shadowing him to get a feel for the work. We had to meet victims in person, ask for their versions of the loss, record their statements, ask for documents, and then investigate with the goal of determining the facts.

At first, it was strange being invited into people's homes or businesses. I was on their turf, a South Florida tapestry of diverse cultures, financial statuses, and attitudes. I smelled incredible home cooking, including many dishes I couldn't pronounce. Some people lived like hoarders, some like humble parishioners, others like drug lords from the movies. Many people were thankful to see an employee from their carrier. Others were instantly defensive: "Are you investigating me!?"

Every SIU investigator remembers their first liar because we take it personally. On my first solo case, I had to travel to the home of a young woman who had reported a home invasion robbery. I was new, so it was awkward when she opened the door and asked me to come inside. She was blonde, in her early twenties. As a newly engaged male, I was nervous to be alone with her in her home. But I took a seat in her living room and stammered through the process, explaining why I had to take her statement.

She did all the things I would later learn could be efforts to curry favor. She grinned, offered me a drink, and sat uncomfortably close. When she launched into her story of the burglary, her eyes began to tear. An abusive ex-boyfriend had stolen her valuables, heirloom jewelry, and expensive wheel rims. (In 1990s Miami, expensive wheel rims were always included.)

I believed every word of it, awestruck at her heart-wrenching narrative. She gazed into my eyes as she wept. As I drove back to the office, I wanted to write her a check for everything she had asked for.

When her ex-boyfriend (who was still her current boyfriend) was arrested for an unrelated drug crime, he rolled on her, offering to testify about how they had orchestrated the insurance claim for money. An agent with the NICB contacted me. From their concurrent investigation, he told me the burglary never occurred, there was no heirloom jewelry, and all the receipts were phony. The young woman confessed to the entire thing and was arrested.

I felt utterly betrayed, stabbed in the back, hoodwinked, and every other synonym for fooled. That woman had sobbed during her painstaking account of a violent partner stealing everything she owned. But it had all been a lie. I was humiliated because I had believed every word of it.

In my career, that wouldn't be the last burglary or the only lie. Thankfully—or regrettably—SIU investigators can become impervious to being lied to.

According to *Merriam-Webster Dictionary*, theft is defined as "The felonious taking and removing of personal property with the intent to deprive the rightful owner of it."[11]

A fake or staged theft is a common way people commit fraud. A tiny diamond ring could be insured for $50,000 to $500,000 or more. If the loss is confirmed, those funds are payable to the policyholder, tax-free.

Hold on, did I just write *tax-free*? That's correct.

I recall presenting at a seminar on white-collar fraud, and several federal agencies had been invited to attend. A young woman from the IRS was seated off to the side. It was evident she had been forced to attend, probably for continuing education hours. As I presented, I heard her clacking away on her laptop, not paying me any attention.

When I got to the part about a person receiving a $500,000 insurance settlement, *tax-free,* her eyes widened to the size of golf balls.

"Did you just say tax-free?" she asked, raising her hand. "Someone received a *half a million dollars* without paying any federal or state taxes on it?"

"Yes, ma'am," I replied to the bewildered IRS agent.

Generally, benefits paid from property/casualty insurance, including injury settlements, are not taxable. The federal government does not tax your settlement funds since they're intended to compensate you for losses that you endured. (There are unique circumstances; please consult an accountant!)

Imagine if a fraudster obtains a jewelry policy for a $50,000 ring. The first month's premium might be around $75. That would include coverage for damage, theft, loss, and disappearance, worldwide. After paying just that first $75, they could report a fraudulent theft and possibly receive more money than many new teachers make in a year—tax-free.

Do you see the gravity of this concept?

In most property insurance policies, "theft" is a specific listed peril. For expensive items such as jewelry, collectables, or fine art, basic policies cap the coverage at a specific amount, such as $1,000. For items that are more valuable, special policies are available with higher limits. These policies require appraisals to prove the items' values.

The following chapters outline types of high-end theft fraud and unique ways perpetrators tried to substantiate them. Before anyone gets any ideas, remember that these offenders were all caught.

Chapter Four
Art Fraud

Would you believe art crime is the fourth-highest-grossing criminal enterprise behind drugs, arms, and human trafficking? [12] According to Interpol, art is an easy way to move stolen assets around the globe. Laundering cash through banks is too dangerous. It's unwise to load your car with drugs or cash. But anyone can put a $50 million painting in the back of a car and drive across four countries.

According to *Newsweek*,[13] a contributing factor to the prevalence of art crimes is that the art trade is generally unregulated. Most countries, including the U.S., do not require verification of transaction records or public listing of art sales.

In an interesting example, the FBI discovered that film director Steven Spielberg owned a stolen Norman Rockwell painting, *Russian Schoolroom*, in 2007. He had innocently purchased it in 1989 from a respected dealer with no knowledge of its origin. It had been stolen from a gallery thirty years earlier.[14] I truly hope that mistake didn't create a financial hardship for Mr. Spielberg.

Unlike in movies, most art crimes do not involve jet-setting cat burglars ingeniously stealing fine art from museums. Instead, most art-related crimes stem from either forging the art or its certification records. Surprisingly, the act of producing fake art is not a crime in itself. The actual crime occurs when someone attempts to pass off the forged art as authentic with the goal of financial gain. That typically involves counterfeit authentication documents.

So how can these crimes meander into the world of everyday insurance?

A criminal could acquire a piece of art (either authentic or not) and then obtain an insurance policy for it. The buyer could assert its alleged value by showing an appraisal or invoice. They may have to pay the first month's premium or wait for the company to confirm coverage, known as "binding" the policy. Once bound, the policy is active.

If the art is genuine and worth the stated value, the criminal might plan to fake its theft. If the art is a forgery or not worth the stated value, the criminal might submit a fake appraisal to falsify what they paid.

Aside from insurers that specialize in fine art for collectors or museums, such as Lloyd's of London, most company underwriters are a few nice folks working in cubicles four states away. They probably haven't had expert training in authenticating fine art. They may skim the documents for accuracy and then bind coverage. After all, the carrier is in the business of selling policies.

A short time later, the devious policyholder reports the art stolen. They falsify a break-in, with incident reports and so on. The company will examine the appraisals or purchase documents, but with no leads on recovery, it may pay the claim—full limits, tax-free.

In my experience with art fraud (or any valuable), the insureds fell into two categories: someone who had innocently bought the asset believing it was legitimate (like Mr. Spielberg) or someone who had purposely insured an inferior item for an inflated value.

Art Fraud on the High Seas

My team uncovered a unique scheme involving art with exaggerated values. Insurance policies might cover fine art up to $400,000 or more per item and up to $2 million for multiple pieces. Insurance agents usually just require an appraisal. That document is the key element in this class of fraud.

Would you believe this scheme originated on major cruise ships?

For those of you who have enjoyed a voyage on a cruise ship, you were probably invited to attend an "exclusive" opportunity to bid on fine art. Perhaps you were enjoying a Mai Tai by the pool when you heard the announcement, "The *limited-engagement* art auction is about to begin on the Lido deck." When you arrived, servers handed you glasses of complimentary champagne as you browsed.

Flocks of sunburned tourists, with a few cocktails under their belt and fun money they'd saved all year, were ready to bid. Charming representatives in suits boasted about bargains if you acted quick— priceless art from renowned artists, up to 40 percent less than appraised value! What an amazing investment opportunity.

The glitch was with the appraisals that accompanied the art. With one of the largest galleries that (still) conducts auctions on almost every major cruise line, the appraisals were signed by the gallery's owner—a conflict of interest? Appraisals should always be carried out by recognized and qualified independent appraisers, not the owner of the gallery that is selling it.

According to *Bloomberg Businessweek*, beginning in 2008, at least twenty-one lawsuits were filed against Park West Gallery, a major player in the cruise industry. [15] In one case, a passenger claimed he had paid almost $73,000 for three Dali prints that he'd been told were worth over $100,000. When the man returned home, he researched the value of the prints to learn they could be worth less than $10,000—and there was a chance they weren't even authentic, according to the complaint.

With a few exceptions, cruise auctions sell reproductions with embellishments (brush strokes). These are known as *giclées*, a high-definition print with signatures or paint added.

During the years of the initial lawsuits, internet reception on cruise ships was almost nonexistent. Prospective buyers couldn't do any of their own research on the art's value. And I'm guessing the free champagne helped lubricate sales. How rampant was the problem? Park West's website states they conducted art auctions at "locations throughout the world, as well as on eighty-five cruise ships operated by Carnival, Celebrity, Disney, Holland America, Norwegian, Oceania, Regent Seven Seas and Royal Caribbean cruise lines."[16]

The lawsuits against Park West Galleries alleged abusive sales practices, promises of investment gains, and even forged signatures of Salvador Dalí.[17]

Mattie King and her late husband purchased the *Divine Comedy* collection from Park West Gallery on a cruise ship in 1999. The collection, consisting of one hundred pieces allegedly worth $150,000, included certificates of authenticity and appraisals, as per court documents.[18] A decade later, when attempting to sell the artwork, King claimed that an expert informed her the signatures might be forgeries. In response, Park West asserted that its own experts had authenticated the signatures.

Mark Jacobs, a New York schoolteacher who was on a cruise in 2009, printed flyers warning others on the ship about the lawsuits against the gallery. According to the *Independent*, Jacobs was escorted off the Jewel of the Seas. They claimed he had violated some unspecified "guest conduct policy."[19] In a statement, the cruise line responded, "The ship's Hotel Director and Staff Captain met with Mr. Jacobs and explained that his behavior was inappropriate and in violation of the guest conduct policy." Jacobs later told a reporter, "One minute I was playing table tennis with my son, the next I was being escorted away by the Oslo police."[20]

Park West insisted the lawsuits were unfounded, but they agreed to a confidential settlement that reportedly included partial refunds and the return of some art. "Those cases were all settled on terms that are confidential but very favorable to Park West," said the company's attorney, Paul Schwiep.[21] They promised to change their practices, including offering returns within forty days and exchanges within forty months.[22]

Even more promising, according to *Artnet News* in 2023, Park West has reinvented itself as a humbled, cleaned-up business. The company says it's established a stringent compliance department that reviews recordings of its auctions to ensure sales are conducted properly. They no longer make promises about the purported value of the art as an investment.[23]

The cruising industry and its art auctions have initiated changes to the benefit of their passengers and customers. But if you bought any fine art on a major cruise line during those questionable years, you may wish to get a second opinion—as always, buyer beware.

On our SIU team, we learned of the above scheme while investigating an art theft case. A gentleman had reported a burglary of his home. Among other things, thieves had stolen six Thomas Kinkade paintings.

During our investigation, his home did show signs of a break-in. A door lock had been defeated. But the first thing our investigator noticed was the man's home did not look like that of a serious art collector. It was a condo, with piled belongings like that of an aspiring hoarder. The six stolen prints were insured for over $20,000 each.

Though we were told each painting was "one of a kind," we found multiple versions of the same pieces online, priced for much less.

We concluded a burglary had indeed occurred. When we asked where he had purchased the paintings, he explained it was during a Caribbean cruise. He then produced the appraisals written by the gallery that had sold them during those problematic years.

A crucial step in the SIU process is to speak with the insurance agent who sold the policies. They might know the customer or insure their family. In this case, the man was a long-time customer who had always paid his premiums on time. The paintings had been insured as fine art, with their values documented by the gallery's appraisals.

We decided to pay the claim in full. The man had purchased the art in good faith, and we had insured it. Our company had accepted the appraisals, and our customer had paid his premiums based on those values for years. We chalked it up as a lesson learned.

A key part of SIU is sharing any lessons from our investigations. In many cases, we alert our personnel and agents to our findings so they can deliver better business in the future. Despite assertions from plaintiff attorneys, it's also proof that SIU departments don't just deny claims. Many times, we clarify the facts to the insured's benefit, even warning the public about bad players.

Unfortunately, when we did pay claims that were fraudulent, it affected all of our customers, who indirectly paid for it through increased premiums.

Chapter Five
Burglaries

People equate the word "burglary" with a financial loss. In my experience with legitimate burglaries, victims also experienced feelings of being violated, helplessness, anger, and fear. We want to believe our homes and businesses are always safe places. But when that security is broken, we feel violated.

Unfortunately, burglaries are also a breeding ground for insurance fraud.

On our SIU team, many suspicious burglaries were on policies that were new versus those of long-time customers. We noted a trend with renters policies, which are valuable but inexpensive to obtain. Currently, for an average-sized home in South Florida (a higher-risk area) a renters policy with $50,000 in property coverage can cost as little as $300 per year, or less than $30 per month. The application can be done online within minutes. There's no proof required for your valuables unless you make a claim.

If it's a brand-new customer—with no other insurance business, such as an auto policy—a reported burglary should receive a closer look.

The Staged Theft

The fraudulent burglaries we investigated fell into one of two scenarios. One: the entire burglary was fake, staged for profit. Or two: a real theft had occurred, but the victim padded the claim with extra items in order to profit.

In the most extreme cases, the criminal had purchased the policy for the sole purpose of faking a theft. They waited a couple months and then reported a major burglary.

The initial step in our investigations was to contact the customer. A good investigator may first do a cursory background check so they have context: How long have they been a customer? How new is the policy? They might use open-source investigation to see how long they've been in the area or if they have a criminal background.

The investigator will introduce themself and explain what documents we need, including a statement. In my experience, if the claim is 100 percent factual, the customer doesn't care. They offer to help with any requests to get the claim moving along. If they seem instantly defensive ("Why do you need a statement?" or "Why do I have to file a police report?"), it could indicate even more reasons to investigate.

It's important to get a record of the loss as soon as possible. Fraudsters might add to their list as time goes on. The police report may state only a television had been stolen. By the time it's reported to the carrier (when they realize their deductible) the loss now includes three laptops and a safe. Another month goes by, and they realize Grandma's silverware is missing and the thief took six Armani suits. (In Miami, people always specified *Armani* suits.)

How It's Committed and How to Investigate

An insurance criminal has to pretend a burglary or theft occurred. It's amazing how many forget a key component: a sign of a break-in. In many of our cases, no door locks or windows were defeated, and there was no damage from crowbars or other tools. The alleged victim might create superficial damage to their doors or locks to make it appear as if they had been compromised. We hired forensic locksmiths who could examine the doors and conclusively report whether the locks had been defeated.

Another cause for suspicion was when the victim had a security system, but it was not working on the day of the theft, or they forgot to turn it on.

Certainly, burglaries can occur without signs of break-in, and criminals know how to bypass security systems, but those are more indicators.

Most policies require the victim to file a police report. Did they? If not, why not? Many fraudsters realize filing a false police report is a crime in itself. In Florida, it's a misdemeanor carrying up to one year in jail. "I didn't think it was necessary," the person might reply. We would then explain it's not too late to file the report, and it's a requirement. Some offenders would brazenly file the police report; others never followed up. They might call to inexplicably withdraw their claim with vague excuses like, "I don't have the time to deal with this."

I always wondered why someone who had suffered a real loss of substantial value would hesitate to file a police report.

In an apartment or business complex, most burglaries are reported to the property manager, security personnel, or the landlord. The SIU investigator will ask them about the incident and for any possible security video.

In any investigation, the SIU personnel will follow the evidence wherever it leads. They will ask the victims where they were before the loss and who they were with. If they name people, our investigator might ask for their contact information to confirm.

I once asked an insured where he was during the time of the theft.

"With two friends at the movies." He shrugged.

"What are their names and which theater?" I responded. "And what was the movie?"

He was a deer in headlights. If the person does not want to give that information, that's another indicator. In my case, he wearily gave first names—then finally last names. It was like pulling teeth. He said he'd have to get back to me with their phone numbers.

As for which movie, he mumbled, "… *Casino*."

"*Casino*?" I frowned. "The one with Robert De Niro?"

"Yes," he replied after a pause.

I had reacted that way because I'm a movie buff and I knew that film was over ten years old at the time. We of course checked with the theater, and *Casino* wasn't playing. We scheduled an examination under oath to ask about a few contradictions. We reminded him we still needed all of his friends' contact information.

About a week later, the man left a phone message stating he'd like to withdraw his entire claim. "I don't have time to deal with this."

It's the same tactic an old high school teacher, Mr. Van Pelt, used. When four students strolled into the classroom late claiming their car had a flat tire, he asked each student to move to separate corners of the room. Van Pelt then asked each student which tire on the car had been flat. Each kid gave a different answer.

Some people don't want to give information about who they were with at the time of the loss. "Why do you have to talk to them?" some have asked. "It was just a guy I picked up." While extraneous personal trysts do occur, these responses could seem peculiar.

With any legitimate losses we investigated, the victims had no problem giving us information to help conclude their claim and get paid.

Authentic Fake Receipts

It may be hard to believe there are websites that create almost every type of fake receipt. You're probably wondering how they exist and for what purpose.

If someone stages a theft, they will need to document the purported values of the stolen items. Today's electronic record keeping has made authenticating receipts easier than ever, but it has made counterfeiting them just as effortless.

At the time of writing this, sites such as Makeareceipt.com, Needareceipt.com, and Expensesreceipt.com are among countless sites that create fake receipts. The sites advertise receipts and invoices for anything from register receipts to travel documents, restaurant receipts,

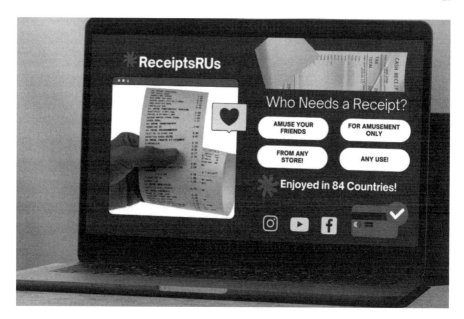

and repair invoices. Some sites add logos from known corporations. One site boasts, "Trusted by thousands of people in 84 countries!" I wonder how they arrived at *eighty-four* countries. Which eighty-four?

How are these companies legal? The sites have dubious disclaimers in fine print. One site states, "Our service is not to be utilized to create fake or fraudulent documents. The user assumes all liability of usage of any receipt." The sites assert the receipts can be used to "replace lost receipts" or to "amuse your friends!" None of my friends would be particularly amused by a receipt.

Astonishingly, the sites even give tips on how to make the bogus receipts appear more real. One site suggests, "Use a thermal printer to print the receipt on real thermal receipt paper. Then put it in the sun for a few hours and you'll have an aged receipt."

I speculate the sites are operated offshore, perhaps from nations with ambiguous laws, and the U.S.'s legal system simply does not have the resources to investigate.

Conversely, a similar fake-documents site that operated in the U.S. was shut down in 2017—not just for allegations of insurance fraud, but the U.S. Federal Trade Commission's complaint asserted the counterfeit documents were used to perpetrate identity theft.

In the cases filed by the FTC, three individuals operated multiple online sites that sold fake documents including pay stubs, income tax forms, and medical statements.

According to Andrew Smith, director of the FTC's Bureau of Consumer Protection, "The sale of fake documents makes it easy for identity thieves and scammers to apply their trade." [24]

One company, Innovative Paycheck Solutions, promoted the sale of financial documents on FakePayStubOnline.com. The site sold fake paystubs for as little as $40 and charged more than $150 for fake tax returns. Another site, NoveltyExcuses.com, sold fake insurance cards, utility bills, and medical absence reports.

The sites claimed the documents were for "novelty" and "entertainment" purposes, but the documents themselves did not state they were fake, according to the complaints.

The defendants were ultimately prohibited from marketing or selling any fake documents or services. One defendant had to pay $169,000 in fines. Another was fined $133,777. To add insult to injury, the fines were suspended due to the parties' inability to pay.[25]

On an amusing note, one niche site I encountered during an investigation produced counterfeit conference documents. You know, when you come home from a convention and you have a stack of C.E. certifications, a glossy program, hotel receipts, and even a laminated name badge. This site falsified all of those items and sold them as a "package." My only guess as to who this site's customer base is would be people involved in affairs, attempting to get extra time off, or in need of an alibi.

A warning for any would-be fraudsters: Unlike a decade ago, SIU teams are fully aware of these sites and know their templates. And they will confirm the receipts with the actual sources.

Another tactic I saw to falsify a receipt could be done on any sales site such as Amazon. Let's say a dishonest person submits a claim for a stolen $40,000 diamond necklace. An investigator will ask for a purchase invoice. It might be another red flag when the insured claims he bought such an expensive piece of jewelry online.

How the "receipt" is faked: The fraudster finds a $40,000 necklace for sale on Amazon (for those of you who didn't know, they sell such expensive jewelry, and even pieces well into the six figures). The person clicks the item, then clicks "add to cart." On the ensuing page, the purchase is summarized: the item's description, shipping address, and payment method, with tax and shipping calculated. It appears to be a full purchase summary. At this point, the culprit prints the page or takes a screenshot. They are cautious to *not* click "place your order;" they do *not* want $40,000 coming out of their bank account. The person then backs out, cancels the order, and exits the site.

To a novice adjuster, the image or printed page might appear to be a genuine invoice. Criminals are preying on overworked and understaffed operations whose investigators are inadequately trained, precisely why companies need ongoing fraud training and strong SIU teams.

Low-tech methods to make fake receipts still exist as well. People buy pads of blank invoice forms at office supply stores. Home computers and printers can create almost any document.

On our team, it was amazing to see how many fake invoices were from merchants that never existed or were allegedly located at addresses that weren't on any map. It's like they had pulled streets out of their imaginations versus studying a real map. Those were easy to discredit, including the use of corporate checks to prove the merchants weren't real.

More brazen fraudsters would use a real company and maybe even steal their logo. Those cases were fun to investigate because whenever we showed a counterfeit document to the merchant, they became incensed. The business owners felt violated by someone using their company, and they gladly cooperated with our investigations—the closest thing to a slam dunk.

I should add that insureds don't always have to have their receipts. Many people don't hang onto them, or the items were gifts or inherited. In those cases, insurers work with their customers for other ways to document ownership, such as through photos or speaking with the gift givers. With today's technology, most large merchants can pull up invoices for large-ticket items such as jewelry, televisions, or computers.

Surveillance—After a Burglary?

Surveillance is a useful tool for many SIU investigations. Due to the high cost of hiring experts for surveillance, it's usually reserved for high-dollar claims or cases with a far-reaching impact such as the investigation of organized crime rings.

But what good can surveillance do once the loss has already occurred? For some large burglaries, we hired surveillance firms to watch the property after the loss—but immediately before our scheduled inspections.

We retained proper surveillance experts that were qualified with private investigation licenses and a full understanding of privacy laws. They needed to be able to establish the authenticity of their videos, with the ability to testify in court if needed.

After the person reports the burglary and has listed the stolen items, an SIU rep will want to visit their property to document the site. My teams would photograph the scenes of the crimes, including where the stolen items had been located. Routine items included televisions, computers, expensive art, and perhaps expensive clothing (back to our Armani suits).

How we used surveillance: For a suspicious case, if our inspection was scheduled for a Monday, we might hire surveillance for the day or weekend before. If the burglary was fraudulent, all the items would need to be moved *out* of the house before our inspection.

Though this tactic was hit or miss, we had countless cases where we observed family members carefully removing the items from the home. Some had rented U-Hauls to load furniture, televisions, bikes, and even cribs (a thief took a crib?).

Many times, we recognized the insured and their family members in the video moving the items—Nana carrying jewelry boxes or teens fumbling with large televisions. It was always amusing to show them the video at an examination under oath to ask what they were doing. We'd ask for the contact information for every person in the video. In one case, we knew they had a self-storage unit, and we asked to inspect it.

In cases where they had hired an attorney to represent them, we weren't shocked when they asked to withdraw their case. Some lawyers quit the

01/18/2024   12:54:03

case, essentially firing their clients. Nothing angers an ethical attorney more than a client who has not been truthful with them.

Even in cases that were withdrawn, if we had evidence of fraud, by statute we had to make a referral to our state's Bureau of Insurance Fraud, or as it's called in Florida, the Division of Investigative and Forensic Services. They could then conduct their own criminal investigation.

Internet as the Adversary

The internet has been a priceless tool to investigate claims. Most carriers' systems are web-based, and there are countless methods of obtaining records and performing background investigations. The internet can also provide valuable open sources.

However, the internet's dark side can pose problems. One of my best investigators, Steve, heard about a website that boasted "How to Commit Insurance Fraud" for burglaries. When I pulled up the site, I was shocked. A legitimate-looking site systematically described how to commit fraud, step by step with bullet points. It started with how to buy a policy for the sole purpose of fraud (walk into an agent's office at 4:55 p.m. on a Friday when the staff is in a hurry to leave).

The specific steps included, "The insurance company might ask you to attend an examination under oath." It advised they should attend because failing to do so could be grounds for denial. The steps were so exact that they had to have been authored by someone with claims investigation experience.

Other steps described how to lie about valuables—to say they were inherited from relatives who were deceased, so it would be impossible to disprove.

Another step recommended saying you *did* save all of your receipts, but you kept them locked in a small safe—which was also stolen. "Create a dead end for the insurance company." The list concluded with large font, "Then you get paid!"

The how-to-commit-fraud site had evidently gone viral because we experienced a spike in burglary cases. When our team began investigating, we were astounded by how many people followed the list verbatim. We could predict what they were going to say next. During EUOs of the insureds, our attorneys had copies of the list so we could follow along with checkmarks.

"I must've left my door unlocked, which is why there's no sign of a break-in." Check.

"I inherited the silverware from my poor dead granny." Check.

"All my receipts were in a safe, which was unfortunately stolen." Check.

At the end of the EUOs, we'd show them the list to point out any steps they might've missed. It was amusing to watch their reactions. We also explained that we had the ability to request their computers' browsing histories.

At that point, their attorneys would ask for a quick powwow at the coffee pot to chat with their client. Some would ask to withdraw their claims. Others would defiantly stick to their stories, only to leave a meek voicemail a few days later asking to cancel their claim.

Regardless of which type of case, whenever attorneys asked to withdraw their client's claim, they would pull us aside with an additional request: Do not report their client to any fraud bureaus. Some tried to make it a contingency with a bold display in front of their clients, "We will withdraw *only* if you agree to not make referrals to any fraud agencies."

"Sorry, we can't do that." Per Florida Statute 626.9891, we had the duty to report any suspected fraudulent insurance act to the Division of Investigative and Forensic Services regardless of whether we paid the claim. The attorneys would still advise their clients to withdraw their claims. Perhaps they believed authorities would view it more favorably if the insurance company never paid it.

As time marched on, more ominous websites appeared offering all sorts of criminal methods. Chatrooms on sites such as Reddit featured users offering advice with almost no regulation. One Reddit forum featured suggestions for how rideshare drivers can make sure their insurance companies don't discover they drive for Uber or Lyft (more on that in Chapter 37).

With the exponential growth of the web—with sites hosted offshore or unregulated—it was impossible to know all the information being shared. But there was no shortage of low-tech methods as well.

Chapter Six
Mysterious Disappearances in the Magic City

On my first day with Miami's SIU, my fiancée (now wife) drove me to the office like she was dropping off a child at school. They recommended I get a ride because I'd be given a company car. At that time, the job was over 50 percent field work, requiring transportation to zigzag across South Florida to investigate cases. After sitting in a cubicle eight hours a day for four years, it sounded exciting to be cruising around the Magic City as an "investigator."

In that era, SIUs were segregated from other departments. We handled confidential investigations using private information. We would meet with police and agents from the NICB and the Division of Insurance Fraud. With organized crime rings, we might have large tree diagrams on the wall of suspects—perhaps local businesspeople. It would not be wise to have that in plain view of everyone.

We weren't 9-to-5 employees. Our jobs could stretch to midnight or spill into weekends. But we also had the freedom to meet our contacts in the field. We might have a strategy lunch with one of our attorneys on glamorous South Beach. On the other hand, we might have to drive twenty miles into the Everglades to search for sunken cars until dusk.

When my wife and I followed the directions to my new office, it led to a leased office on Don Shula's golf course in Miami Lakes. We lived forty-five minutes north of Miami, and the whole area seemed like another world. We only visited Miami a few times a year to enjoy concerts, Miami Heat games, the cafés of South Beach, or Versailles in Little Havana. The thought of this being my new workplace seemed surreal.

My wife was less than thrilled. It was the early '90s, so we had both witnessed the Miami of the 1980s. Along with pink and blue neon were visions of cliché drug dealers from *Miami Vice* and *Scarface*. Miami's drug war had been splashed in the headlines with a record number of murders in its wake. While out at Coconut Grove one evening, my wife and I witnessed people snorting coke from their car's dashboard at a stoplight. So, she had a distorted vision of the people I would be investigating.

For those reasons, we continued to live almost an hour north of my office. It helped create a separation between my career and my home life. I wouldn't have to worry about bumping into someone whose claim I had denied—or who had been arrested—while out with my family.

When I arrived at my new office, my new boss Tom—an excellent, happy leader— introduced me to the team of six investigators. I was Luis's partner anytime he had to go out into the field. In the meantime, they gave me a stack of cases to review to understand how various investigations unfold.

One of the first types of cases I studied was called "mysterious disappearance" claims. In addition to sounding enigmatic, I learned they were among the hardest to disprove. But Luis had a knack, and he taught me some tactics that my teams would use for decades.

Whenever someone reported a suspicious claim under their personal articles policy (PAP), the challenges were significant. However, our SIU team boasted a commendable success rate. Here, "success" is defined as either compensating the customer when indicators were cleared, or proving fraud or the insured withdrawing their claim when they weren't legitimate.

PAPs were invented to offer higher coverage for expensive items. They're used to cover costly jewelry, collectables, valuable equipment (cameras, tech devices), and fine art. The items are covered worldwide, so when you go on vacation, even internationally, property such as your wedding ring or laptop is fully protected.

However, some features of the policies make them attractive for insurance criminals. First, they usually have no deductible. Second, they are "valued policies," meaning you're paid the face value without any depreciation. And finally, among the listed perils such as theft or fire is "mysterious disappearance." That's an elegant way of saying, "I lost it and can't find it."

Therefore, a criminal does not have to risk staging an elaborate burglary, theft, or fire. They simply have to say, "I can't find it."

If someone insures a $50,000 ring, even if it is tarnished and scuffed, and they claim they can't find it, the insurance company might issue a $50,000 check with no deductions for depreciation, deductible, or taxes.

The term "mysterious disappearance" is the aspect exploited by criminals. How can you prove someone can't find something? If the owner says she left her ring in a bedside drawer and now can't find it, we're not going to search her home. We have to take her word for it. I knew SIU investigators at smaller carriers who believed such cases weren't worth investigating.

Our team did not share that mindset.

The Devil is in the Details

We had an effective system for investigating mysterious disappearance cases. As a disclaimer, a majority of those claims were valid and promptly paid. If someone had been a customer for years and suddenly reported a missing ring, it probably wouldn't come to our SIU team.

However, if it was a new policy or for someone we had never insured before (we'd say, "They walked in off the street"), we might take a look. If they were recently unemployed or had filed for bankruptcy, it might come to us. If the lost item was not commensurate with their income, we might investigate. I recall a young couple who were janitors. Though that is a noble profession, it seemed odd they both had new matching Rolex watches that went missing on the same day.

Our technique to investigate seems pragmatic. During a recorded statement, we'd ask them everything about the day the item went missing and then examine every part of their response.

People love to talk, and they fill awkward pauses with even more words. That's an old approach, whether it's a police officer, an attorney, or an SIU investigator asking questions: the long pause. When the interviewer hesitates—perhaps to check their notes—a guilty party may find the silence uncomfortable. They believe if they add more details or people to their narrative, it might make it seem more real.

"What were you doing before you realized your ring was missing?"

"I was in a rush because… I'd just left my brother-in-law's house to visit my friend. By the time I got home, I realized my ring was missing. I immediately called my mom/sister/friend to see if they'd seen it."

We would respond, "Please provide the names, phone numbers, and addresses for your brother-in-law, your friend, and your mom/sister/friend."

Long pause. "Why do you need all that?" or, "I forgot their number" or, "I forgot my friend's last name" (people have said that.) Or, "My mom/sister/friend just left the country on a long trip."

One of the principal duties outlined in insurance policies is their duty to cooperate with our investigations. We would ask them to gather all the information we had requested and inform them we couldn't conclude our investigation until they did.

Ask yourself: If you lost an expensive item and the company asked for contact information for a friend you had been with, would you care? My friends and family would be eager to help me.

But the criminal is at a crossroads. They may have to coach their friends and family to back up their story. Are their friends 100 percent dependable? Are their friends willing to lie for them, perhaps under oath? Even if the insured hires an attorney and files a lawsuit, those same friends and family will have to answer the same questions in sworn depositions.

Or the fraudster might decide to walk away from the claim. I called it the "meek retreat." Rather than overtly withdrawing their claim, they would email or call us after hours to leave a message, "Sorry, I found my ring. I remembered where it was. You can cancel my claim."

In a memorable case, Mrs. Insured reported her $20,000 wedding ring missing while in the Florida Keys. My investigator was an avid fisherman, so he knew the area. The insured said she and her husband had been snorkeling for lobster with their three friends. When my representative asked which hotel they had stayed at, in the event the ring might be there, the insured replied, "None." They had driven just for the day (eight hours roundtrip). We asked for the names and phone numbers of each of their three friends.

Mr. and Mrs. Insured were reluctant to give their friends' names and numbers. "They're very private people." When we asked to see the toll charges for their drive to the Keys, the insured explained they had driven on "back roads" to avoid tolls and save money.

My rep and I studied our maps to see if any such route was possible. It was conceivable if they took roads that meandered through the Everglades for an additional hour. We scheduled our insureds for EUOs to get their stories under oath.

When we arrived at the office Monday morning, we had a voicemail from that couple. They had called Sunday night when we were closed. Mrs. Insured said she was so embarrassed, but she had found her diamond ring; it had been stuck inside her dive glove all along. "Please cancel my claim. Sorry!"

That was $20,000 saved with a fifteen-minute statement by asking all the right questions.

I had a case for the theft of sports memorabilia, an autographed Dan Marino Miami Dolphins football. Mr. Insured made the mistake of telling me how "devastated" his teenage sons were. "They would gaze at the ball every day. They almost cried…"

I perked up and asked, "Your two teenage sons saw the ball every day?"

"Yes," Mr. Insured said, frowning. "Why?"

His sons were between the ages of seventeen and nineteen years old, mature enough to cooperate with our investigation. When I requested their statements to ask about the last time they had seen the ball, Mr. Insured had a sudden epiphany: he wanted to search for the ball one more time. "Maybe they let their friends borrow it."

He miraculously found the ball. He wasn't about to bestow his fate to the reliability of two teenagers' capacity to recite the same script, nor reveal to them that their daddy could be a liar.

The easiest stories to discredit were from anyone who inadvertently involved their job in their statements. "I had just left work when I noticed it missing" or, "I had met with my boss before I got home."

We would reply, "Where do you work, and what is your boss's name and phone number?"

Jaw drop. "My job? Why… do you need that?"

"So we can verify the timeline. Your boss might help us confirm the time of the loss."

Insurance criminals do *not* want to involve their boss or coworkers. Anyone who ventures into the world of insurance fraud out of desperation can't afford any interaction that could affect their livelihood. Again, any of my past managers would have been happy to help me, and I would have been grateful.

The opposite of the meek retreat was the angry withdrawal. Invariably their words would include how busy they were: "I'm too busy to be dealing with this!" or, "I don't have time for this nonsense!"

Would you be too busy to follow up with someone to receive $20,000 that you rightfully had coming to you (tax-free)?

Video—or Lack Thereof

"Eyes in the sky" have been a useful tool in our mysterious disappearance cases, even if they didn't capture the act. A new investigator asked me, "What good is video if it *doesn't* catch anything?"

CCTV (closed-circuit television) includes security cameras found on many corners, at banks, places of business, and so on. If you've ever traveled to the United Kingdom or some other countries in Europe, they seem to be on every corner (coincidence that they have lower crime rates than the U.S.?) Each year in the U.S., there are more cameras to provide security and safety. Businesses usually maintain the video for a specified amount of time before recording over the data.

We would visit scenes to look for available video—perhaps from a parking lot, a merchant, a lobby, or someone's residence. If there was no direct video, there might be cameras close by. In a mugging case, we were disappointed there was no video in the parking lot. However, my investigator realized the adjacent McDonald's drive-thru had a camera pointed right at the parking lot. (Turns out that insured was never mugged.) The proliferation of doorbell cameras has helped as well.

The point wasn't always capturing the alleged loss on camera. That's a highly coveted but infrequent scenario. Many times, just the fact that a camera was present was enough. Our team had success disproving theft and disappearance claims just by having a camera in the vicinity, whether the cameras captured anything or not.

How, you ask? In one case, the insureds reported they were moving cross-country. The wife had *all* of her jewelry, worth tens of thousands, with her in the car. When they had stopped to eat at a Cracker Barrel, she brought the bag of jewelry inside. She explained she'd felt safer having the jewelry with her instead of in an unattended car. That was a credible response. She said she had placed the bag at her feet while they ate, and then the entire bag had mysteriously vanished.

When my investigator visited the restaurant, he discovered the insureds never reported the incident to the management. Business owners and management are usually helpful with our requests because they'd like to avoid any liability. My investigator was disappointed to learn they had cameras in the retail area but none where the insureds had been seated. It seemed like a dead end, but it was all we needed.

We scheduled our insureds for examinations under oath to ask them to clarify a few details. They had a difficult time explaining why they never reported such an expensive loss to the management. We then asked them to state precisely where their table had been located. Mrs. Insured repeated how the large bag of jewelry had been at her feet before it vanished.

We were intrigued when our attorney skillfully asked, "Are you aware the restaurant had security cameras that were functional that day?"

Long silence. "No, we did not realize that."

"Well, they did," our attorney replied, "and the management has been cooperative with our investigation."

After a pause, the couple asked to conclude the examination. They said they wanted to search their belongings one more time for the missing items.

The question our attorney asked was not deceptive. He had merely asked if they were aware the restaurant had cameras. It was a simple yes or no question. Honest victims might have replied, "Great! What did it show?"

The policyholders called a few days later, ecstatic that they had found their bag of jewelry buried in their luggage. "We're so embarrassed. Please close our claim."

That wasn't an anomaly. That same question startled other fraudsters who weren't fully committed to their schemes. In a stolen boat case in Key Largo, a man told us he had seen the thieves through his rear window and knew the precise time.

Our attorney asked, "Are you aware your neighbors across the canal have a security camera aimed directly at your dock?"

His question was legitimate. During a neighborhood canvass, our investigator Steve had discovered the rear neighbor had a camera aimed toward our insured's home, but it hadn't been operational. Our attorney's question was genuine.

Same result: After a slight delay, the insured asked to withdraw his claim. I guess he wasn't that friendly with his neighbors.

Switcheroo Schemes

Another tactic criminals use to commit mysterious disappearances or theft claims is similar to the fine art schemes previously discussed: insure an item of lesser value for a higher value—like a shell game, swapping a fake for the real thing.

In Miami, one of the most common examples was Rolex watches. The two-tone gold and stainless Datejust Rolex had become the Miami cliché for wealth since TV's Don Johnson sported one while chasing dealers in his Ferrari and/or speedboat.

If you found ten people in a crowd wearing Rolexes, eight of them would probably be phony. In my youth, fakes were common at flea markets. They looked perfect but would only last about six months. Thanks to the internet, counterfeits from overseas were plentiful, ranging from basic phonies for $50 to over $200 for models with "real Swiss-style movement." For an extra charge, the sites could include "original" boxes, bogus sales paperwork, and warranties. (Remember the phony receipt sites?) The phony boxes we observed were impressive hard cases, and the warranty paperwork would appear authentic to a novice. The websites use key words such as "replica" Rolex, as well as replicas for many other valuable brands.

Imagine a rookie insurance agent receiving that watch and phony sales paperwork at 4:59 p.m. on a Friday. Some might write that policy in minutes. The deceitful customer would pay their first $50 premium before the watch is reported missing over the weekend. Some insurers pride themselves on how fast they pay claims and even use replacement services that can ship a new watch to their home within days. That's a $50 investment for a brand new $25,000 watch delivered to their doorstep.

I found it interesting that different people would rehash the same story: They lost the jewelry while swimming at the beach. With the Rolex cases, they went swimming at the beach, and it "fell off." We'd ask how a watch could just fall off. Was there a faulty clasp? Shrug: "It was a big wave, I dunno..."

They were clever enough to not add witnesses. They were always alone and just decided to go for a quick swim. They rarely reported them missing from hotels or businesses because there might be video. Hotels avoid liability by offering safes. A housekeeper could get fired. Burglaries require police reports. So, losing it somewhere you would never find it (like the vast ocean) sounded good.

But there was a flaw in their plots that few laypeople know about. Rolex tracks serial numbers with the precision of IRS auditors. It maintains records when its watches are sold between individuals, given to pawn shops, or refurbished by jewelers. Rolex also keeps records of stolen watches. If you're tempted to buy a used watch for a price that seems too good to be true, you can check with Rolex.

Our investigators were able to find out if purported serial numbers were genuine. Some numbers didn't even resemble an authentic number. Or sometimes the actual watch assigned to the given serial number had been owned for twenty years by a Hank Neebler in Albuquerque.

In one unfortunate case, our customer had purchased a Rolex from eBay. When he received the watch, he took it to his jeweler to be serviced. The shop contacted him, stating police had confiscated the watch. When the shop had entered the serial number, it had come back as stolen. The watch had been stolen in Germany the previous year. The jeweler had a duty to contact the police. Fortunately, the insured contacted the seller, who refunded the money.

Diamond schemes were similar since "moissanite" became popular in the late '90s. Jewelry containing moissanite is almost indistinguishable from real diamonds to the naked eye.

In the late 1980s, the North Carolina firm Cree Research, Inc. developed a commercial process for producing moissanite. In 1995, Charles & Colvard was the first company to manufacture and sell synthetic moissanite under a U.S. patent.[26] Almost overnight, the gem became an alternative to diamonds at a fraction of the cost. To distinguish between a real diamond and moissanite required a specific diamond tester from an experienced jeweler.

If a fraudster were to find a jeweler careless and feeble enough, they might write an appraisal for moissanite believing it was a real diamond.

With any of the above, our SIU team would perform our due diligence: request appraisals, validate them at the source, request proof of payment, and ask insureds to attend EUOs to explain any inconsistencies.

I learned something interesting when I took a statement from a wealthy older woman. The beautiful, silver-haired lady was an affluent Palm Beach socialite. She told me all her rich friends own duplicates of their "show jewelry." For any pieces that they enjoy flaunting at functions—such as diamond necklaces, rings, bracelets or jewel-encrusted broaches—the women owned two sets: the genuine item and an exact copy. They only wore the *copies* in public.

"No one wears the real ones in public," she had said. "It's much too dangerous."

The jewelry that we insured was authentic—but locked away in safe deposit boxes, never to be worn. It was as if the moment they receive jewelry as a gift, they whisk it away and lock it up to never see the light of day. Then they parade reproductions of the same items to the world.

"Everyone does that, dear," she had said, grinning at my naiveté for not knowing about her world.

For years I wondered how many stolen counterfeits we had paid for, when the actual items were safely protected in vaults.

Ominous Sources of Funding

In 2020, one of our projects uncovered an organized crime ring that used jewelry claims as a means to fund more severe crimes.

We caught the reckless offenders because they kept reporting the same exact jewelry stolen again and again. Their mistake was using highly identifiable items, reported to multiple carriers at the same time, using the same photographs. If insurance criminals were geniuses, they would have pursued other livelihoods.

Efrain, one of my best investigators at finding connections to larger networks, brought the first case to my attention. A man had reported being mugged late at night while walking home from a nightclub. The jewelry included a square solid-gold medallion depicting Jesus's Last Supper. Another gold pendant was of a large lion's head. The combined value was well over $50,000.

I couldn't imagine someone wearing that much jewelry while walking alone at 2 a.m. from a bar, but to each their own. The man submitted appraisals and invoices from where he had purchased the jewelry in New York. The invoices declared "paid cash" to prevent a credit trail.

The clincher was when another SIU rep on our team received a case from a different person who had reported being mugged, gold chains stolen, including the Last Supper and lion head pendants. They submitted the same photographs—not just similar, but the *exact* same photos.

In Florida, we have the legal ability to request file materials from other carriers. If we discover someone has made prior claims at another company, using Florida Statute 626.989, our investigators can ask those companies for copies of their file material, and they're allowed to provide them (with certain exceptions).

Efrain discovered other people had reported similar claims around the state. By contacting his SIU peers at other companies, he confirmed the items were the same: a gold Last Supper medallion and the lion pendant. He then obtained copies of the other company's files. Each person had submitted the same photographs, with matching invoices from the same shop in New York (that didn't exist), each made out to a different person, "paid cash."

Though it was comical how they all claimed to have paid cash while being unemployed and had carelessly used the same photographs, we learned the group had much more sinister ties.

When we submitted our case to the Division of Insurance Fraud, the special agent was aware of the group. Working with detectives from Miami P.D., we discovered the gang was part of a Caribbean crime organization. The insurance claims, valued at over $50,000 apiece, were channels to fund their operations, which included drug dealing, arms trading, and murder.

The gang had discovered insurance fraud was a faster, safer way to generate funds. Imagine getting hundreds of thousands of dollars without using a gun, targeting companies that pride themselves on how fast they pay. And the money was perfectly laundered since the funds were issued by respected carriers.

Criminals had begun to wonder, "Why deal drugs?"

PART THREE –
ARSON FOR PROFIT

Chapter Seven
The Little Havana Years

Around Christmas 1998, I was promoted to be a manager of the Miami SIU. I was thirty-two years old and married, with a two-year-old toddler at home. I still lived in Coral Springs, a quiet suburb of Fort Lauderdale.

My wife Anthea was thrilled with the promotion but concerned about where I was assigned for my first management job: Little Havana, nearly an hour south of Coral Springs.

To say I was a naïve gringo would be an understatement. I had not grown up in a Latin community and didn't speak any coherent Spanish. But I knew a lot about fraud schemes affecting the people in the area, and I was one of only a few who had applied for the job—and there was a reason for that.

A year earlier, our company had decided to set up shop in Miami's Little Havana. Since 1962, Little Havana has been a working-class Cuban exile neighborhood west of downtown Miami. It's distinguished by its street life, restaurants, music, political passion, and cultural events such as the *Calle Ocho* festival and the Three Kings Parade during the holidays.

The architectural style is reminiscent of its namesake, Havana, Cuba: a mix of old and new Mediterranean-style bungalows, Spanish architecture, Art Deco courtyard apartments, and mom-and-pop corner *bodegas*. And the best Cuban cafés I've ever visited.

But like urban areas of any large city, portions of Little Havana were known at the time for high crime, drugs, and poverty.

My company had decided to buy a small building in Little Havana. When local sellers realized one of the largest carriers in the world wanted to buy, the prices soared. Transparency about our company name was a curious choice since some businesses use separate entities to buy property more discreetly. When Walt Disney wanted to buy swampland in the 1960s, he used shell companies to hide his identity and keep prices from skyrocketing.

Our company purchased an older two-story building at a price that was far from a bargain. They then needed to decide who would staff it. The company placed an insurance agent on the first floor to offer services to the community. It wanted a claims team to work on the second floor, but there were few volunteers. People either lived too far away or were concerned about safety in the area.

Someone decided, "Let's put an SIU team there."

When I got the promotion and learned it would be in Little Havana, I felt like Kevin Costner's Lieutenant Dunbar in the movie *Dances with Wolves*. He was promoted but sent to the farthest outpost in the frontier.

My company paid another fortune to renovate the building with modern upgrades. When I arrived, the interior was state-of-the-art. My predecessor Gerry introduced me to the neighborhood. It didn't look like a high-crime area. Though it was a dated urban neighborhood, little old *abuelas* walked on the sidewalks with umbrellas to block the sun. There was a Cuban bakery next door that smelled heavenly, with fresh ham and cheese *croquetas* and guava pastries for less than a dollar.

Our building had a fenced parking lot and security cameras. We could hop onto State Road 836 to be in downtown Miami in five minutes to meet our attorneys, or at lunch in South Beach within fifteen. I inherited a team of SIU investigators I had known for years. They were experienced, and we had excellent working relationships.

Every morning, I had to beat the rush hour traffic from home. I'd leave so early that I could be in my office with a Cuban coffee by 7 a.m. The SIU investigators worked primarily on the road, so they'd come and go throughout the day to discuss their cases. I loved my new gig.

La Gran Apertura (The Grand Opening)

The office had another unique feature: Very few local or corporate managers ever wanted to visit. Perhaps due to the stigma of urban Miami—especially with visitors from the Midwest who had only seen Miami on television—they must've envisioned something worse than what it was. So, with no visitors, I managed my team with little oversight. I could communicate with my boss electronically, and if anyone over my paygrade wanted to visit, they'd give us two weeks' notice. It was like the military needing to coordinate a USO tour.

Our new building had an almost comical ribbon-cutting ceremony. The invited guests included local politicians and management from our regional office in Central Florida. The festivities were set up outside, within our fenced parking lot, including a lectern for speaking and tents for a catered buffet.

As we were making final preparations for everyone's arrival, one of the employees noticed some neighbors from the adjacent apartment building had hung their laundry, including bras and underwear, on our fences to dry. We had to send a bilingual employee to ask them to please remove the panties and undergarments until after our event.

Though it's a trite cliché, our parking lot had actual roosters. An entire family of hens and brash roosters would screech to remind us we were on their turf. Several of our reps had to continuously wrangle the fowl out of our staging area like Rocky Balboa chasing chickens.

The invited VIPs had no plans to stay overnight. They had flown in to be ushered into town cars, with tickets to fly home immediately after the event. For any potential press, the company asked our SIU team to stay out of the spotlight, instead wanting to focus on the agency downstairs that was there to serve the fine folks of the community. Our jobs were to chase away roosters, keep any bras off the fences, and make sure the shrimp and pasta salad were covered from the blazing sun.

As esteemed speakers took turns at the podium to express how marvelous it was to have us in the area, SIU rep Steve approached me with wide eyes. He pointed at several homeless men who had wandered into our parking lot. They were entering the buffet line, shuffling along with the guests.

"What do we do?" Steve asked with a shrug.

To avoid any potential scuffles, we decided to let 'em stay. They might as well get some food. The vagrants smiled and said nothing as they heaped their plates with shrimp, chicken, and pasta. We were truly one with the community.

When the hoopla was over, the invited VIPs waved as they marched toward their cars. By pure coincidence—and as multiple witnesses can attest—there was a deafening boom. A block away was an overpass for the highway leading from downtown to Miami International Airport. Two semi-trucks had crashed into each other within blocks of our office.

When the VIPs spun their heads toward the clamor, they saw smoke. Not realizing what they were seeing, they dashed to their cars, and the wheels screeched like officials fleeing the U.S. Embassy in Iran. We had very few outside visitors to our office after that.

For the next five years, our SIU team loved our upstairs office. We called it our "tree fort," where we were able to freely conduct our everyday efforts. There was enough fraud for job security. We could visit our attorneys downtown within minutes. We had lunches at Cuban cafés that loaded our plates for $7. We could hold office celebrations in Coconut Grove. I had a wonderful boss an hour away whose actual name was Don Johnson. He was a knowledgeable man who had SIU experience and was compassionate with family needs.

During that period, my wife became pregnant with twins. Our SIU staff organized a marvelous baby shower luncheon at the office, complete with all of her favorite Cuban delicacies.

Though I look back with affection, I realize our brains have a way of erasing any difficult times. As I reminisced with my former SIU colleagues in preparing for this book, I have been reminded our little tree fort wasn't always filled with fun, triumphs, and laughs.

Havana Hardships

Within our exciting world of investigating insurance crimes in the early 2000s, our office endured a few incidents that tested our spirits.

Though sweet little grandmothers walked the sidewalks by day, the neighborhood could be different at night. Several company cars were stolen despite our barbed-wire fence. Once, we found our stolen van abandoned one block behind our building. When Steve and I went to retrieve it, we discovered it was filled with thousands of dollars' worth of satellite equipment. We presumed a thief just ditched the vehicle for whatever reason.

When a young woman, Sonia, interviewed to be on our team, she was caught in a shootout behind our office. She departed in her car by taking a rear shortcut. At an intersection, she heard gunfire. A car of thugs had made an abrupt stop in front of her, and a team of armed federal agents approached from behind. A cop shouted for her to "get down!" She did so, and the gunfire continued as the feds pursued the criminals.

Fortunately, Sonia was not injured. Everyone was worried she would never come back to work. I would have bet she'd never venture anywhere near our office again. To our grateful surprise, she wanted to work with our team, and she went on to be one of our best investigators.

Just a few weeks later—still jumpy with paranoia—we all heard a thunderous blast behind our office and the faint crackle of gunfire. We sighed with relief when we called the police. They told us Hollywood director Michael Bay was filming the movie *Bad Boys II* with Will Smith at an abandoned boathouse on the Miami River, two blocks behind our office.

Thankfully, our building had an alarm system, but it was monitored by corporate security 1,300 miles away. Since I was the only "manager on duty," anytime the alarm was triggered, they would call me first.

I would get calls at home at 3 a.m., and a voice from Illinois would say, "The alarm has been activated. Do you want to drive down to check it out? Or should we send the police?"

"Hmmm. Let me think about that," I would reply, in bed, an hour away, with my wife, newborn twins, and a four-year-old.

"Why don't you go ahead and send the police."

Which is what they did, and it was usually just kids throwing something at our building.

Martes Muerto—Dead Tuesday

In 2000, the local saga of Elián Gonzalez seized the nation's attention. Five-year-old Elián and his mother had fled Cuba in rafts to come to the United States. During their perilous journey, his mother had been killed. Fishermen found Elián nestled in an innertube off the coast of Florida. The Coast Guard rushed him to a Miami hospital for dehydration and minor cuts. With his mother dead, his closest relatives were a great uncle and his family, who lived in Little Havana, in a small house a few blocks from our office.

Elián entered a brutal custody battle waged between his father, Juan Miguel, who was still in Cuba, and his extended family in Little Havana. An international tug-of-war raged on, splashed on the news, which enraged our local Cuban exile community.

We could hear the incessant drone of helicopters above our office as the legal proceedings unfolded every day. I would approach my car to head home and see countless news choppers hovering over Elián's interim home. When protests flared, we would have to reroute our commutes.

On April 20, 2000, a judge revoked the uncle's custody, clearing the way for Elián to be returned to his father in Cuba. In the pre-dawn hours of Saturday, April 22, Border Patrol agents stormed Elián's house. When no one opened the door, they forced their way in, using mace. An Associated Press photographer clicked the infamous photo of an agent retrieving the horrified boy from a closet. That raid and photograph ignited a fuse that escalated protests.

On April 25, 2000, I decided to alert my company's upper management about possible violence. Infuriated by the federal removal of Elián, exile leaders had demanded a work stoppage they called *Martes Muerto*— Dead Tuesday—to take place on April 25, 2000, ending at midnight the following day.

"We are trying to do an act of what we term passive noncooperation that will produce a dead city," said Ramon Saul Sanchez, leader of the exile group Democracy Movement. They called for all Little Havana's shops, restaurants, businesses, and markets to be shuttered.[27]

I feared there could be retaliation if we kept our office open. Being so far removed from our local news, we had to bring our Midwest carrier up to date. Since the media had labeled it a "peaceful protest," a decision was made to remain open, which I ultimately agreed with. Most of our SIU investigators worked in the field, so I planned to stay in the office with our three female support staff. One woman expressed that she did not feel safe, and I told her to absolutely stay home, "off the books." If there were repercussions, I could handle it.

Aside from someone throwing an immense crowbar through my office window (which I still treasure to this day), the day was nonviolent. Untold numbers of people in the 800,000-strong Cuban exile community had not gone to work that day. Many of our favorite places such as Versailles restaurant and Sedano's Supermarkets had closed. On the flip side, it made driving in the area easier. The neighborhood was so empty that I almost expected to see tumbleweeds.

There was one unforeseen side effect. Every afternoon, our support staff enjoyed their daily shots of *café Cubano*. They were probably addicted to the caffeine because they got the shakes and almost panicked when they realized the local cafés were all closed. Vowing to find them coffee at any expense, I drove my car in concentric blocks away from Little Havana in the pursuit of their javas. I finally found a 7-Eleven five miles north that had Cuban coffee. When I returned to my caffeine-dependent staff, I felt like a hero.

Less than five months later, our entire team sat at our conference room table aghast, with tears in our eyes. Like everyone else in the U.S., we witnessed the tragedy of September 11 on television. The phones were silent, and no work was completed. We returned home to our families, realizing nothing in the United States would ever be the same.

But the next day, the fraud resumed.

Chapter Eight
The Fire Triangle

We endured many events in our Little Havana outpost, both in our lives and on the job. I was already familiar with many types of fraud, but there was one I hadn't led yet as a manager. When a "total burn" was called in, it was all hands on deck. No claim is more complex or volatile.

Our company had a phenomenal SIU school to teach us how to investigate arson cases. It was similar to the FBI's Quantico, which uses a fake town, "Hogan's Alley," to train its agents in crime scenarios. For our class, the company would acquire an actual farmhouse in rural Illinois. They would fill the house with evidence and clues, douse it with gasoline, and then burn it.

For the two-week training, our teams had to solve the fictional arson case. We had to rake through debris to search for evidence. The instructors had hired SIU managers from around the country to act as the homeowners, witnesses, and experts. The company flew in attorneys for the imminent mock trial, complete with a judge and jury.

After days sifting through fake personal items and questioning witnesses, we would return to our hotel to work together on laptops. We had to work night and day to solve the case, and no day was less than twelve hours.

The arsons were staged with painstaking detail. Phony records to indicate a bankruptcy had been scattered within the debris. Our instructors once bought five-gallon jugs of gasoline at a fuel station using all pennies to pay for it—and then dropping all the coins on the floor. That way, when we interviewed the local gas stations to ask if they could recall any unusual gasoline purchases, the merchant would always remember it.

After we had survived the class and solved the crime, we all flew home exhausted and with a sense of satisfaction—and a souvenir photo of us posing in front of a blazing home being prepared for the next class.

But like the Quantico town that used rubber bullets and actors, handling an arson case in the real world was vastly more grueling.

The first "total burn" I was involved in was a large two-story Miami home worth a half-million dollars (well over a million today). The homeowner said he and his family had been vacationing in the Keys when the fire occurred. Fortunately, they also brought their three dogs.

A neighbor had seen smoke in the middle of the night. When the fire department arrived, it was a total loss.

One of our first tasks was to hire a certified origin and cause (O&C) expert. These specialists arrive at the scene and work with the fire departments to investigate how the fire started. These forensic experts have credentials beyond the talents of our team. Our job was to investigate the facts surrounding the entire case, utilizing the expert's findings, to arrive at a conclusion.

I must preface this by stating the field of fire investigation is one of the most complex forensic sciences due to the evidence altered or destroyed by the fire itself. Certified investigators adhere to strict standards published by the National Fire Protection Association (NFPA). It would require an entire series of books to describe the scientific and legal technicalities.

With our new fire, we quickly noticed two red flags. First, the homeowner was reportedly out of town at the time of the fire. This included his grown children and relatives who lived with them. Most legitimate structure fires require human intervention, such as a fire while cooking or from cigarettes. It was fortuitous that everyone was gone at the time of the fire.

The second indicator was that they'd brought their three dogs with them. That would've been quite the road trip, and this was before the proliferation of dogs staying at hotels. Arsonists usually make sure their pets stay out of harm's way.

With any arson case, we had to prove the three sides of the "fire triangle": motive, means, and opportunity. If we couldn't prove any one side, it'd be almost impossible to make a case for arson or insurance fraud. There was no room for error.

Motive is the "why." With insurance fraud, the motive is usually financial gain—money, the root of all evil and so forth.

Could arson ever have a non-financial motive? Absolutely, with such things as hate crimes, revenge, or retaliation. In those non-financial scenarios, insurance could still provide coverage. Example: an angry ex-business partner burns your house down.

In my years of experience, most arson cases involved someone planning a big payday. Perhaps their business was going bankrupt, their home was

in foreclosure, or they had lost their job. Maybe it'd be faster money than trying to sell their property during an economic downturn.

The other two sides of the triangle, "means" and "opportunity," are about how the fire occurred. "Opportunity" implies if the suspect had an occasion to burn the property. Were they in town? Did they have keys or access? Did they have an alibi? Maybe they hired a third party to start the fire. "Means" indicates if there was evidence of an intentional burn such as an ignitable fuel, a staged kitchen accident, or an explosive device.

The strongest cases of arson always had a solid triangle, such as the insured was in the area around the time of the fire, he had recently lost his job or was going through a divorce, and gasoline samples were found in the home. Cases that straightforward happened all the time.

If we were missing one element, such as motive, it'd be a tough case to pursue. What if the suspect was wealthy and had zero financial motive to burn their own home? If one of Jeff Bezos's vacation homes burned, that would not be the best case to take to trial with an arson for profit defense.

For our Miami fire, all local SIU investigators were summoned for the "dig-out." Once the fire department had concluded its efforts and our expert had finished documenting the damage and taking samples, our team arrived to inspect what was left.

Getting dirty at the scene was the best training—hands-on. We had to wear old clothes and respirators or face masks due to potentially dangerous soot (e.g. asbestos). We thoroughly documented every room, including drawers and closets. There may be salvageable belongings. Clothes could still be in the closets. We might recover some sentimental items.

But this fire was unusual. Though the home was completely charred, telltale signs of fraud were evident right away. Sometimes it's not what you see, but what you don't see.

Chapter Nine
The Dig-Out

When I arrived, senior SIU investigators and experts were already on the scene. I learned a lot from their experience as we walked from room to room.

The two-story home was destroyed but safe enough to go inside. The debris was over a foot deep, some of it mud due to rain and water from the fire hoses. The area smelled like smoke, burnt plastics, and the rot of God-knows-what critters had perished.

My first observation of something amiss was in the living room. There were no pictures on the walls—no framed portraits, paintings, or family photos—and no charred remains of any pictures. The authorities told us that the walls—aside from soot—were still exactly as they were when the fire had been reported.

So, what does that have to do with arson? If someone plans to burn their own home, they tend to remove items that are expensive, irreplaceable, or sentimental before they torch it. In this case, when we requested past photographs of the interior, the living room had been filled with family portraits—everything from wedding pictures to the kids through the years. Those pictures had been removed prior to the fire. Had they taken the pictures with them on vacation?

What else was missing? A good reason for a statement is to ask what valuables were lost in the fire and where they were located. There is one possession that's expensive, difficult to replace, and almost impossible to destroy: a gun. As you can imagine, many Miami residents own firearms.

Mr. Insured had included guns on his list of destroyed items. When we asked where they had been stored, he was dismissive, replying he always kept his Glock 19 and Smith & Wesson .38 pistols in his bedside drawer in the master bedroom.

Our first "dig out", West Miami, April 1995

So, I knew exactly where to dig for the guns. The guns should have survived the fire. An average house fire burns at about 1,100 degrees Fahrenheit, which isn't hot enough to destroy most metals. If items are small and stored in a safe place, their chances of survival increase. Other items that can survive fires include diamonds, filing cabinets, safes, silver (melting point of about 1,800 degrees), and stainless-steel items (2,700 degrees).[28]

I easily located the master bedroom and the bedside drawers. I raked through the debris to find no guns. They would have dropped straight down. I tried the other dressers and photographed my findings. This meant no guns were present at the time of the fire. So, did Mr. Insured bring his guns on vacation? If so, why was he claiming them as lost? More good questions during an EUO.

When I checked the closets, I almost laughed. They were filled with smoky clothing, shoes, and purses, but these particular items were a huge red flag. The homeowners had claimed expensive items including designer dresses, Christian Louboutin shoes, leather bags "from Italy," and of course the Armani suits. Evidently, the arsonist had not realized the clothes in the closets might remain intact. The items I observed were ridiculous.

Arsonists have been known to buy clothes from thrift shops like Goodwill or Salvation Army. They place them in their closets and drawers, hoping they all burn into heaps of unidentifiable cinders. This arsonist had made two mistakes: One, the closed closet door had kept the clothes from burning. Two, they had purchased absurd decoy clothes: lime-green pantsuits from the '70s, orange and plaid polyester business suits, Halloween princess dresses, vinyl purses, and Walmart sneakers. It was like the home of circus clowns. More good photos for an EUO.

Arsonists have used this same tactic to adorn entire homes: second-hand furniture, old lamps, rugs, and cheap art swapped out in a home before burning it. One burned home actually had those black velvet paintings of dogs playing poker. One could then deduce, if the homeowners had removed all their expensive items *prior* to the fire, they probably needed help doing it, along with a place to store it all. Did any neighbors witness any loading or trucks? We all have neighbors who watch everything like hawks.

When we inspected the kitchen, the smell made us cringe. The food in the freezer and refrigerator had been rotting for days, and no one wanted to remove it. Our newest rep had to hold her breath and photograph the contents, not as some sort of cruel initiation, but because when we would ask people what they had lost in their fridge, they'd usually tell us Kobe beef, lobster, and bags of stone crab instead of Jeno's frozen pizza, Bud Light, and Hot Pockets.

One key piece of evidence in the kitchen was the stove. We lifted our cameras to document the controls. The burners had all been turned on prior to the fire, set to "high." The most violent flames can't rotate a knob—unusual if everyone was on vacation.

Richard Wickliffe (left) and Chris Hunter (right), April 1995

Another reason we called the scene a dig-out is because we would use shovels to rake debris so the bare floors were visible. Ignitable liquids such as gasoline can create visible damage to the floor in the shape of a puddle, with distinct burn marks in the shape of a pour. These "pour patterns" are indicative of a fire started with a flammable liquid. The patterns can include "trails," long lines of damage as if someone had gone from room to room pouring the fuel in order to spread the fire throughout the home.

Pour patterns and trails aren't enough to prove arson against the insured, but they are more indicators, and our experts had collected samples for analysis.

In our case, we did indeed observe pour patterns on the concrete floor that had been under carpet. More significantly, we found the patterns in multiple rooms, meaning the fire had *multiple points of origin.*

A fire's point of origin can help indicate possible arson. If the fire began in more than one room, it would mean two or more separate fires.

Applying logic, what are the odds of two natural fires occurring at the same time? It'd be like lightning striking the house in two places. Did the fires start in unusual locations such as the middle of a large room or in a closet?

With any fire, we never automatically presumed it was arson. The vast majority of our fires were accidental, such as kitchen fires, electrical fires, or smoking-related fires. But if the case came to our SIU team, it meant there were already other indicators.

We had to rule out all natural and accidental causes. Combined with a financial motive, many courts have held the exclusion of accidental sources was a solid basis for arson. In every case we took to trial, our experts were always asked if they had ruled out all potential non-arson causes.

Another necessary disclaimer: Most of the fires we investigated turned out to be valid, payable claims. As I have told countless plaintiff attorneys, it's much easier for us to pay a claim and move on. Keeping a file open for years—with all the associated expenses—was never a goal.

With our fires, the most frequent non-fraudulent causes included:

- Electrical fires from damaged wiring, overloaded circuits, or faulty appliances
- Smoking-related fires: falling asleep while smoking or improper disposal of cigarettes or cigars
- People (kids) mishandling matches, candles, or fireworks
- Lightning, especially during dry months

With this particular Miami fire, our experts had ruled out all accidental or natural sources. We discovered multiple points of origin for the fire. Samples tested positive for a "Class 2 petroleum distillate" (gasoline). We had proof that pans on the stove had also contained flammable fluids. In addition, we had evidence of misrepresentation of the value of their clothing, furniture, jewelry, and belongings.

That was only the beginning. We proceeded to request sworn statements from all family members. We checked for bankruptcies and tax liens. We conducted neighborhood canvasses for anything peculiar the neighbors might have noticed.

Per Florida Statute 626.9891, if we suspected *any* variety of fraud, we had to report the case to state and local agencies, including the Division of Insurance Fraud and the NICB. They could then involve law enforcement, which could initiate concurrent investigations.

Mr. Homeowner was going to wish he had just put his house up for sale.

Chapter Ten
Bad Actors

No one has ever accused an arsonist of being a genius. According to an older 1987 study in the *FBI Law Enforcement Bulletin,* the majority of profiled arsonists had a below-normal IQ, falling somewhere between 70 and 90 (a score of 100 is considered average). About one in four fell below the 70 IQ range. Seventy-two percent were males, and 56 percent had marginal or less income.[29]

I have no reason to dispute those figures. I call it the fallacy of superhero villains; if they were such masterminds, they would be able to make the same amount of money doing something legitimate.

Some arsonists were creative. Many were weak souls who had become desperate. Some were careless fools who could have killed themselves or others. A few were downright heinous.

For my first Miami fire, the case was textbook. We were able to prove fraud with a litany of offenses. Mr. Insured had filed for bankruptcy and had been four months behind on his mortgage (motive). Our experts uncovered multiple points of origin, and samples tested positive for gasoline (means). Though his family had gone to the Keys for vacation, Sunpass toll data and cellphone records showed Mr. Insured had commuted to and from Miami for work (opportunity). The next-door neighbor had seen the family loading a U-Haul several days before the fire (even more opportunity).

The fire marshal ruled the fire as arson, triggering a criminal investigation. By the time we asked the insured and his wife to attend examinations under oath, they had hired an attorney. Due to the pending criminal case, their attorney told us they wanted to "take the fifth" and not answer any of our questions.

The man had evidently watched too many TV crime dramas. He did not realize the Fifth Amendment privilege against self-incrimination did not apply to civil matters such as our insurance investigation. It's almost uniformly held across the nation that an insured can't avoid the contractual duty to attend an EUO by demanding Fifth Amendment protection. Our insureds "taking the fifth" to dodge our questioning was a breach of their cooperation duties, adding another cause for denial.

At their attorney's advice, the homeowners withdrew their claim before we could get statements from all family members, which I'm certain would've proven amusing. Imagine getting a bunch of teenagers and grandparents to recite the same story. I had also been looking forward to showing a jury enlarged photos of all the garish clothing and belongings found in the house.

Their attorney probably believed by withdrawing their claim, it would make our company appear to be less of a victim to soften the criminal case. "The company never had to pay..."

However, the fact his client committed arson was enough for a conviction. Arson is a first-degree felony in Florida, punishable by up to thirty years in prison and a $10,000 fine. Our company was still a victim because our policies protect mortgage companies. Despite their withdrawal and our fraud defenses, we still had to satisfy their six-figure mortgage. There was still over $100,000 in equity denied to the insured, which he would never see.

As for any feelings of frustration that we still had to pay over six figures for such a brazenly fraudulent claim, that's the point of this book. We are all paying for the fraud.

New Kitchens for Plantains

Our team didn't get many full-home arsons in the Miami area. My theory is because of the high values and poor opportunity. Home prices were high, so it'd be much easier to just sell the house. And South Florida is so crowded, including countless zero-lot-line communities, that it'd be impossible to start a fire without having a dozen witnesses.

That didn't mean we never had fire cases. Kitchen fires became the fraudster's favorite scheme to give their home a facelift. The fires were small, easy to fake, and could cause exponential damage. The best part of the scheme: no fire department involved.

How many of us grew up in a home that looked like *The Brady Bunch*? Lime-green mica kitchen counters. Mosaic floor tiles that haven't been produced since the '80s. Cheap laminate cabinets. How would you like a new, updated kitchen (and all the adjoining rooms) for the price of frozen French fries?

Correction: In Miami, it was always fried plantains. North of Miami-Dade County, it was French fries. I'm not being facetious.

The ploy started with the homeowner reporting a kitchen fire. They would tell us they had been frying plantains/fries when they had to suddenly step out, either to run to Walmart or to pick up Champ from soccer. But when they left, they forgot to turn off the stove. A fire from the pan ensued. Flames traveled up to the roll of paper towels, then to the cabinets to destroy the entire kitchen.

"When I got home, I acted fast," they would say, trying to sound responsible. "I keep a fire extinguisher in the kitchen, so I was able to put out the fire myself. Thankfully, I didn't have to call 911 or the fire department."

Then they would add, "But the pan was so hot, I dropped it. It chipped the tile floor, so that needs to be replaced. That tile hasn't been made in decades, so it can't be matched. And that tile runs throughout the entire house, so…"

It wouldn't end there. "The thick smoke got sucked into my air handler and then blown back into the entire home, ruining my clothing, bedding, drapes, carpet…"

So, for the price of a frozen box of whatever, the homeowner's claim is for new kitchen counters, cabinets, stove, new tile throughout the house, painted walls, new carpet, drapes, designer clothing, *Armani* suits…

Fraudsters must have meetings to share schemes with each other because the same set of facts were reported time and time again: plantains… Ran to Walmart… I put the fire out myself…. The entire deception was contained indoors, so there were no nosy neighbors or witnesses. The homeowner "admitted" to being at fault: "careless me…" No fire departments got involved, so no official reports or investigation.

It may be a small consolation, to the best of my recollection, we proved arson or fraud in many of those claims. The same fire triangle and SIU investigation applied. There was always a financial motive, opportunity was already admitted, and they usually added fuel to ensure the fire would be sufficient to cause the needed damage.

In one case, my investigator asked the insured where the culprit frying pan was. Mrs. Insured replied it was so damaged, she had tossed it onto the patio. We were able to retrieve the pan and test the residue. It came back positive as a Class II combustible liquid. She had to explain why she had fried plantains in kerosene.

The Fire Merchant

In the mid-2000s, the entire ruse was revealed when a rogue public adjuster was arrested. In a perfect world, public adjusters are licensed professionals who policyholders hire to assist with the claims process in exchange for a commission, such as 20 percent of the insurance settlement. An example might include an elderly insured who doesn't understand the claims process. The public adjuster (PA) would help them document their claim.

However, as with many professions, there are bad apples who can give the rest a bad name. Unscrupulous PAs have been known to stage entire claims for profit or inflate actual claims to increase their commissions. Friends of mine who work as ethical public adjusters strongly dislike those who tarnish the reputation of their profession.

With the kitchen fires, the arrested PA testified about his role in the scheme. He explained he would go door-to-door, reciting his pitch to homeowners, something as direct as, "How would you like a new kitchen?" He would then promise to handle the entire claim with the insurance company, telling homeowners they had "nothing to lose."

The PA would create the fires for the homeowners. He would tell them to leave the house while he started a fire on the stove. He would wait long enough for the flames to create suitable damage, then put out the fire with an extinguisher.

That wasn't the inventive part. The PA demonstrated to authorities how he created the smoke damage. He would make a torch with an oily rag on the end of a stick. He'd light the torch, which created black smoke. He'd then raise the stick to each air vent on the ceiling so it would leave blotches of soot. He would repeat the process for every vent in the house to fake that smoke had allegedly "blown" into each room.

After learning about this tactic, SIU teams began to counter it by simply removing the air vent covers and testing the inside of the ducts. If swabs from the interior tested negative for smoke, how could smoke have blown out?

Arguably one of the most criminal public adjusters in Florida to date, Jorge Espinosa Sr., was sentenced to 20 years in prison in 2018 for intentionally setting homes on fire. Prosecutors said Espinosa had torched homes and caused water damage for the sole purpose of filing fraudulent insurance claims. He had even recruited homeowners to assist in the schemes.

He operated the arson scheme with his 35-year-old wife and his son, Espinosa Jr. Ironically, his son was once a Miami police officer who left the force after shooting an unarmed teenager in the back, according to the *Miami Herald*.[30] Espinosa Jr. was also a public adjuster and would reportedly carry a gun in his waistband. He would lift his shirt to anyone reluctant to help with their plans so they could see he was armed.[31]

Espinosa Sr.'s wife, who was also a public adjuster, and his son were arrested along with twenty others, as well as complicit homeowners who had been looking to profit.

The Espinosas had hired what they called "fire chasers" to infiltrate neighborhoods and knock door to door, looking for any homeowner willing to destroy their own house, or at least enough to remodel a kitchen.

A Craigslist job posting for a "fire chaser" promised that candidates with the ability "to perform and deliver in a high-pressure, cut-throat environment of fire chasing will be given serious consideration."[32] The ad promised a possibility of earning up to six figures in the first year: "$1000 a week is just a start." The job always paid in cash to avoid federal income taxes.

Espinosa Sr. pleaded guilty to 28 counts of arson, racketeering, conspiracy, organized schemes to defraud, and multiple counts of insurance fraud. He was also ordered to pay $1.9 million in restitution. The arrests were the result of "Operation Flames and Flood" carried out by the Florida Fire Marshal's Office and the Miami-Dade Police's arson unit.

Miami State Attorney Katherine Fernandez Rundle said in a statement, "Insurance policyholders were Espinosa's real victims."[33] Espinosa made more than 50 false claims with more than 14 insurance carriers. Authorities said the schemes had cost insurance carriers and policyholders over $14 million in losses.

Our company had been a victim of Espinosa's conduct for years. SIU teams from multiple carriers had contributed data to help authorities with their investigation. In similar cases, homeowners would roll over on the public adjusters, confessing to the entire scheme. They had no allegiance to these strangers who had come knocking on their doors offering something for nothing. And if the homeowners weren't arrested for insurance fraud, they were left with charred kitchens they would have to repair on their own dime.

The next time someone comes knocking, consider, *if it sounds too good to be true...*

Chapter Eleven
The Rogues Gallery

Though some schemes can seem almost ludicrous, the act of committing arson is a dangerous and sometimes lethal crime. Some offenders were much worse than others.

As I have reminisced with investigators and colleagues, our most memorable cases stand out because of their creativity or absurdity. However, there were a few that could summon nightmares.

Burned Alive

Our SIU team investigated an arson case where the perpetrator misunderstood the flammability of gasoline fumes—and this can serve as a cautionary tale for the next time you or your children are tinkering in your garage or workshop.

Liquid gasoline itself does not ignite; it's the fumes that can explode. Gasoline vapors are denser than air, so they sink and collect at the lowest point. An open flame is not necessary to ignite gas vapors; a single spark can cause the vapors to ignite.

This can be hazardous for an amateur arsonist.

How many movies show the hero or villain walking away from a gasoline-soaked home or vehicle? As they toss a cigarette over their shoulder, it twirls in slow-motion before igniting the fuel, creating a path of flames to race along the surface, climaxing into a mesmerizing fireball.

Just like people "taking the fifth," aspiring fraudsters seem to watch a lot of movies. So, can a cigarette ignite a pool of gasoline? The brief answer is "not exactly."

Variables with the fumes, airflow, and the temperature of the cigarette are hard to calculate, but the probability is low that a blaze would result from tossing a cigarette into a puddle of gas. In one study, researchers attempted over 2,000 different scenarios between a cigarette and gasoline, and not a single attempt resulted in the fuel igniting. [34]

Theories as to why it doesn't work include the rapid formation of ash on the cigarette, fumes drifting away from the area making ignition impossible, and the fact that cigarettes are at their hottest when the smoker inhales a drag.[35] A cigarette, when not inhaled and tossed in the air, rapidly loses heat.

On our team, stories about accidental gasoline fires demanded further investigation. People used excuses such as, "I fell asleep while smoking near a gas can." When we asked one man why he had gasoline in his home, he replied he'd been cleaning motorcycle parts in his living room.

In one horrendous criminal case, a man claimed he "accidentally threw gasoline on his girlfriend" while she was smoking and she burst into flames. That was proven by experts to be impossible. Thankfully, she suffered only minor burns, and he went to jail.

However, using a lighter is another story. It seems most fraudsters used cigarettes in their tales because it sounded plausible and accidental. A lighter seems more deliberate. But combine a lighter with a poor understanding of fumes, and it's a formula for disaster.

Back to our perpetrator who misunderstood the flammability of fumes. Our SIU team received a claim for a full-home fire. This case was different because the homeowner had to be rushed to the hospital with third-degree burns to 80 percent of his body. It was uncertain if he would survive.

Despite the unfortunate condition of the man, we needed to know the circumstances surrounding the fire. Since he was unable to communicate, we contacted his wife, who was also on the policy. We learned she lived at a different address; they were separated with an impending divorce. As we proceeded with our investigation, fraud indicators began to emerge.

We discovered it was a combative divorce. Her husband had filed Chapter 13 bankruptcy in an attempt to halt child support payments (not realizing bankruptcy does not relieve someone of child support obligations). Second, their house had been up for sale for a year without any bites. The house needed a new roof and air conditioner and was in an overall state of disrepair. Not least of all, the wife told us her husband had threatened to do something "drastic."

The wife hired an attorney. They knew of the "innocent co-insured doctrine," also called the innocent spouse doctrine, which means the intentional acts of one insured will not affect coverage for the "innocent" co-insured. For example, if a husband decides to commit insurance fraud and the wife is a law-abiding citizen who knows nothing about it, she is still protected. This would apply to the children's belongings as well. After all, what did they do wrong?

Florida courts have held the intentional misbehavior of one insured can only apply to the innocent co-insured if the policy clearly states that.[36] We honored the innocent co-insured doctrine and worked together with the wife and her attorney to continue our investigation.

The fire marshal had concluded the fire was arson. Collected samples had tested positive for gasoline, which had been used to start and spread the fire.

When the burned homeowner had healed to the point of coherence, the state prosecutor was granted permission to question him. Our SIU investigator Eduardo was invited to attend for any questions relating to our investigation.

The attorneys and Eduardo had to meet the insured in his hospital room. The man was bandaged from head to toe like a mummy. Eduardo described the scene as disconcerting. He could only see the man's bloodshot eyes. The man was propped up in bed and answered each question with a pained slur. With little more to lose, the man confessed to starting the fire. He had doused the home with gasoline, room to room, then stood at the door with a lighter.

Unlike a cigarette's inability to start a fire, the sparking mechanism in a lighter can be disastrous in the presence of gas fumes. A person would be safer walking through a gas station with a lit cigarette than igniting one with a lighter while standing near a puddle of gasoline.

Ironically, our homeowner had planned to light that cliché cigarette to toss into the house. But by the time he stood by the door, the invisible fumes had surrounded him. When he flicked the lighter, his entire body was engulfed in flames.

Despite any sympathy we had for the man's condition and his immeasurable pain, we had to investigate the case on its own merits. We denied the claim as an intentional, fraudulent act (arson). The state arrested him for the crimes of arson and reckless endangerment, topped with the additional charge of insurance fraud.

His innocent wife was paid for her portion of the contents, and their mortgage was satisfied.

Ritual Sacrifices Gone Wrong

To set the ominous scene: Imagine an investigator entering a charred building to find symbols written in blood, with animal carcasses including beheaded roosters and a goat's head nailed to the wall. In South Florida, specifically Little Havana, we investigated such fire scenes where something unnerving had occurred.

Santería is a religion that has been practiced in South Florida for decades. Santería, Spanish for "worship of saints," is a blend of the African religion of *Yoruba* and Roman Catholicism. It developed in Cuba in the late 19th century, and now over 100,000 people practice the religion in South Florida.[37] Though it's shrouded in mystery, its ceremonies can include animal sacrifices, specifically to cure a loved one's illness.

"They believe that by offering the blood or energy from an animal, that the animal is taking on the illness of that individual," Tori Lockler, a professor of religious studies at the University of South Florida, told the *Tampa Bay Times*.[38]

Some Santería rites involve leaving the animal carcasses at a cemetery, delivered to specific graves to summon help from their deceased relatives.

I have friends who have visited their loved ones' graves in Miami to find the remains of headless roosters scattered on the ground. They were understandably horrified, regardless of the religion's legitimacy.

In even worse cases, graves have been robbed for human bones to be used in rituals. Acts of vandalism at Miami's oldest cemeteries have not only disrupted the remains of the deceased but also affected the preservation of historic sites that had been neglected for years. At Miami's Lincoln Memorial Park, the cemetery for some of the area's most prominent past leaders, three graves, including one of a child, were broken into for bones.[39]

In a notable incident in the upscale suburb of Coral Gables, just a few miles from our office, neighbors complained about shrieking goats. When police conducted an armed raid on the home, they found goats, chickens, and pigeons being slaughtered for a ritual. The police detained the worshipers for three hours until the State Attorney's Office said the ceremony was not illegal.[40]

In Miami, it was deemed the U.S. Constitution protects the humane killing of animals in religious ceremonies. In 1996, the U.S. Supreme Court ruled that animal sacrifice for religious purposes was protected from prosecution. However, county authorities can require that worshipers perform a sacrifice humanely, and properly dispose of the carcasses, rather than dumping them in cemeteries.

Our SIU team came across Santería rituals because they can involve candles and fire. We entered fire scenes in Miami that contained evidence that a Santería ceremony had taken place. We found goat heads and beheaded roosters with their legs wrapped in ribbons. Many of the worshipers—who were also our paying customers—were forthright during statements about what they had been doing at the time of the fire.

In other words, accidentally destroying their home with candles and burning herbs had not been part of their plan. Authorities deemed it accidental and not arson—therefore, it was a payable claim. Our company was not about to go to trial to wrangle with Supreme Court rulings regarding freedom of religion.

Some consequences of these rituals were much more tragic. Similar to the case described previously, the practices have resulted in people burning themselves or dying.

One woman accidentally burned herself alive during a Santería ceremony. A friend of the victim, who had witnessed the incident, told police that the woman had anointed her nude body with a flammable cologne. The perfume "Florida Water" is commonly used in rituals associated with Santería, Wicca, and Voodoo practices. It is a citrus cologne with an alcohol content as high as 75 percent.

After the woman covered herself with the elixir, according to her friend, she made the sign of the cross using a lit candle. However, she held the candle too close to her body, igniting the fumes. Her entire body burst into flames.

Two police officers on patrol heard screams coming from inside the building, according to the *New York Post*. They kicked down the door to find the woman dead. Her friend said she had been performing a Santería cleansing ritual to be cured of an undetermined illness.[4142]

The Most Heinous Yet

We investigated one case where the arsonist was monstrous to an unconscionable degree. To this day, the man's scheme still makes me cringe.

It started with the same drill: The bankrupt homeowner wanted to torch his house to make his debts vanish. He had removed all his expensive property and clothing, but it's what he left behind that was horrific: two dogs.

Earlier in this book, I wrote, "Arsonists usually make sure their pets stay out of harm's way." Key word: *usually*.

If it's a red flag when someone takes their pets *away* from the house before torching it, a more diabolical arsonist might surmise he would appear innocent, perhaps even sympathetic, if his pets perished in the fire.

In our case, after firefighters extinguished the blaze, they had to gently inform our tearful insured that his pets had not survived.

In fact, the homeowner kept reminding us that he had lost his beloved canines. During every encounter and statement, he'd break into tears about how he would never see his dogs again. He had held them as newborn puppies.... He had trained them.... They were his best friends.

Our SIU investigator was also overcome with emotion. As a compassionate animal lover, she asked the man questions for her own curiosity. What kind of dogs were they? Did he have pictures of them? How old were they?

Suspicions slowly began to emerge. The man couldn't get his dogs' names straight. He **had no** pictures and couldn't identify their species. "They're just mutts." Other indicators appeared as well. The man had been unemployed and on the verge of foreclosure. He said he had been alone at a bar at the time of the blaze but couldn't remember which one.

When our investigator conducted a neighborhood canvass, the man's next-door neighbors didn't know he had any dogs. In today's society, even if people aren't friendly with their immediate neighbors, they usually know if they own dogs.

We regularly used public record searches during our investigations. Based on the man's curious demeanor about his pets, we brainstormed one public record we had never requested before: from Miami's Animal Services Department.

For transparency about medical and safety records of dogs and cats, the county provided records upon request. We located two county animal shelters within a ten-mile radius of the insured's home. After formal queries at both locations, our worst fears were confirmed. The homeowner had adopted two dogs from a local shelter several days before the fire. He had purchased them with cash and declined to pay for any optional vaccinations.

Our entire team was revolted as we assembled the pieces. Our insured had acquired two dogs for the sole purpose of burning them inside his house to avoid suspicion.

As investigations from the police, fire marshals, and SIU converged, the authorities became equally enraged with the same conclusion. Defenseless animals, which wanted nothing more than to be accepted into a loving home, had been adopted by a monster. The State Attorney's Office threw the proverbial book at the man, who was jailed for the maximum sentence.

Despite our teammates' diverse personal beliefs, we all agreed there would be no punishment too harsh for this man.

PART FOUR –
ORGANIZED CRIME
GROUPS

Chapter Twelve
Tonight's Episode Featuring...

Our company produced a monthly video program called *Claims Video News,* shared throughout the country to profile interesting cases and inspirational company stories. The show's producers had begun to hear chatter about some of our team's bizarre and intriguing projects.

My area boss Don Johnson called me to say corporate had approved our request to help U.S. Customs at Port Everglades. When we submitted a proposal to be part of the unique project, it caught the eye of the *Claims Video News* team.

The theft of high-end vehicles was on the rise. To fuel the problem, people were unable to afford their overleveraged cars and gas-guzzling SUVs. People wanted their vehicles to vanish, and thieves wanted them.

The thieves exported many of the stolen vehicles overseas. Fort Lauderdale's Port Everglades is one of the busiest container ports in Florida and ranked among the top twenty busiest in the U.S.[43] Sixty-one percent of its cargo was linked to Central and South America.

"Drug lords are taking your vehicles," a U.S. Customs agent said to me bluntly. He told us luxury vehicles were too expensive to legally import into South America. It was cheaper and easier to have thieves steal them in Florida, then have them smuggled into Colombia. They would conceal the vehicles in shipping containers, falsely recording them as something else.

There were exorbitant taxes and duties to import a legitimate vehicle into Colombia. In addition to the cost of a vehicle, there was a 35 percent import tariff, plus a 16 percent consumption tax.[44] So, a $50,000 vehicle would cost an honest buyer over $75,500.

In our fraud world, "owner give-ups" were on the rise, where a vehicle owner wanted to get rid of their car through illicit means. Maybe they couldn't afford it, or it was a lease with excessive miles. The owner paid a thief to make it vanish, then they fraudulently reported it stolen.

U.S. Customs and Border Protection asked for our help to inspect cargo containers. Agents with the National Insurance Crime Bureau (NICB) invited multiple carriers' SIU teams and asked us to search outgoing containers headed for South America.

It was a win-win for U.S. Customs; they had to do the job anyway, and we were excited to do the work for them. We all thought it was fun, like a field trip, and we would order lunch for everyone. It was also a great opportunity to connect with our SIU colleagues from other companies.

The *Claims Video News* team from our corporate office thought it would make a remarkable story. The host of the series was a company employee who looked like a textbook image for "handsome broadcaster." The man, "Lyle," was tall with impeccably coiffed hair. Lyle took his job seriously, and he indeed would have been the perfect anchorman.

We were told Lyle and his crew would be arriving in Miami to profile our team working hand-in-hand with U.S. Customs. His crew included two consultants whom I had met in SIU school (remember the training at the burning farmhouses?) and two camera people.

It was fun having them visit, especially watching the culture shock. Lyle and his team were from the Midwest, and it was their first time meeting us at our Little Havana office. For the morning welcome reception, I wanted to offer things they couldn't get at home, including Cuban coffees, guava pastries, and *pastelitos de carne,* which were spicy, meat-filled pastries.

We scheduled an introductory meeting in our conference room. Lyle swaggered into the room, surrounded by the others like an entourage. I understood how the man could command the camera. We brought out refreshments as we outlined our day.

As Lyle was holding court with his stories, he bit into a *pastelito de carne.* He instantly recoiled and spewed its contents all over the table. We all paused, uncertain if he was choking.

He shouted, "There's hamburger in my donut!"

Lyle ended up loving the local pastries and wanted to bring a box back home.

After snacks and Cuban caffeine, we drove the crew to visit the Division of Insurance Fraud office in downtown Miami. The camera crew wanted shots of the skyline, probably envisioning the Miami of TV and film. The city is a vibrant metropolis with unique experiences unlike anywhere in the U.S., with its food, nightlife, and beaches. But locals also know downtown can be another story. Unlike pedestrian cities with around-the-clock commerce like New York or Chicago, downtown Miami pretty much exists for the business sector, Monday through Friday, 9 to 5. With vagrants and street crime, a visit beyond those hours could be risky.

When we parked off NW 2nd Avenue, the camera crew wilted. They readied their cameras only to realize the scene was unworthy of their glossy program—just a few figures sleeping under trees and empty grocery bags waltzing down the sidewalk, caught in a breeze. Perplexed, they asked me where all the Art Deco was. I promised to take them to South Beach after our field trip.

Our day at Port Everglades was exhilarating. Over the years, we benefited from having valuable contacts in local police, as well as agents from the FBI, ATF, Secret Service, the State Attorney's Office, and even the Coast Guard. This project introduced us to men and women with U.S. Customs and Border Protection, who would go on to help us with future cases.

At the port, in the shadow of stacked cargo containers, the Customs agents smiled at our arrival. Teams of civilians were there, eager to do part of their jobs for them. They split us into groups and led us to outgoing containers. A few of our reps remained on the sidelines with laptops to check vehicle identification numbers (VINs) for any recovered vehicles.

Taped to each container were manifest documents to identify its contents. Some listed textiles, building supplies, or clothing. An agent would snip the nylon security tie, open its doors, and we'd check the container's contents. Nine out of ten contained what they were supposed to.

However, roughly every tenth try, we would find a vehicle that wasn't expected to be there. One was covered by mattresses. One SUV was hidden behind bales of hay. We would crawl to read off the VIN through the windshield. Many of the vehicles had already been reported stolen.

When we ran the VIN for a gorgeous red Porsche, it came back as insured with our company. It had just been reported stolen from a mall two days earlier. But here's the clincher: That container had been at the port for two weeks. That meant the insured had been told to "wait a few days" before reporting it stolen. They hadn't counted on people inspecting the containers.

In another case, a pristine black Denali SUV hadn't yet been reported stolen. We called the insurance agent from the port with instructions to contact us immediately if the owner reported it stolen. That case would come straight to our team.

The *Claims Video News* crew relished the operation. Lyle got *exclusive* interviews with our brave U.S. Customs agents. They caught vehicle recoveries on film. The camera guys captured long shots of Fort Lauderdale and the surrounding cruise ships.

Lyle and his crew featured the story in their next edition. The episode involved professional thieves, illegal cargo, and working with U.S. agents, all surrounded by Florida's beauty. It came off like a gripping episode of *Dateline*. The same crew returned a couple years later for another one of our team's projects. It was fun bringing a copy of the episode home to show the family. My wife gaped, "That's what you do all day?"

As much as we enjoyed the port, I had moments of clarity. Career criminals had been involved with these thefts. Even if a person had paid someone to make their car vanish, it required organized thieves to ship them. *Who did they work for?* Someone had to mastermind the crimes.

I should also mention that I am five feet, seven inches tall. At that time, I was one of the youngest and shortest men on the scene. When they needed someone to crawl into a tightly packed shipping container, who do you think they chose?

"SIU Rich, you're on deck!" a Customs agent yelled, pointing into a pitch-dark container.

Rather than pause, I dove right in. I climbed over boxes and bales like Spider-Man, excited to look for hidden vehicles.

"But be careful," the man then shouted. "Drug lords sometimes put booby traps in these things."

I froze, mid-crawl. *Drug lords set traps?* I heard the echo of the agents' laughter behind me, not completely sure if they were kidding.

I had no proof the vehicles were really going to drug lords, but I had no better explanation. These were lavish cars and ominous black SUVs, arranged to go to *someone* in South America who had serious funds and influence. Were our investigations crossing lines with cartels? If so, they would not be the only organized crime groups we would encounter.

The realization that fraud was being exploited by organized criminals wasn't new, but it had become more prevalent. Our police contacts relayed unnerving accounts of Russian organized crime expanding into Miami. Former drug dealers had discovered they could earn more money without using a gun. Even darker crimes such as human trafficking had slithered into our SIU.

I didn't discuss those parts of the job around the dinner table. But it was one of the reasons why the work could never be described as boring.

Chapter Thirteen
Little Moscow – The Russian Mob

As we investigated large thefts and injury cases, a new trend developed. Some fraudulent claims seemed to be coordinated by known crime rings. Organized Eastern European crimes (the preferred term for "Russian Mafia") had begun to eclipse other organized crime in South Florida. And according to the *National Institute of Justice Journal*, "Fraud is the most common type of crime among Russian criminals in the United States." [45]

Within law enforcement, the term "Eurasian mafia" became the most common label since "Russian mafia" would be inaccurate, as the groups also included Ukrainians, Georgians, Belarusians, and Chechens.

For the state attorneys who prosecuted our cases, ordinary citizens who submitted inflated claims out of desperation were no longer a top concern. The growth in organized activity had become a more significant and costly threat.

"Eurasian organized crime is our number-one priority," an undercover FBI agent from the Miami office said. [46] North Miami Beach, where many reputed ringleaders had relocated, along with many honest and hardworking immigrants from the former Soviet Union, had earned the nickname "Little Moscow."

Their innovative crimes first entered our awareness with cases that seemed modest. They weren't multimillion-dollar heists. People were reporting expensive jewelry and watches stolen while out at nightclubs. The cases came to our team when the victims said they couldn't remember what had happened or who they had been with when they were robbed. And though watches may seem small in scale, they included Rolexes for over $25,000, and even Patek Philippes for over $100,000 each. This was in addition to their credit cards being depleted.

Before we understood the gravity of the players, I investigated one of the cases on their turf. I visited one of their infamous Russian nightclubs, alone.

A wealthy man had reported his $80,000 Piaget stolen after meeting a lady at a Miami nightspot. I figured an upscale club would have security video. The man told me where he sat at the bar and the timeframe. My plan was to convince the club's management to show me the video, presuming they were conscientious businesspeople.

In prior cases, we'd had luck with managers of clubs sharing their video, even at less-reputable gentlemen's clubs. In the *Jesus and the Last Supper* jewelry case, we had visited a strip club, and the management was happy to share the video because they wanted to dodge any liability. Any time one of our investigators went to such an establishment, I always recommended they bring a second employee as a witness to avoid any odd accusations.

However, when I decided to visit this Russian "nightclub," I naïvely believed it was just a dinner club, so I went alone without mentioning it to my coworkers or wife. The Zolotoy club was closed on weekdays, so I decided to visit unannounced on a late Friday afternoon, hoping management would be on the premises.

When I arrived at the Zolotoy, I was perplexed at the location: a forty-year-old Art Deco strip mall. There was a gourmet market at the far end and a variety of boutiques in between. The Zolotoy looked like the latest tenant in a large space that had been other stores previously. It had blackened windows and posters advertising Russian musicians scheduled to play on weekends.

Despite their hours, the front doors were unlocked. I decided to walk in, and as I did, I was awestruck. The cavernous interior didn't match the outside. The lofty second-story ceiling had been painted black to appear infinite. From it hung enormous chandeliers, with sheer drapes to divide the room into separate areas. The floors were covered with vast Persian rugs.

As my eyes adjusted, I saw the walls were wine-red with gilded moldings. Ornate cabinets displayed priceless *Fabergé* eggs and crystal vodka bottles.

I flinched at a voice as a man approached. He was bald and pale, and I recall a spiderweb tattoo on his neck. I smiled and offered my business card, probably stammering that I was trying to confirm the facts of the theft. He frowned at the card and mumbled in a thick accent to follow him. *Should I call my wife first?* I wondered.

The man led me to a smaller, private room and told me to wait. I absorbed the space: leather booths and red and gold walls. It was adjacent to the kitchen, where I could hear the clamor of dishes.

Two men finally emerged. They looked like twins, both in their thirties, with shaven heads and wearing all black. They smiled but had cautious eyes. I made it very clear I wasn't any sort of cop. I explained my stolen watch case and asked if they had security video.

The men gazed at my card and mumbled to each other in Russian. I probably just bobbed my head at my surroundings. It's odd how our memories can retain tiny random details. For some reason, on a wall among priceless framed oil paintings was a poster of actor Mark Wahlberg, the iconic '90s black and white Calvin Klein ad with him in his underwear.

The man who seemed to be in charge finally spoke. In broken English, he told me their cameras had not been working. He uncoiled a smile and said, "Nothing bad happens here. All girls who visit here are good," implying our customer must have been lying or drunk.

At that point, the other man stepped behind me. He began to massage my shoulders. I recall the sound of his gold bracelets clinking by my ears and the burning aroma of his cologne.

I stood upright and turned. I muttered that I had to go; I was late for a meeting. I thanked the men as I marched toward the door. They just stood and I could hear their chuckles. It was odd to say the least—the men as well as the entire club.

As Little Moscow grew, other clubs opened nearby, offering elaborate ambience, Russian cuisine, and entertainment. One restaurant, the Tatiana, even showcased a caged tiger that was paraded through the dining room. Its cabaret shows finally stopped using the tiger after complaints of its poor condition, along with a viral petition that had gathered 150,000 signatures.[47]

Of course, the vast majority of Russian establishments in South Florida are legitimate. My wife and I enjoy their cuisine, and we've attended dinner shows with our friends of Russian and Ukrainian heritage.

In fact, in our SIU department, we promoted a new investigator who was fluent in Russian. The young man had a mother from Russia and a father from Cuba. His name was Sergei, and the locals called him Sergio. He proved to be immensely valuable in translating advertisements for local clinics and organizations. Additionally, Sergei introduced us to Russian and Ukrainian lunch establishments and businesses. But with our unique SIU cases, our team crossed paths with people and enterprises on the other end of the spectrum as well.

If I had known at the time what we would later discover about these crimes, I would have never visited the Zolotoy club alone. We had begun to see patterns: all the theft victims were men, in upscale lounges, specifically in Miami's South Beach, Fort Lauderdale, Palm Beach, and Boca Raton.

One burning question: Why did all the victims ask us to not tell their wives?

Attack of the B-Girls

The intriguing Russian racket had become known as the "B-Girl" scheme. With any reported robberies of jewelry or watches, our flags went up anytime the victim declared, "I woke up and couldn't remember anything."

Another curious detail included the victims asking us, "Can we please keep this claim private?" They didn't want their wives, family, or friends to know anything about it.

The B-Girl (bar girl) cases were also examples of crimes where the insureds were actually innocent—of committing insurance fraud anyway.

At the height of our investigations, six reputed members of an Eastern European network and ten B-Girls were charged with conspiring to seduce and fleece gullible Miami visitors by stealing their jewelry and draining their credit cards at private nightclubs.[48]

To initiate the scheme, Russian criminals had leased properties on Miami Beach to turn into bars and nightclubs. They flew in "B-Girls" from Eastern Europe—mostly from Latvia and Estonia—with ninety-day visas. The young ladies could be described as alluring, probably aspiring models. The mob rented apartments for the girls, and by night they would send them out to hotels and lounges in trendy upscale areas. In our cases, it was primarily South Beach.

The ladies "hunted" in packs to entice male visitors. They targeted men at bars who appeared successful, usually based on expensive clothing, jewelry, or watches. The ladies would persuade the men to bring them to "private clubs," where they would order bottles of over-priced champagne, Russian vodka, and caviar. The nightspots had stylish names such as Caviar Bar and Stars Lounge.

The FBI's arrest affidavit stated, "The clubs are not open to the public and operate solely as a front for fraud." [49] According to authorities, the girls received a 20 percent commission for bringing in customers.

In our cases, an inordinate number of victims seemed to be airline pilots. My guess is they were ideal targets. It was a lucrative profession, they would only be in town for a brief period, and they wouldn't want to risk their livelihoods or family status by reporting the crimes.

All of the victims suspected they had been drugged. We never received any forensic proof because the men refused medical treatment, perhaps out of humiliation. At the clubs, some girls would physically assist their victims in signing credit card slips. The girls propped the men up long enough to force a signature.

But why was this scheme big in Florida and not widespread in other areas? The Russian mob was preying on Florida's liberal "innkeeper laws" that require customers to pay a disputed bill up front to the merchant, and then take up any dispute with their credit company.

As a large, service-oriented state with countless restaurants and bars, Florida designed its laws to protect merchants from tourists who might run out on a tab and then flee on the next plane. Florida Statute 509.151 was designed to protect businesses from just such scenarios.[50] Based on that law, if a customer refuses to pay, even at a shady Eurasian vodka bar, the merchant can call the police and have the patron arrested.

In a B-Girl scenario—if a victim was coherent enough to dispute their bill—they would think twice when police arrived with a genuine threat of taking them to jail. If the victims filed formal grievances with their creditors, the banks could initiate their own investigation with the merchants. The bars might respond with evidence including receipts with the victim's signature, copies of their driver's license, or the worst case: security photos of them kissing a young lady.[51]

It's an almost perfect crime. And, ultimately, insurance would compensate the victims.

A case that helped publicize the scheme was when a prominent Philadelphia meteorologist claimed to be a victim of two B-Girls on South Beach. His case followed the exact pattern just described, and he used his media status to bring attention to the unique scheme.

In 2012, John Bolaris relayed his story on TV's *20/20* and in a *Playboy* article, which ultimately cost him his job as a weather forecaster in Philadelphia. Unlike most mortified victims, he decided to make his case public, including a lawsuit against his credit card company for not believing his story and destroying his credit.

He vaguely remembered meeting two "beautiful girls" on South Beach who wanted to do shots of Russian vodka at a private club. He recalled getting into a cab with them to go see a painting their friend was selling for charity. Bolaris had a hazy recollection of "signing something" and later riding in another taxi with a large painting at his side.[52]

Bolaris woke up the next morning fully clothed in his hotel room with a new painting and no memory of what had happened. He felt even more ill when he received a call from American Express informing him that over

$43,712 had been charged to his card, including caviar, a $5,000 bottle of champagne, and $2,480 for the painting.[53]

American Express refused to reverse the charges because a manager from the nightclub named Stan Pavlenko (later arrested) supplied them with photos of Bolaris at the bar using his own credit card.

Exasperated, Bolaris contacted the FBI, who launched a full investigation into Eastern European criminal activities in Miami clubs. They used a detective from Miami Beach Police, who went undercover as a dirty cop to gain information.

The cop got close to Alec Simchuk, who ultimately fled to Eastern Europe. Simchuk operated many of the targeted clubs. The FBI learned how Simchuk had coached his ladies to get the men drunk and toss out their own drinks. The clubs then charged the victims exorbitant amounts for drinks as the bar forced them to pay using the innkeeper laws.[54]

After more than a year and $1 million investigating the case, sixteen suspects, including bar managers and almost a dozen B-Girls, were arrested when they attended a fake birthday party thrown by the undercover detective. However, Simchuk and several of his ladies had already fled to their native countries.[55]

WANTED
BY THE FBI

ALEC SIMCHUK

Aliases: Olec Simchuk

DESCRIPTION

Date of Birth Used:	10/10/1966	Hair:	Balding
Place of Birth:	Russian Federation; Russia	Eyes:	Green
Height:	5'8"	Sex:	Male
Weight:	160	Race:	White
Occupation:	Unknown		

"B-Girl" ringleader wanted after fleeing to Russia

C FBI - Courtesy United States Attorney's Office for the Southern District of Florida

As a result of Bolaris's lawsuit, American Express repaid him over $43,000 from the bogus charges, plus an undisclosed amount in damages.

In an interesting twist, a year after the ringleader Simchuk escaped the country, he mysteriously returned to surrender—with a broken leg as a result of threats from the mob.

Simchuk had initially fled to Russia, which has no extradition treaty with the United States. Nearly a year later, he showed up on a flight to Miami with a broken leg. According to reports, Albert Takhalov, who was also convicted in the B-Girl case, had threatened Simchuk and his wife.[56] Russian criminals broke his leg to hinder his return to the U.S., where he intended to confess and provide testimony against his associates.

Prosecutors agreed to a lighter sentence because he had returned voluntarily from Russia. Simchuk pleaded guilty to charges of wire fraud and conspiracy to defraud the United States. He received a relatively lenient sentence of three years in a federal prison.

Altogether, 12 individuals involved in the scheme admitted their guilt, with the majority of the "B-Girls" subsequently deported. According to a court filing, two of the girls, Julija Vinogradova and Marina Turcina, testified pursuant to plea agreements to reduce their sentences.[57]

Accused "B-Girl" 24-year-old Marina Turcina of Latvia
© FBI - Courtesy United States Attorney's Office for the Southern District of Florida

Accused "B-Girl" Valeria Matsova, 22, of Estonia
© FBI - Courtesy United States Attorney's Office for the Southern District of Florida

Despite the arrests, our SIU team dealt with similar thefts over the years that followed the same pattern: our male customer met a woman at a bar, then woke up missing his valuables and suspecting he had been drugged. I'm certain most of the cases were orchestrated by organized crime. Some were perhaps copycat schemes. But in all the cases, we paid the claims, as our insureds had been the swindled victims.

Staged Injury Rings

According to a U.S. Senate hearing before the Subcommittee on European Affairs, "Eurasian organized crime enterprises have been identified in cases which include insurance fraud, generally staged auto accidents, and medical fraud involving false medical claims." [58]

Our team was aware of accidents staged for the purpose of creating fake injury cases. We had begun to uncover evidence that many cases were linked to larger organizations. It had become so prevalent and costly that our company—and most other carriers—created new SIU teams for the sole purpose of investigating organized injury rings. The specialized teams were designed to work alongside our traditional SIUs.

My team continued to investigate all varieties of fraud. If we discovered an injury case that had links to known players, we'd refer it to the organized activity team. As we worked in the field—old-school, knocking on doors—their specialized reps conducted investigations through data. To keep up with vast groups of conspirators, analytics had become an essential tool to track known parties, suspicious medical clinics, and even attorneys.

Unsurprisingly, Florida contains many dubious medical clinics, operated by an elusive mix of physicians. Many clinics seemed to have fewer visitors per day than they billed us for. Some were just "pain clinics" that scribbled prescriptions for narcotics for repeat customers.

An organized "ring" existed if we uncovered a pattern of accidents, sometimes involving the same passengers, attending the same clinics, represented by the same attorneys.

The above is a heavily abridged overview. Organized-activity investigations spanned years and required volumes of data, especially considering Florida's Personal Injury Protection ("PIP," or "no fault") coverage. Currently, PIP insurance is mandated in twelve states to pay for injuries from auto accidents regardless of fault. So, disreputable attorneys and clinics view it as a free $10,000 per person, regardless of who is at fault. Ten thousand dollars times eight people per car, plus a dozen lawsuits equals millions in tax-free proceeds for orchestrating fender-benders in parking lots.

With that much ostensibly laundered money at stake, could more devious parties be masterminding the rings?

During my tenure, in 2011, indictments for over a hundred people were filed against suspects in Miami, with associates in Los Angeles and Denver, for fraud involving staged accidents, in addition to extortion, money laundering, and smuggling firearms. Suspects were in every corner of South Florida including Miami, Sunny Isles Beach, Hallandale Beach, and Hollywood.

John Gillies, Special Agent in Charge of the FBI Miami office at the time, said, "The impact on Eurasian Organized Crime is not just from the sheer number of arrests today but from disrupting their criminal influence in our community." [59]

Three suspects from Russia and Armenia were charged with committing fraud using South Florida chiropractors and medical clinics. According to the FBI, a Hallandale medical clinic and a "family" chiropractic center paid individuals to refer them patients from staged accidents. The clinics billed insurance carriers for treatments that either they did not perform or were medically unnecessary.[60]

Bill Kuhn, former Special Agent with the NICB, told me, "The latest trend with Russian clinic ownership is they're now smart enough to keep their names off the corporate paperwork." They learned names that appear Slavic in origin could bring unwanted scrutiny. They had begun to use proxy owners for their clinics.

To illustrate the extent of the mob's influence, Miami's ringleaders had a bond with "Armenian Power," a violent Los Angeles crime organization with ties to gangs in Armenia and Russia. The Armenian Power leaders were suspects in fraud crimes that spanned from Los Angeles to Las Vegas and Miami.

Members of these groups were not rookies. Some had spent time in the Russian military, and the groups had distinct chains of command. One group's crime boss, Konstantin Grigoryan, had been a colonel in the Soviet Army.[61] His Russian-Armenian ring was caught billing insurers for over $20 million through sham medical clinics.

In the case of the Miami arrests, the alleged ringleader, Aram Khranyan, had meetings with a "thief-in-law" in Miami and Las Vegas. The term "thief-in-law" refers to a member of a select group of high-level criminals from the former Soviet Union. They receive tribute from other criminals in exchange for protection.

With the mobs' hierarchy, local bosses work for a thief-in-law from their homeland who acts as a "general," guiding their businesses and resolving disputes through violence. The general is also called a "*vor*" in Russian, a term from Stalin's labor camps for criminals. These layers hindered many investigations because the mob's chain of command could be 6,000 miles away.

Why the growth in organized injury fraud? Because it's faster money (courtesy of your insurance) and results in shorter prison sentences, if caught. Injury fraud could net the groups $30,000 a day, risking just a modest prison sentence—if they were ever convicted. A drug dealer would need to work weeks to earn that much, while risking life in prison.

The Economist called our beautiful Miami the "capital city of medical fraud." [62] Our company was billed for equipment and treatment that patients never received or didn't require. The groups enlisted desperate residents to participate in crashes for kickbacks. They recruited homeless people to obtain insurance policies and use their Social Security numbers on fraudulent invoices.

According to the Department of Justice, "Runners often recruited such individuals from soup kitchens and local welfare offices and coached them on what to say on various medical forms in order to make it falsely appear that the medical tests to which the defendants intended to subject them were medically necessary." [63]

In a parallel New York case, fraudulent clinics targeted the poor— people desperate enough to undergo needless surgeries in exchange for small payments. Patients would ask for food during meetings with their complicit attorneys. According to the DOJ, "Many of the patients did not have sufficient clothing to keep them warm during the wintertime and had poor-quality shoes." [64] The criminal organizers didn't care about the well-being of their participants.

They also targeted elderly people. Police received reports from family members who had feared their grandparents were missing, only to discover they had been picked up by a van and taken to bogus clinics to have their Medicare information recorded.

With loopholes in Medicare rules at the time, criminals with violent records—in one of our cases a convicted murderer—were able to obtain Medicare supplier licenses. Our Miami suspect, who had spent fourteen years in prison for second-degree murder, opened a business in Hialeah as a medical supplier. Applicants with felony records could only be rejected if their convictions were ten years old or less.[65] Investigators eventually suspended his license, but the clinic had already received tens of thousands of dollars in fraudulent billing.[66]

Russian brothers David and Michael Smushkevich led an organized injury ring that had spread from Los Angeles to Florida. Thirteen defendants were charged with the conspiracy estimated at $1 billion, considered the largest of its kind. [67] They used mobile labs to conduct unneeded tests on patients they had recruited. One brother was sentenced to twenty-one years in prison for fraud and money laundering. He was ordered to return $50 million in assets, pay $41 million in restitution to insurance carriers, and pay a $2.75 million fine.[68] His brother flipped, testifying for the prosecution, and received only probation. Authorities believed most of the estimated $80 million they had stolen was hidden overseas.

Auto Theft and Chop Shops

My SIU peers in California helped investigate a Russian theft operation similar to many we encountered in Florida. The ring's members included laborers from Ukraine and Western Russia. The younger members specialized in auto theft, while the senior members operated fraudulent body shops. The group sold the stolen vehicle parts to other Ukrainian and Russian criminals.

To highlight the fallacy that insurance crimes are victimless, by the time the group was arrested, their rackets had evolved into extortion, prostitution, weapons trafficking, and narcotics. According to the California Office of the Attorney General, group members were carrying firearms and had become increasingly violent.[69]

Their auto shops were actually chop shops, sites that mimic body shops to disassemble stolen vehicles in order to sell the parts. With most vehicles, the opposite of the adage is true: The sum of the parts is greater than the whole. A vehicle's many parts, sold individually, will bring in more money than trying to sell a single stolen vehicle.

The Russian ring also sold vehicles out of state with fraudulent salvage titles. Similar to our Florida vehicles being shipped through Port

Everglades to South America, the California ring shipped stolen vehicles through West Coast ports to Eastern Europe and Russia.

So how did these menacing players and schemes affect our team?

Kim, an intuitive investigator who was on our team for over a decade, had been investigating a clinic tied to suspected staged accidents. She requested examinations under oath of the two young Russian female passengers.

Only one woman showed up at our attorney's office for the examination. Kim described her as beautiful, dressed nicely, with a long blonde braid. The woman was vague when she explained how she and the other passenger worked for the driver, who was also from Russia.

When our attorney asked why her friend hadn't shown up for the examination, she replied, "She fell out of a window and is dead."

Our attorney and court reporter froze at how bluntly the woman had replied.

She went on to explain that both of them had been staying at an upscale Miami hotel when her friend mysteriously "fell" over the balcony of a high-level window. She did not elaborate, except to add that it was under criminal investigation.

Needless to say, Kim and our attorney were rattled but proceeded with the investigation. No other parties cooperated from that point forward, and the case was closed without payment. The fates of the surviving woman who testified and the driver are unknown.

When I recently spoke to the attorney we had hired for the case, he vividly recalled the woman. She told him she used to be a Russian police officer. He described her as "tough," and she testified coldly, particularly about the other woman falling to her death. According to our attorney, the medical clinic in question is still in business. Due to the players involved, our former attorney asked me to not publish his name.

In another case, we wanted to conduct a medical clinic inspection. Chris, an eager and innovative rep who I worked with for twenty years, visited the clinic to see if it was equipped to do the volume of billing we had received. We would often make impromptu visits to these places only to find an empty storefront or a tiny office with no equipment, yet they were heavily billing us.

Chris entered the clinic unannounced to see all their equipment still

wrapped in plastic. He was approached by two Russian gentlemen who were not pleased. They shouted at Chris and began to corner him around the office. He was able to flee, but when he entered his car, the men surrounded the vehicle and began to pound on the hood, shouting in Russian. Chris lifted his camera and began clicking photos of the men. When he dialed the police, they finally left.

I was shocked when Chris returned to the office and told the story. We had to file an internal threat report, but Chris's photos of the men came out great. When we shared the pictures with law enforcement, we learned the men had been boat painters one week, and the next week were operating a multimillion-dollar clinic.

As for me, I published an article, "The Russian Mafia: A Rising Threat of Fraud and Violence," for *SIU Today* magazine. I also posted it on my website, which provided monthly reports of where reader clicks originate, usually just from friends or family around the country. I was shocked to see a spike with hundreds of readers from outside the United

States. When I checked to see where, it indicated "Russian Federation." Numerous people 6,000 miles away were reading my article—and it did not paint a favorable picture.

I made the mistake of telling my wife, who was not overjoyed. "Now the Russian mafia knows about you—from your insurance job?!"

Chapter Fourteen
Gypsies in the Palace

As a different type of organized group, the word "gypsies" may conjure several images. One could be a now-offensive term for people who originated in India and now live in Europe, who travel from place to place in small numbers. Another might be the cliché Hollywood vision of mysterious people traveling in wagons, telling fortunes or cursing anyone who wrongs them.

Or, in our SIU world, it's an admittedly passé term for organized groups who travel town to town for the sole purpose of committing fraud.

This is another example of parties committing fraud who were not our policyholders. Our customers were innocent victims of these deceptive schemes, and in most cases, we paid for the fraud. Your neighborhoods could be targets as well.

I used to think of theft as the robbery of just tangible property. I soon learned people could suffer the loss of their hard-earned cash and dignity through fraud—innocent targets scammed into paying for goods or services that were either fraudulent or didn't exist at all. It was even more infuriating when criminals targeted the elderly, the uneducated, or people whose first language wasn't English.

One group of nomadic grifters are known as "Travellers" or "Irish Travellers." (*Traveller* with the double "l" is the British English spelling of the word). They've gone by other names such as the "Irish Mob" or "White Gypsies." They've been known to travel throughout the southeastern United States, committing fraud on unwary targets before moving on to other areas.

I had first learned about "gypsy" or Traveller activity during a class at the annual FIFEC (Florida Insurance Fraud Education Committee) Conference. Considered one of the preeminent insurance fraud conferences in the nation, it's an annual fraud training seminar, supported by the Florida Division of Investigative and Forensic Services and SIU

departments from almost every insurance carrier.

When the class profiled "gypsy" schemes, my eyes widened. Our team had investigated many of the same scenarios, but I had no idea such a prolific and organized group had orchestrated them.

The Irish Travellers' lineage hails from the Emerald Isle, as one of Ireland's oldest and most disparaged minority groups, known for their wandering lifestyles, unique dialects, and dubious traditions. Ironically, in the U.S. they are not recognized as a distinct ethnic group by the U.S. Census, and Irish-Americans have never accepted them as their own.[70]

Due to their elusive nature, the number of Irish Travellers could range from 7,000 to 30,000 in the U.S., primarily in Georgia, Florida, Mississippi, South Carolina, and Texas. They move with the seasons, traveling north in the spring and returning south for the winter. Their primary trade is repair work and labor, which is often the basis for their fraudulent activities. In recent years, Travellers have also accumulated fortunes through corrupt life insurance schemes.

Repair Rackets

I'm confident there are honest, hardworking members of the Irish Traveller community, but the cases we investigated mirrored crimes committed across multiple states. In fact, according to law enforcement, the Travellers have a finite number of surnames that keep recurring such as Gorman, Carroll, Jennings, Daley, McDonald, and Toogood (apologies to anyone with one of those names). The schemes were very similar, as they stalked trusting communities.

Examples of their scams are important to know as consumers and homeowners. After I learned some of their tactics, I witnessed a few attempts in my own neighborhood, including my own home.

One common scheme involved roofing, particularly targeting the elderly. The Travellers just showed up at the insured's home and began working. They demanded payments that authorities later deemed to be "exorbitant in relation to the work or supplies." [71] The poor quality of their work would often lead to additional repairs and extortion. In other cases, they'd show up, offer a low price for a project, and later escalate the costs. If the victim paid once, the criminals would return to bleed more

money out of their naïve prey.

On our team, we received claims where roofs had been half completed and our customer had already paid thousands. We covered the losses as vandalism but had no recourse as the culprits were long gone. We encouraged our insureds to file detailed police reports of the suspects.

One scheme invaded my community when men knocked on our door claiming they had been hired to apply asphalt to a neighbor's driveway. The man told me they had leftover asphalt and would do our driveway for $1,000 cash. Victims of this ploy would soon discover the guys would either vanish, or they'd cover their driveway with cheap paint that would wash away with the first rain. I declined and warned my neighbors.

I knew to drill them with questions: "Which neighbor were you working for? What's their name?" "Do you have a business card?" "Why not?" Swindlers hate questions.

A more amusing scheme—which I no longer chuckle at—occurred when I was home one day. A man knocked on my door claiming he had frozen meat in his truck. He claimed to be a restaurant supplier who had ordered too much, or some other convoluted story. He offered to sell me meat—steaks, seafood, chicken—at suspiciously low prices.

I wondered who would buy meat from a stranger's truck? And what type of meat could it possibly be? Where did it really come from?

Just like with the asphalt guy, I told the man to get lost. But it was daunting to know these organized crooks had infiltrated our community, preying on our family and neighbors.

In a 2017 North Dakota case, a man named Patrick Gorman (recurring surname) appeared at the home of a fifty-seven-year-old widow. Gorman offered to put asphalt on her driveway and a shed for $10,000 to $15,000. After completion, he told the woman she owed $65,000. When she replied she didn't have the cash, Gorman took her horse trailer as a "down payment," insisting she still owed him $40,000. The woman was forced to withdraw cash from her savings to pay the man. The asphalt had "cracks and weeds growing through it within a short time." [72]

In 2019, two different Gormans arrived at the home of a ninety-five-year-old widow, offering to do roof repairs. The widow and her daughter had found them on Craigslist and had not checked their credentials. They paid the Gormans $6,700 for work they never performed.

Also in 2019, Gorman General Contracting (see a trend here?) billed an elderly man for over $1.9 million for a series of repairs. The man was a rancher living alone in secluded North Dakota. The man's payments to the Gormans totaled almost $2 million for repairs that they either never performed or performed poorly.

Lesson: warn your family and friends, especially older people or anyone whose first language isn't English, to always ask questions or call the police if laborers just "show up" at their homes and begin working.

Be wary of workers knocking on doors offering services. Though they could be legitimate (e.g., tree trimmers driving through your neighborhood), always check their licensing and insurance. Honest workers usually put that information prominently on their trucks and business cards. When hiring services from any marketplace sites such as Craigslist, always check the workers' licensing and credentials.

And don't ever buy meat from a guy in a pickup truck.

Life Insurance Crimes

Life insurance policies are a leading moneymaker for these organized groups. When the Travellers' daughters have their First Holy Communions at around eight years old, the families sometimes provide dowries that include life insurance policies on someone who was "thought to be short for the world."[73] In other words, they might die soon.

In a South Carolina case, authorities found an eighty-five-year-old woman with fifty-two policies in her name. Thirty of the beneficiaries were known Travellers, even though the woman had no children. Another man, who also had no children, had twenty-seven insurance policies listing Traveller children as beneficiaries.[74]

For investigators, one difficulty with detecting life insurance schemes is that neither the insured, nor their relatives, may even know about the policy. After the person dies, the Traveller beneficiaries collect the proceeds.

Could these groups infiltrate the insurance industry itself? In 2018, a South Carolina insurance agent, Douglas Wade Williamson, was sentenced to five years in prison for his part in a vast fraud scheme that ran for years using his own insurance agency.

According to Assistant U.S. Attorney Jim May, members of the Irish Travellers turned to insurance fraud as a "major source of wealth." [75] Williamson's agency had sold more than 400 life policies to Travellers with a value over $54 million, payable to non-relatives. Approximately one in every four policies Williamson sold was fraudulent. He wasn't a Traveller but conspired with members of the group and earned commissions on the sales. [76] More unsettling, the average time between the policy application and the death of the insureds was only 4.8 years.

In a more sinister case, a housekeeper had $5 million in life insurance coverage she knew nothing about. She was brutally murdered by the policyholders, who were also the beneficiaries.

Seventy-two-year-old Anita Fox had been hired to clean a Colleyville, Texas, home when father-and-son Travellers Bernard and Gerard Gorman stabbed her to death. The Gormans had acquired the life policies from Fox's daughter, who was unable to afford the premiums.[77]

The Gormans tracked Anita Fox for days to learn her daily routines. In one of the homes she cleaned, they broke in to stab her seven times in the chest, back, and head.

According to Police Sergeant J. Garner, the Gormans decided to murder the woman because "she was too healthy" and "wasn't going to die anytime soon."[78]

By the time authorities caught up to the elder Gorman, he had died of natural causes. The son, Bernard Gorman, had fled and was arrested in—of course—Florida.

PART FIVE –
BOAT CRIMES &
SMUGGLING

Chapter Fifteen
"Everyone's a Drug Smuggler..."

After five wonderful years at our Little Havana hideaway, it was time to move. With changing management over that time, the placement of SIU teams fluctuated between being "out of sight, out of mind" to being one among the people.

Around 2005, the company decided to sell our beloved Unity Boulevard Office (the name was crafted to soften any urban stigma). My team and I were relocated to a standard claims office, placed in a vacant center row, surrounded by daily adjusters.

Gone were the days of talking aloud about our colorful cases. No animated tales of goat heads in Santería fires. We had cases with former professional athletes that had to remain hushed. No more tree diagrams of suspected organized criminals on our walls. Management believed we could be an asset, present in the office to help review cases and assist with training.

It was fine with me; it was twenty minutes closer to home. The office didn't have any roosters, and the eighty-person staff enjoyed cookouts and potlucks. I discovered another plus: The staff made Cuban coffees every afternoon and passed them out—most of us depended on it.

Let me explain. When I was working Hurricane Andrew cases in the early '90s, our company had flown in employees from all over the country for extended tours of duty. The locals quickly introduced them to the ritual of afternoon Cuban coffee.

Miami runs on coffee. Cuban coffee, called *coladas,* has been referred to as "jet fuel" and the original Red Bull. Chef Anthony Bourdain called it "liquid crack." But most gringos did not realize it's not an espresso, nor is it served in a normal-sized cup.

A *colada* is an extremely strong espresso with spoons of sugar added. It's served in a large Styrofoam cup with a stack of four or more thimble-sized cups. The thick, syrupy coffee is poured into the tiny cups to pass around and share. One cup can serve four to six people.

First-timers always think you're supposed to drink from the big cup. Not a good idea, especially if you have any cardiac issues.

Dave, an upbeat manager from Georgia, had been managing hurricane teams in Miami for a year. Immersed in the culture, he had learned to love his morning and afternoon Cuban coffees. But when Dave returned home to Atlanta, he began to experience severe headaches every afternoon. When they persisted, he underwent a litany of medical exams including MRIs of his brain. His worst fear was that he had a brain tumor.

Mercifully, Dave did not have a tumor. He was diagnosed with severe caffeine withdrawal. His year of drinking continuous Cuban coffees had come to an abrupt halt.

One day while enjoying *café Cubano* in our new office, Steve approached. He and I would go on to work together for twenty-five years. As a personable Miami native, he was tall and bearded, and ladies often described him as a jovial teddy bear. In addition to being a top investigator, Steve knew almost everyone. He was friends with fire marshals, police officers, FBI agents, Coast Guard officers, and workers at every marina who witnessed *everything*. He could pick up the phone and get anyone on the line.

However, Steve was rarely politically correct, nor had he mastered the elusive art of "corporate speak." At leadership meetings, if they asked the crowd for their opinion, Steve would certainly raise his hand to give his view on things. As some managers cringed, I knew he spoke from the heart about things everyone else was scared to say, and it was *always* for the company's benefit.

Steve entered my office and said, "We gotta tell corporate to stop insuring these three models of boats immediately."

I sat upright because he was usually on to something. "Why?"

"Only *drug smugglers* buy these three boats."

That was a pretty substantial allegation. I replied, "So no pleasure boater or fisherman would possibly buy one of these boats?"

"Nope." Steve was also a boat specialist and an expert fisherman. He categorically knew more about boats than our underwriters.

Curious where all this was coming from, I asked him to explain.

Steve unraveled the histories of the three boat models. The vessels had been designed by former drug smugglers from the 1980s who were now earning (and laundering) money as boat manufacturers. The boats were conceived with smuggling in mind.

In photos and diagrams, Steve pointed out how the three models had cargo spaces that were excessively large for the size of the boats. They had very little deck space, so they were not ideal for fishing. They were built for speed with massive—sometimes triple or quadruple—engines.

The boats were types of "go-fasts," built to carry large loads of something, then go as fast as possible.

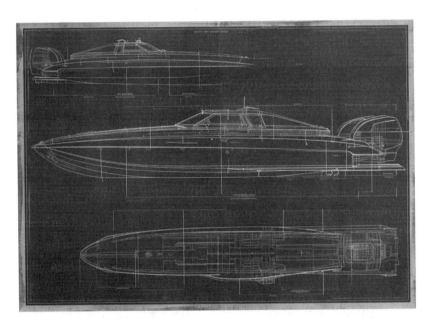

It was plausible, if not believable. I decided to rearticulate Steve's assertions to my boss with a tad more corporate tact. My manager liked Steve and also knew he was usually right. But we couldn't just march to corporate and exclaim, "Only *drug dealers* use these boats, so don't insure them!"

My boss wondered if we could get the same information some other way. Using analytics, we pulled data on any cases involving the three boat models. We were amazed to see a significantly high number of thefts, realizing the value for each boat was over $100,000. A high percentage of the thefts came from new policies from people we had no other business with. Essentially strangers had paid only a few months' premiums, then made claims for over six figures each.

Next, we were able to obtain arrest information from our friends in law enforcement and the Coast Guard. A majority of the seized smuggling boats included the same three models.

It was compelling information. We were granted a presentation to our state's underwriting department. We never referred to our customers as "drug dealers," but using the data, we were able to illustrate that insuring these three boat models created highly adverse risks.

Miraculously, our underwriting department—for one of the largest carriers in the world—agreed to no longer insure these three models based on our presentation.

I'm not naming the three boat manufacturers (Steve reminded me there are now six manufacturers) as their nefarious origins are not public knowledge, yet they are well known in boating circles. In addition, the companies constantly change their brand names and resell their various boat designs as different models. It would require constant effort to avoid insuring these specific vessels forever.

Bad Guys Have Bad Days Too

For one of the notorious boat models used (and designed) by smugglers, I'll rename the brand "Traitor" boats for the sake of this case. When Steve received another Traitor theft case, he scheduled a meeting with the boat's owner, Hugo. While seated with Steve in one of our small, windowless statement rooms, Hugo reached into a bag and placed two separate stacks of $10,000 cash on the desk.

"What's that for?" Steve asked, puzzled.

Hugo pointed to one stack, "Ten grand for any cop who finds my boat." He then touched the other stack, "This ten is for you if *you* can find my boat."

Steve replied, unphased, "I'm not in the business of locating boats."

It was clear the man wanted his boat back. If it was a real theft, there was something very valuable onboard that he wanted returned.

In a rare move, Hugo told us he had security video of the thieves taking his boat. But Steve would have to come to his warehouse to view it. To play it safe, Steve asked one of our teammates, Albert, to accompany him. Albert had a calm, cool demeanor and agreed to ride along. He was a sharp investigator, and it usually took a lot to fluster him.

They drove to Hugo's warehouse in Medley, a bleak industrial area in west Miami. When they arrived, Steve noticed several Traitor boats parked outside on trailers. When they entered the warehouse, they were surprised it was more like a secret "man cave." On the first floor was a small office and another parked Traitor boat. But when Hugo led them upstairs, it looked like something out of *Scarface*. It had dim lighting, a full bar, mounted televisions, and a king-sized bed. To the side, Albert saw a man wearing sunglasses passed out on a black leather couch.

The boisterous Hugo proceeded to a gun case to show off an assortment of firearms. At that point, Steve turned to exit, claiming he had forgotten his phone in the car. Albert's eyes bugged at the thought of being left alone in Hugo's bizarre lair.

Steve's actual plan was to go outside to get his camera. He wanted to take photos of the Traitor boats, including their hull IDs and serial numbers, to share with his Coast Guard friends. He tried to hurry to avoid suspicion—and to not panic Albert more than necessary.

Meanwhile, upstairs, still seated across from Hugo, Albert described to me an excruciatingly long silence before Hugo finally uttered in Spanish, "Tell the gringo to get back up here."

To Albert's relief, Steve huffed back up the stairs. Hugo then showed them the security video taken during the early-morning hours. To their surprise, the video indeed depicted shadowy figures stealing his boat.

The next day, Steve shared his photographed boat ID numbers with his Coast Guard pals. They verified the boats had been legally purchased and registered—but they had unsettling information about Hugo: He had been in prison for shooting two Miami police officers. It was back in the 1980s, and Hugo hadn't known the men were cops. The officers were undercover during a botched drug deal in South Beach. Hugo had shot the men, who miraculously survived their wounds. Hugo—our loyal policyholder—had served twelve years in prison.

07/08/2020   05:12:06

Fatefully, Hugo's stolen boat appeared to be a legitimate theft. We paid the man for his vessel—but not for whatever precious cargo had been onboard.

As my area manager Don Johnson used to say, "Even bad guys can have bad days."

During this period, Steve was alarmed to discover a spike of nineteen Traitor boats recently insured with our company. When he researched, he discovered the same local insurance agent had written all nineteen policies, almost back-to-back. We wondered how one agent could sell so many boat policies that were such dangerous risks. The agent was located in a quiet suburb forty miles north of Miami.

When Steve contacted the agent's office to use his charm to fish for answers, one of the employees eagerly offered to help. I recall the man's name because it was easy to remember: Elvis. He was also concerned about the influx of boats insured by their office. Elvis revealed the reason why: His boss was personal friends with the owner of Traitor boats. The agent would leave stacks of insurance applications at the Traitor Boat showrooms in Miami and the Keys. Customers who purchased the boats were coerced to insure them with the same agent.

Coincidentally, around this time, I had been invited to speak about fraud to a group of insurance agents. My presentation included information about the dubious boat models, and I disclosed the fact that we had errantly insured nineteen of them. After my lecture, a respected agent approached me to ask if I knew which agent had sold the nineteen policies.

I paused, probably uneasy, and had to reply, "It was you."

Shortly thereafter, we discovered Elvis no longer worked at that agency. Our informant was gone. We reported our findings to the agency leadership, but with no real proof the man had done anything wrong, nothing happened.

Postscript: Out of those nineteen boats we insured, ultimately ten were reported stolen, seven were reported as sunken, and one was burned—senseless losses valued at nearly $2 million.

Paper Boats

Allowing karma to take root, one day over lunch, a friend from Steve's law enforcement circle informed him that a Traitor dealership was selling fraudulent sales documents for $20,000 cash. A person could buy "purchase records" for a Traitor boat—but without the boat. It would include registration documents and a photo of the vessel. As an additional service, if the buyer told Traitor when the insurance company wanted to inspect the vessel, they would tow a boat to their home. When the inspection was over, Traitor would bring the boat back and give it new ID numbers for the next sham purchase. The scheme included fraudulent loan applications as well.

The buyers were told to "wait about a year," then report the fictional boat stolen: a $20,000 investment for a $100,000 return, tax-free cash.

Steve managed to secure an invitation to *quietly* observe a Miami Theft Task Force meeting when he learned they were investigating Traitor boats. After mutely listening to the group speculate, he believed they were barking up the wrong tree. He exclaimed, "You know, Traitor is selling fraudulent sales paperwork."

An officer frowned at the civilian visitor, "No, they're not."

In true Steve fashion, he replied, "Yeah, they are."

Everyone's heads turned. Steve proceeded to tell them about his police friend who had proof, including copies of the fake invoices and sham loan documents.

A new investigation ensued that would result in the arrests of multiple Miami residents associated with the boat company. According to the United States Attorney's Office, they were charged with bank fraud and money laundering in connection to fraudulent boat loan applications.[79] The Florida Division of Insurance Fraud's concurrent project called "Boatscam" resulted in seven arrests for the scheme totaling over $12 million.[80] The owner of the boat manufacturer was sentenced to prison, and the company went out of business.

As a side note, Steve was one of the nominees for Investigator of the Year by the Florida Insurance Fraud Education Committee (FIFEC) as a result of his far-reaching boat investigations. (First place went to Carol Price LaDuke, a colleague and friend whose investigations tackled staged accidents and criminal medical providers—more on that world in Chapter 25.)

I wanted Steve to introduce me to his friends with the Coast Guard and sheriff's office in the Florida Keys. The Keys, a string of islands stretching over 100 miles off the southern tip of Florida, are known as a destination for fishing and boating, as well as a haven for smugglers.

When law enforcement realized our interests overlapped, they began to include us in their task force meetings. They invited us to their offices to see evidence firsthand. We learned the smugglers' schemes and discovered how our company—as well as other carriers—had been unintentionally helping fund smuggling operations.

For years thereafter, Steve and I presented at multiple conferences about how smugglers exploit insurance companies for their criminal trades. We pointed out weaknesses in the industry's procedures and policies, and how to investigate more quickly.

And we discovered the smugglers' new cargo was more horrific than narcotics.

Chapter Sixteen
Targeted by Human Traffickers

If insurance companies inadvertently helped facilitate smuggling operations, that really implies the policyholders did—meaning you, through increased premiums. Are we all unwitting accomplices?

As I saw it, the central problem with boat insurance was any company that sold "agreed value policies." That meant the "total loss" value of the boat policy would never decrease due to years or depreciation.

Boaters will tell you nothing depreciates faster than watercraft. With usage, boats are worth less every year. However, with valued policies, if the owner insured their boat for $100,000 and then rode it rough for a decade before it was stolen, the policy would still pay the full $100,000 (though it was really worth $20,000).

How is that good business? It seemed smugglers understood that glitch as well.

At the time, smugglers were targeting major carriers for coverage before pursuing their activities. They needed boats with unfailing speed, ample fuel tanks, and large cargo areas.

Certainly not everyone who owned one of the described models was involved in illegal activities. Our company had long-time customers who were boat enthusiasts. However, it was crucial to be aware of the trends, especially with any first-time customers.

The Traffickers' Scheme

The smugglers' methods followed the same pattern. They approached an innocent "straw buyer" to purchase the boat. The naïve buyer was chosen for their clean record, no arrests or major violations. Some were seventy-year-old grandmothers from Hialeah. The smugglers gave them enough money for the down payment for a boat that could cost from $70,000 to over $180,000. In almost every case, the buyers would've never been able to afford such vessels.

After the purchase, the smugglers would instruct the buyer to obtain theft coverage from an insurance agent. They would give them enough money for the first few months' premiums.

The smugglers then told the buyer they might be "borrowing" the boat soon. I can imagine conversations such as, "By the way, don't worry if your boat goes missing from your backyard on Tuesday night."

The smugglers would then use the new vessel for their corrupt deeds. If the boat returned, then all was well. If it didn't, the buyer reported the boat stolen, making a claim for the full limits, which was usually more than what they had paid for the boat.

Our team learned it wasn't just drug smuggling. The new trend was human trafficking. There was more money, with less severe penalties.

The smugglers made their runs of human cargo between Florida and Cuba. Our SIU partners in other southern coastal states investigated similar schemes between the U.S. and Mexico.

As an illustration, imagine a $110,000 boat with less than a $400 monthly premium. The policyholder paid for only one month, but we would pay the full value, six figures, tax-free. It would require 275 honest policies to offset just one claim.

The Monroe County Sheriffs in the Keys taught us that foreign governments can confiscate the smugglers' boats with no recourse. If Cuba captured a boat, the U.S. would not start a war over it. The Coast Guard had witnessed the Cuban military using Florida-registered vessels for its own use. Cuban hotels had boats registered to the U.S. available for rent to tourists. It was a safe bet we had paid for many of those boats, and we would never see them again.

If U.S. authorities did recover a smuggling vessel, they had little value after we had already paid the limits. Some smugglers discarded their boats after only three or four runs. The vessels were operated so rigorously that the fiberglass hulls and engines would break down. Boats were recovered abandoned in the mangroves with "spiderweb" cracks throughout their hulls. Smugglers considered the boats virtually disposable because they use our money (your money) to buy another one, and so on as the cycle continues.

The Plague of Human Trafficking

Refugee smuggling was on the rise because of less severe penalties than those for drug trafficking. A smuggler could pack twenty-five migrants into a boat, with each paying $10,000 cash to come to America. It's only ninety miles between Key West and Havana, and most runs were done at night. The smuggler could earn a quarter-million dollars cash per run, with almost zero risk.

And the smugglers had a built-in alibi: If they were ever caught by authorities, they'd declare they had "saved" the refugees while fishing. They'd say they were out trawling when they came upon these defenseless refugees on a raft. So not only were they *not* smugglers, they were heroes! But in one case, that story fell apart when we discovered one of the refugees was the boater's cousin.

Cuban nationals continue to risk their lives to cross the Florida Straits to come to the U.S. Prior to 2017, before President Barack Obama did away with the "wet-foot, dry-foot" policy, Cuban migrants could remain in the country if they touched U.S. soil. Many refugees attempted the voyage in flimsy, homemade rafts they call *rústicos*. With severe currents, poor navigation, and sharks—reminiscent of Elián Gonzalez and his mother's tragedy—the criminal niche of human smuggling flourished.

Our Coast Guard friends told us traffickers were charging $10,000 per person to be packed into overloaded boats. Those who didn't have money or relatives in the U.S. to pay the exorbitant fees would sometimes sell everything they owned. Even today, flyers in Cuba have appeared with people selling their homes to earn the cash, sold complete with "everything inside." [81]

Smugglers would deliver their human cargo near any U.S. shore and then flee. When the refugees were found, they would never betray the smugglers, perhaps under threat. They would allege they had arrived on rafts, yet they showed no signs of sunburn, dehydration, or fatigue.

Today, if the migrants are caught, they are returned to Cuba, where they might face unimaginable penalties. Despite the multiple hazards, these oppressed people risk everything to start new lives in our nation.

A more ominous concept is human trafficking in exchange for abhorrent acts. With few migrants able to pay the $10,000 cash fee, they agree to such things as forced labor and sex work. Arrested members of injury fraud rings have testified they used refugees with their staged accidents. A fourteen-year-old girl told one of our SIU investigators that she had to be part of four auto accidents before she could be "free."

With an increased focus on human trafficking, Florida Statute 787.06 went on to state, "The Legislature finds that victims of human trafficking are subjected to force, fraud, or coercion for the purpose of sexual exploitation or forced labor." [82]

The Department of Justice conducted a study in three areas of the U.S.: Florida, Chicago, and Washington, D.C. The first two areas were considered trafficking "hotspots." Their report confirmed human traffickers were engaged in a wide range of crimes. "Investigating other crimes (money laundering, car-theft, organized begging, prostitution, weapons charges, document fraud, labor law violations, etc.) can illuminate a case of trafficking." [83]

In a Miami case, criminals paid a Cuban national $10,000 for just his signature before he was sent back to Cuba. The offenders used his information to appear as the owner of a North Miami Beach pharmacy that robbed $695,000 from insurers within two months. Two other Cuban nationals, who'd had multiple convictions, were charged as leaders in a 48-person, multi-state ring that stole $500 million in prescription drugs from insurers. [84]

Many staged auto accidents we investigated included passengers who had been in our country for a year or less. Some had been in multiple car crashes, and a few had suffered real injuries. The criminal ringleaders have zero regard for the safety or welfare of the refugees.

I recall a summer date when I visited Key West with my family, July 8, because it was my birthday. On that day, we heard a report that the Coast Guard had seized a smuggler's boat carrying thirty-one refugees. But during the high-speed chase, a twenty-four-year-old female, Anay Machado Gonzalez, died when she smashed her head against the hull of the boat.[85] Another pregnant passenger was transported to a hospital with injuries. The smugglers had ignored the Coast Guard's order to stop, with no concern for their passengers.

In May 2021, the Coast Guard pulled eight Cuban migrants and two bodies from the Atlantic after their boat capsized off the coast of Key West.

After searching by air and sea for over 120 hours, the Coast Guard called off the search for the eight missing people who were never recovered, and presumed dead. [86]

The bottom line: There are minimal penalties for first-time human smugglers compared to zero-tolerance punishments for narcotics smugglers. And the criminals further protected their hefty investments by insuring their voyages to fund their ongoing operations.

Smuggler's Island

We discovered a small island off the coast of Florida that served as a hub for human smuggling. Bimini, the westernmost island of the Bahamas, is only nine square miles in size. Its primary draw is Resorts World hotel, clubs, and casino. On holidays and weekends, thousands of people navigate to the island to enjoy its turquoise water and nightlife.

Bimini's constant boat traffic continues to help enable smuggling. Located just 52 miles from the Florida coast, it's the shortest direct route. During peak times, its shores are filled with pleasure boats, yachts, and Jet Skis. Rather than using speed boats, some smugglers have hidden migrants inside large yachts that look like tourist boats to avoid suspicion.

Migrants from Cuba, Haiti, and the Dominican Republic can charter private boats to the Bahamas. Upon arrival, they work to earn enough money to afford their final journey to the U.S. via smugglers.

The U.S. Coast Guard and the Bahamas Defense Force admit their fleets aren't large enough to capture every boat. Smugglers avoid using lights at night to minimize visibility. Successful smugglers are experienced navigators with years at sea. An anonymous smuggler told *VICE World News* that the best traffickers are "people who can orient themselves off a compass alone or by looking at the stars on clear nights."[87]

The roots of illegal trafficking run deep in Bimini's economy, passed down through generations due to its proximity to Florida. Some smugglers had trafficked cocaine in the 1980s before shifting to the human cargo trade, enticed by the quick cash. According to the anonymous smuggler, "As long as you get the money, you do what you got to do."[88]

How We Investigated

Our team relied on the mantra, "Does it make sense?" If we received a theft of a $100,000 powerboat, does it make sense the owner is a sixty-five-year-old seamstress from Opa-locka? Maybe. It at least demanded further investigation.

We encountered boat owners who had never owned a watercraft before. So their first foray into boating was an 1,800-horsepower go-fast? In most cases that were proven to be fraudulent, the owners had no prior business with our company—no autos insured, no home insurance or renters policies. When we asked how we were so fortunate to gain their business, they'd say, "I drove by and saw your sign."

When our team visited the agents who had sold the policies, many told us they didn't know the applicants; they had just "walked in off the street." One agent who had sold a policy to an older woman insuring a powerboat remembered a "large man" had come in with her. The man had kept his arms crossed and whispered answers to the woman for the application.

I asked, "Did you think to ask her who the man was?"

The agent blinked, "No…"

That woman paid one month's premium, and our company paid over $120,000 when the boat was reported stolen a few weeks later.

One tactic while conducting EUOs of the boat owners was to have them sketch a diagram of the controls. We asked them to help us understand how the vessel operated and where various electronics were located. Not only were these owners unable to explain anything about their boats, when we asked one woman how she started its engines, she replied, "By pulling a string."

In most cases, the boat owners were insolvent or poor, certainly unable to afford a new boat with a $100,000-plus price tag. Again, does it make sense?

We asked them the following questions: "Have you ever owned a boat before?" "Where and how did you obtain the boat's down payment?" "Who is the primary user?" "Have you had any boat training?"

One aspect overlooked by many fraudsters was the vehicles needed to tow the boats. These heavy vessels require large trucks to tow them such as F-250s or large SUVs. What kind of vehicle did they have? In one case, a new applicant only had a Honda Civic. We asked, "Did you plan on pulling your thirty-eight-foot cigarette boat with your Civic?"

During meetings with our agents, we explained smugglers might insure their boats with faraway agents in non-coastal areas. For example, one Miami boat owner had an agent in Thomasville, Georgia. Perpetrators quickly learn which agents and companies are easy targets, and word spreads fast.

We recommended personal inspections of the boat. Shouldn't we see what we're insuring? Many smugglers remove the "Bimini top"—the open metal and canvas structure over the cockpit—to create a lower visual profile and enhance speed.

Does the boat have only handheld electronics instead of installed devices such as GPS? Smugglers have been known to throw handheld devices overboard when caught to conceal where they have been.

A Coast Guard agent told me an amusing story about a smuggler who had thrown his GPS device overboard when he was caught. The man didn't realize it was a floating, waterproof model. The agent simply scooped up the yellow GPS with a net, and it showed the vessel had been to Havana and back.

Any aspiring smugglers—or anyone attempting boat fraud—are hopeful the insurance employees are not boat experts. Agency and underwriting personnel should request sales paperwork to help verify the value versus taking the owner's word for it. If an applicant buys a boat for $70,000 then obtains a $100,000 policy, they could earn a quick $30,000 cash profit if the boat is stolen. One idea I suggested was to require a valuation from a certified appraiser and then have the boat reappraised every three years.

Today, I'm pleased to see more carriers selling boat insurance policies that are not stated value policies. In the event of a claim, depreciation would apply, hopefully decreasing its allure for fraud.

Dangerous Players

There were other concerns that transcended the problem of fraud alone. Feeding the human trafficking machine was certainly number one. But there were other risks that these ruthless criminals rarely considered.

Smuggling vessels carry hundreds of extra gallons of gasoline for their voyages. Law enforcement in the Keys have called the boats "rolling firebombs" as they're towed on our highways. Imagine the exposure on our roads if there was a major collision or if the boat ignited. Making it worse, there are loopholes in the laws regarding the transportation of fuel if it's in approved containers.

Our friend Lieutenant Anne Ramirez with the Monroe County Sherriff's Office invited Steve and I to attend their taskforce meetings in the Keys. We had befriended Ramirez when they had recovered boats that belonged to our company. The meetings included Coast Guard, U.S. Border Patrol, and police. Our SIU team was a new addition after they realized our mutual interests. It was a win-win to attend the meetings.

During one meeting in the Keys, Ramirez invited Steve and me to their evidence hangar on the island of Marathon. We drove to their aviation

department on a sweltering summer day. Beyond barbed-wire security gates, they led us inside a cavernous hangar. When my eyes adjusted, I saw seized narcotics planes, smuggling boats, and private jets like something out of *Narcos*.

One officer showed me blood droplets that were still on the carpet of a small jet, He chuckled, "Wonder what happened there?" On boat trailers were confiscated smuggling vessels. Just as described, the boats had their tops removed and no installed electronics. Smugglers had painted some dark blue or gray to obscure their visibility.

Lieutenant Ramirez and her team showed us daunting proof we were dealing with *very* bad people, perhaps worse than our Russian mob foes. Items seized from smugglers included shotguns, tasers (for unruly passengers), nylon zip-ties (for uncooperative passengers), twelve-inch Bowie knives, and an assortment of semi-automatic weapons.

It was the first time I had seen fuel "bladder bags," which are collapsible rubber bladders used by the smugglers to carry gasoline. Bladders can be filled with fifty to a hundred gallons of gasoline and stuffed into cargo holds, just inches from their human freight. The sobering part: The bladders are government approved for fuel transportation, so there's nothing illegal about that.

Weapons siezed from a smuggling vessel
off the Florida Keys

Courtesy Monroe County Sheriff's Office

The officers described items found on boats that could indicate they had been used for human smuggling. They included food to assist large groups like bread and sports drinks. When they mentioned diapers and baby food, I was naïve, wondering if the smugglers had some shred of compassion for their passengers. The officer scoffed, explaining it was strictly to keep any babies from crying. He added, "They'll threaten to throw a kid overboard if it cries."

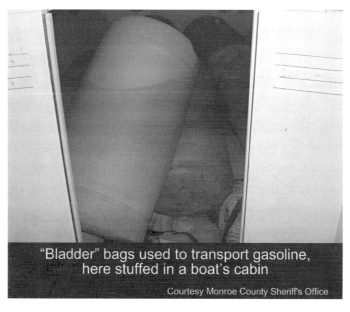

"Bladder" bags used to transport gasoline,
here stuffed in a boat's cabin

Courtesy Monroe County Sheriff's Office

They described an example of how callous smugglers were with children. The Coast Guard had sharpshooters that would attempt to shoot a boat's engines if it tried to escape. In one pursuit, the smuggler held a toddler in front of the boat's engines to keep authorities from firing.

All these barbaric tales served as a poignant reminder that some of these criminals were ostensibly our policyholders.

We continued to attend Lieutenant Ramirez's quarterly meetings in the Keys. We were amazed how beneficial it was to share a few raw bar lunches with Coast Guard officers and law enforcement. They were great people, and we learned valuable advice for our own cases.

Smugglers were also stealing boat trailers and engines to replace the ones they had worn out. Boat trailers were easy to steal, and to conceal any ID numbers, there was a loophole in the law where the thieves could register the stolen trailers as "homemade" with the state.

We also learned of an increasing problem with stolen Jet Ski-type watercraft. The small watercraft are easy to steal, and owners and tourists rarely have them properly secured. Despite their size, they're costly, many over $20,000 each.

When I asked why a smuggler would want a Jet Ski, the cops explained they sell them for funds, often on Craigslist for suspiciously discounted prices. It was so rampant that Ramirez had one officer whose job was to monitor Craigslist, Facebook, and other online marketplaces for boat engines and Jet Skis. Our company also observed an uptick in these stolen watercrafts. Let this be another warning to not buy things from online marketplaces when the price seems too good to be true.

As a result of our new alliances, whenever authorities seized watercraft of any kind, we would receive personal calls and emails if any belonged to us.

Despite abolishing wet-foot, dry-foot policies, the human trafficking problem is not going away. The U.S. and Cuba are confronting the highest number of migrants to leave the island by boat since 2017. Over 6,000 Cuban migrants were interdicted in 2021 while attempting to cross the Florida Straits in small boats, a sixfold increase from the previous year. Between just October and December 2022, 2,982 Cubans were interdicted at sea.[89]

Our post-COVID era has made people even more desperate. Widespread oppression from the Cuban regime, an economic crisis worsened by the pandemic, and food shortages have forced more Cubans to flee. Trafficking from Haiti has also increased due to its own political crises and increasing gang violence.

Shockingly, according to the U.S. Embassy in Cuba, due to some strange omission, Cuban law does not explicitly prohibit labor trafficking as defined by international law. The Cuban government does not have specific procedures to identify victims of forced labor.[90]

The crisis of human trafficking—used to fuel unconscionable crimes including forced labor, sex crimes, and insurance crimes—will not be diminishing anytime soon.

Chapter Seventeen
A Race Against Future Crimes

How often do you learn of a crime before it happens, and then have the ability to stop it before it occurs? No, this isn't science fiction like the movie *Minority Report*, where police predicted crimes before they took place. We were given a real opportunity.

There's a common myth told within law enforcement that turned out inherently true: Organized criminals have "lists" of where your property's located in case they want to steal it. Imagine a menu of items they could take from you anytime they wish.

During our days searching containers at Port Everglades, we heard stories about thieves having databases of vehicles listing the makes, models, and colors. They also keep records of the homes where the vehicles were parked. In theory, a crime boss could "order" a vehicle for himself. Perhaps he wanted a pearl white Denali with alloy rims. The thieves would check their database, locate the requested vehicle, then steal it.

The notion of criminals cruising our neighborhoods, watching us, and knowing our habits and property was unsettling. Then, one day, we received a call that confirmed "theft lists" were real.

Through our contacts in the Keys, Steve learned they had an informant working with boat thieves. The man had obtained a list of twenty-one boats targeted to be stolen within days. They were high-performance boats, some worth over $175,000.

We were given a copy of the theft list. It contained the boats' makes and models but did not reveal any names or exact addresses. It only gave the crossroads where the boats were parked. We needed to immediately ascertain if any of the boats were owned by our customers.

Timing was critical—six of the boats had already been stolen within the first seventy-two hours. How many criminals were working from the same list? Were any of our unwary customers going to be visited by professional thieves?

The race was on. Steve drove to each listed intersection in hopes of locating a boat. If he found one, he used his laptop at the scene to run the address and obtain the resident's name. We then checked our company's system to see if we had insured the boat. It was a tedious process considering the number of boats—now down to fourteen and counting.

If he came upon a boat that we didn't insure, we alerted our SIU partners at other companies. By the end of the day, Steve had driven to each listed intersection, spread across Miami-Dade County, to search for vulnerable boats. When he completed his list, he returned to our office. "So, what do we do now?"

We decided to not contact our customers directly to warn them that "thieves might be on the way to your home!" We chose a less panic-inducing approach. We called it something like "customer safety check" calls. We contacted their insurance agents to assist with phone numbers and other information about the owners.

Next, we called each boat owner to check on the security of their property. We did mention a spike in thefts across South Florida, and we recommended they check the locks on their boats and trailers. We suggested they keep their vessels parked behind fences or park a vehicle in front of it. The agents' staff assisted with interpreting for Spanish-speaking customers. It was a group effort, and the customers seemed appreciative.

Did it work? None of the boats on the list that we insured were stolen. This is a perfect example of the benefits of developing relationships with outside agencies. If we hadn't had friends in law enforcement, it's uncertain whether we would have received the list so quickly, and it was a credible threat that thieves were going to visit some of our customers.

Thanks to our valuable contacts and fast work, we were able to prevent the thefts of vessels totaling deep into the six figures. We may have prevented thieves from surveying our insureds' homes, and at least two arrests were made.

Lesson: Always be aware when it comes to you, your family, and your property. Regardless of what kind of property, make sure it's properly secured. With trailered boats, make sure the trailers are locked or other obstacles are blocking them such as secured fences or other vehicles. You never know who's watching.

Chapter Eighteen
Thinking Outside the Barnacle

Whenever we interviewed a prospective new investigator, a key attribute we looked for was creativity. No two cases were ever the same, and there were no templates on how to handle an SIU case. With the elaborate ingenuity of the culprits, our reps needed to be just as inspired.

On any given day, we may need to locate witnesses for thefts, participants of organized activity, a motive for arsonists, or the identity of smugglers. In each of these predicaments, the rep had to consider, "How am I going to do this?"

We searched for cameras at the scenes. We used forensic locksmiths who could tell us what key was last used to open a lock or start a vehicle. We hired handwriting experts to determine if signatures were genuine. We had the water tested for chlorine in flooded vehicles, which would indicate someone had flooded the car with tap water from a hose.

However, the single most creative way we proved fraud was for a burned yacht case.

Our customer reported waking up in the middle of the night because he had felt "radiant heat" coming from his backyard. When he looked out at the dock behind his Miami Beach condominium, his sport fishing yacht was engulfed in flames. The forty-foot InterMarine boat with diesel engines was insured for over a quarter-million dollars at the time.

We inspected the boat three days after the fire. It was half-sunken at the dock, with its top third sticking out of the water at a 45-degree angle. In addition to fire damage, we observed a stained line around the vessel where the waterline had been. Below the line was muck and organic growth.

We didn't need to be Mensa candidates to know it had been partially sunken for a long time. With the thick growth, it looked like a derelict vessel had been dredged up by a storm then set ablaze.

However, our insured insisted he had gone boating with his girlfriend a week before the fire. He told us they'd fished and swam without any mechanical issues.

Then we uncovered a possible motive to set his own boat on fire. The man's textile business in Venezuela was going bankrupt. His Miami warehouse was in the process of foreclosure. When we pushed for more information, he refused to cooperate. He hired an attorney and sued us for "denying" his claim.

Of course, we had not denied his claim. We had just begun trying to clarify irregularities. Now we had to push forward with our investigation to defend the lawsuit.

We hired an origin and cause expert for the fire. He observed the distinctive pour patterns on the boat's deck. Samples tested positive for a Class 2 petroleum distillate (gasoline) that was nowhere near the fuel tanks. It was ruled arson, which meant it was intentionally set by human hands—but not necessarily by our insured. He and his attorney could argue it was vandalism. We needed a stronger reason "why" the man would destroy his own boat.

We hired a mechanical engineer to examine the engines. After a thorough inspection, the engineer determined both motors had been non-functional for an extended period before the fire.

Considering the evidence, we surmised the insured had previously blown his engines due to improper maintenance. The repair costs would have been exorbitant. Since the line of sludge on the hull was above the waterline, we knew the boat had been half-sunken or abandoned for a while. He then set it ablaze as the final step before collecting his $250,000.

Steve, our unofficial boat specialist, visited our customer's condominium and spoke to a security guard. The man told him what we suspected: The boat had been sunken for over a year. The condo board had issued warnings to our insured to either move the boat or he'd be fined $1,000 per day.

It wasn't a shocker that no one had removed the boat. South Florida has hundreds of derelict sunken boats. State, city, and county agencies point their fingers as to who should remove them. It's an enormous expense, requiring a barge and crane, with fees as high as $500 per foot, and then the costly storage. If the boats don't impede navigation, they might remain sunken for years.

In this case, we had a strong list of circumstantial evidence, including proof it was arson, mechanical problems prior to the fire, and financial distress. But it would be the *coup de grace* if we had scientific evidence of how long the boat had been sunken.

I give credit to Steve and my predecessor Gerry for conceiving a genius idea. During the inspection of the boat, they had documented the murk and growth on the hull above the waterline. It included colonies of barnacles.

None of us were marine biologists, but we all guessed barnacles required time to grow. If you sank a boat on a Saturday, there wouldn't be barnacles the size of quarters by Wednesday. But none of us were qualified to testify about how long it took to grow barnacles.

What do you do if you're not a marine biologist? You hire one.

Fortuitously, one of the nation's leading marine laboratories was just a few miles from our Little Havana office. The Rosenstiel School of Marine and Atmospheric Science was the marine laboratory of the University of Miami. It's one of the nation's foremost institutions for oceanographic research.

Steve cold called the Department of Marine Biology. When he reached the chair of the department, the woman was instantly intrigued. As he began to describe our case and observations, including the muck and barnacles, the woman kept saying, "Go on, tell me more." When Steve finished, she said, "I love your job!" She said she knew the perfect biologist for our needs.

The next morning, Dr. Alexandra, PhD, a professor of marine biology, called us. We explained our unique request. She was fascinated, and stated that she had never heard about any of her colleagues being asked to help with an insurance investigation.

Our request was simple: for her to examine photos of the barnacles found on our recovered boat. She could also visit the salvage yard to inspect the organisms firsthand, then provide a written opinion about how long it would have taken for the barnacles to grow.

We had to inform her there was a high likelihood our case would be going to trial. Some people are not comfortable giving testimony in a courtroom. Not only does it require expertise, but the person needs to present well, be able to speak in layman's terms to a jury, and be likable overall. We thought Dr. Alexandra would be perfect, and she agreed to help. In fact, she thought it was an exciting opportunity.

Before any case goes to trial, the plaintiff and defense attorneys must disclose their list of potential witnesses and experts. If the insured's attorney had read our list, he would have been aware we had a marine biologist as an expert. Under the Rules of Civil Procedure, any expert expected to provide testimony at a trial can be deposed. For some reason—perhaps they were overly confident in their case or too frugal—they never deposed Dr. Alexandra, which meant they had no clue what she was going to say in trial.

I attended the trial along with Steve, Gerry, and our attorney, Michael. As chance would have it, Mr. Insured did not present well to the jury. He appeared harried, babbled when he spoke, and his attorney had evidently never coached him on how to dress for trial. He wore the same wrinkled, mustard-yellow suit every day. He looked like he'd just rolled out of bed.

When it was time for Dr. Alexandra to testify, she was riveting. She was mid-thirties, blonde, and appeared relaxed, smiling at each juror as she described the lifecycle of barnacles.

Dr. Alexandra explained that barnacles are one of the oldest living animals in the world. They're members of the marine invertebrate class *Maxillopoda,* small crustaceans that attach to the surfaces of rocks, sea walls, boats, and other marine animals such as sea turtles.

Our attorney showed the jury enlarged color images of barnacles found on the boat's hull above the waterline. He asked Dr. Alexandra how long they had been there. With poise, she replied that, based on their size and circumference, they were nearly two years old. She added, "In fact, these are some of the largest barnacles I've ever seen."

For emphasis, our attorney asked, "So, the insured's vessel had to be in this half-sunken position for nearly two years for those barnacles to grow to that size?"

"Absolutely," Dr. Alexandra responded. There was no doubt in her reply.

The insured's attorney had brought no expert to counter her opinion (nor would he have been able to find one that matched her qualifications). For cross examination, the opposing attorney stood at his podium, shuffled his notes for what seemed like an eternity, then said he had no questions.

It took the jury less than an hour to render their verdict.

We had a tradition: Whenever a case was given to a jury to deliberate, we would walk with our attorney to Cacique, a Cuban café across from the Miami-Dade Courthouse, to get coffee. It'd give us time to unwind and talk about how we thought we did. Before we could even finish our coffee, Michael was notified the jury had reached a verdict.

The jury ruled in our favor. The insured had committed arson on his own boat to collect insurance proceeds and had lied about the condition of the vessel.

When we thanked the jurors after the trial, the foreperson told Steve, "We had a unanimous decision in five minutes but were embarrassed to come out that soon."

Dr. Alexandra thanked us for the opportunity. Neither she, nor anyone else in her department, had ever served as an expert in trial before, so there was no precedent for how much to charge us for her services. She eventually sent us a bill for $750, which we gratefully paid.

As an aside, Dr. Alexandra went on to become one of the foremost barnacle experts in the United States, and an international advocate for the protection of endangered staghorn coral.

PART SIX –
VEHICLE FRAUD

Chapter Nineteen
What You Know

Inspired by my stimulating job, combined with all the time I had to daydream during my hour-long commutes, I began to write crime fiction.

There's an old adage for writers, "Write what you know." I knew about creative crimes, and the local news provided fertile ideas to get the ball rolling. Sadly, in South Florida, the news always seems to start with finding a body in a canal. Add to that organized crime moving south to enjoy the weather, strange reports of B-Girls, and the fact Florida is somehow involved in every national scandal from election fraud to 9/11 (its organizer rented an apartment in my hometown, Coral Springs, and trained as a pilot on Florida's West Coast).

Needless to say, I would never have writer's block. My first published thriller was inspired by a true story I heard on the radio while commuting. A young couple had found a bag containing a fortune in cash while boating off the coast of Key West. When they turned it in, the police were so impressed with their honesty that they allowed them to keep the money if no one claimed it in ninety days.

With that kernel of a plot, my mind raced. Who had lost the money? It had to be bad guys; *honest* money isn't found in duffel bags in the ocean. More importantly, wouldn't the criminals be furious? Since the story was splashed on the news, couldn't they track down the young couple to get their money back? And so I wrote the most nightmarish version of what could happen.

And guess what subplot found its way into the story: smugglers using stolen boats to traffic human cargo. Also, a detailed scheme using sham owners, high-speed chases in go-fasts, and helpless refugees used for even worse crimes. As a writer, I had an arsenal of experts to consult, from sheriffs in the Keys to agents from the U.S. Border Patrol and the Coast Guard.

I entered my manuscript in an Amazon crime-writing competition where readers voted. Though my book didn't win first place, it was a third-round finalist out of thousands of entries. As a consolation prize, *Tropical Windfall* was published through Amazon in 2014, and readers still seem to enjoy it to this day.

I never considered myself a qualified expert in anything, but as I accrued years of experience, news outlets began to call for their articles. What I tackled on a daily basis was evidently interesting, yet foreign to most of the public.

The first reporter to contact me was Elise Ackerman with the *Miami New Times.* She was doing a story about a surge in auto theft and the associated fraud. In my interview, I explained theft tactics and chop shop schemes. I described people sinking their cars in canals and thieves shipping stolen vehicles through our ports—just everyday events.

I presumed very little of my yammering would be used in the article. They were going to interview people much more accomplished than me, including detectives with the Miami Theft Task Force. However, I was shocked when I opened the paper to see the opening line, "Insurance-claims specialist Richard Wickliffe has seen just about every auto-theft insurance fraud Dade County con men can dream up." [91]

Based on the positive response, I discovered insurance fraud was interesting to the public. Though it wasn't as provocative as some of our larger cases, auto fraud made up a majority of our outgoing funds. Over 50 percent of our business came from auto insurance, so consequently over half of our SIU cases involved vehicles.

Since auto damage and injuries came from collisions, fraudsters became experts at staging accidents. For thefts, vandalisms, and fires, criminals were equally well versed in how to steal, fake thefts, and destroy vehicles.

It wasn't long before our friends with *Claims Video News* would fly back to Miami. When my boss learned that corporate was drawn to another one of our projects, he was amazed they would fly down twice in as many years. He joked it was only because it was December. It was about 15 degrees Fahrenheit at the corporate office, versus a sunny 85 in our backyard.

Either way, "Operation Rainbow Sheen" was a visually perfect project for video. It showcased new tactics to combat theft, working alongside police, surrounded by the beautiful outdoors.

None of us could have predicted how a simple auto fraud story would uncover so many stolen vehicles, or a corpse.

Chapter Twenty
Operation Rainbow Sheen

Police departments would occasionally approach us for donations toward mutually beneficial projects. They figured we had the money, and our teams were chasing many of the same crimes.

One example was when law enforcement would ask for the donation of a "bait car" to use in sting operations. After insurance companies settle total loss claims, the carrier becomes the titled owner of the vehicle. So we had many recovered theft vehicles that were titled in our name, completely functional, and not being used by anyone.

The police would ask to lease one of our vehicles to use for their operations. They might leave the car in high-theft areas, then monitor it with the goal of catching thieves.

If I received a request that seemed valuable, I'd forward it up the chain for approval. I would sell the potential for positive results, such as the arrest of thieves in our community. But we had to be cautious with the contracts to avoid liability issues. Imagine loaning a car to the police and

they hit someone. Once all the conditions were ironed out, it created a nice photo op to deliver a car to the police, and we would wait for any notable results.

One day while having a lunch of *vaca frita* (a Cuban dish made with shredded skirt steak, topped with sauteed onions with a squeeze of lime, served with black beans and rice) at La Caretta, an agent with the Auto Theft Task Force told me they were seeking donations for a project. At the time, hidden cameras that could be monitored from elsewhere were expensive. City budgets wouldn't pay for it, so they figured they'd ask us since we insured so many stolen cars. My proposal to our corporate office would state, "If we recover just one vehicle insured with our company, the value will exceed the donation."

The project became instantly more intriguing when we were told the Environmental Protection Agency was getting involved.

"The EPA?" I thought I had misheard. "Why are they involved in auto theft and fraud?"

South Florida has over 2,200 miles of canals and waterways within 1.5 million acres of land. [92] Our southern counties also border the Everglades, a 7,800-square-mile natural wetland. That much area provided a lot of placcs to hide or destroy vehicles. Fraudsters began sinking their cars in remote canals to ensure they would never be found.

Environmental groups became concerned when they realized *thousands* of cars were deteriorating in our waterways, releasing gasoline, motor oil, and battery acids into our fragile ecosystem. When sunken cars were winched out of the water, they would leave behind a multicolor oil slick, hence Operation Rainbow Sheen.

That added twist of so many cars polluting our beautiful environment was the final selling point. Our company agreed that the project would be enormously beneficial.

Police planned to hide a camera on a utility pole near a canal in west Miami known for frequent dumping. Neighbors across the canal had reported seeing people sinking vehicles late at night. The police would monitor the camera from a van a mile down the road. If they witnessed someone sinking a car, they would intervene. When they obtained the culprits' information, they would call us to see if it was one of our customers or vehicles.

I obtained approval for a donation to purchase what we called the "pole-cam." After corporate agreed, the *Claims Video News* team was ready for another Florida field trip. Lyle, two SIU consultants, and their video crew arrived in sunny December. It was so picturesque, the film crew wanted to drive to Key Biscayne so they could have a backdrop of the Miami skyline while I described the spike in fraudulent vehicle thefts.

With the recession of the early 2000s, many people could no longer afford their lavish cars. Their SUVs guzzled fuel that was skyrocketing (over $4 per gallon in 2012). Locals tried to project certain lifestyles by driving heavily financed luxury cars. We encountered people earning minimum wage with $1,000 monthly car payments just so they could be noticed in a BMW.

Vehicle leases were a recipe for fraud. Early lease contracts were brutal and almost impossible to terminate. The irony was that for people who had poor credit or no equity, their contracts were even worse. There were exorbitant penalties for exceeding 12,000 miles per year. People would sign anything to be seen at a valet station driving something plush.

Lenders seemed to be accepting every applicant. Here's the complication: Many insurance policies at the time had to protect the lienholders no matter what. If the claim was denied for any reason—including fraud—we still had to pay off their loan. So, insurance was a perfect instrument for fraudsters to get out from under a vehicle loan or lease.

How many times have you heard "no credit checks!" or "no money down!" or the dreaded "no payment for three months!" This created what I called the summer party car. Imagine a deceitful young person hearing those ads. They could buy or lease a cool car for the summer—after all, no money down and no payments for three months! They party every night in the car, with all their friends, up and down Ocean Drive.

When summer's over and the car's trashed, they drive fifteen miles west to any canal and sink it. They report the car stolen, and when it's not recovered, their dependable insurance company pays off their loan. Cue my refrain: "We all just paid for that car."

Our canals were filling up fast with newer vehicles. Criminals had no clue they were dumping cars on top of other cars. In some canals, cars were stacking up like a game of Jenga.

The *Claims Video News* team was thrilled to wear their tropical casuals in December. They observed the pole-cam hidden beside a remote canal. It was the perfect visual setting: an area that fringed the Everglades, so we had a vista of cypress trees and sawgrass as far as the eye could see. They were ecstatic when they captured a few alligators on film.

Police shared compelling night-vision video of men pushing cars into the canal. Perpetrators had been arrested and charged with insurance fraud. They either confessed to dumping the vehicles (with added counts for environmental crimes) or they testified against our insureds who had hired them to make their cars vanish.

As an added holiday bonus, law enforcement invited us to a "canal dive" the next day, allowing the crew to film police divers locating cars for removal. Similar to when we helped search containers at the port, our entire SIU team was invited to assist. The dive was located at an infamous canal just miles from my home, north of Fort Lauderdale.

We met the next morning, ready to film the day's harvest of recovered vehicles. Having grown up in the area, I knew the canal well. It ran for seven miles along a rural road called Loxahatchee "Lox" Road that led to the Everglades. It was a notorious dumping area, with sparse nearby homes for potential witnesses.

And we would all discover why the desolate stretch had been called "cursed" since I was a kid.

Chapter Twenty-One
Ghosts of Hillsboro Canal

Canal dives were like an exciting school field trip for our entire team. When we arrived on the grassy banks of the canal that morning, there were a half-dozen Palm Beach County and Broward County Sherriff's Office cars and a couple tow trucks waiting for the day to begin. We were wise enough to bring several boxes of donuts (not an imprecise cliché), sunscreen, and lawn chairs. It would be a full day.

The Sheriff's Dive Teams were a bold group. Their job was to respond to emergency situations in underwater environments, including the sea, lakes, and the Everglades. They provided underwater search and recovery, locating drowning victims, diving accidents, and submerged boats and vehicles.

While speaking with a diver, I cringed to learn they required numerous vaccinations to protect themselves against infective bacteria from potentially hazardous water. They might submerge in water containing sewage, toxic chemicals, or fuel. Their wetsuits covered every inch of their skin, with hoods and masks that sealed their ears and faces. Though our surroundings were beautiful, the canal water was the color of Snapple iced tea and contained God knows what.

The twenty-foot-wide Hillsboro Canal ran alongside the narrow Lox Road, terminating at the swamp of Loxahatchee. When I was a kid, my dad would take us to the end to fish and watch airboats heading out for the day. Years later, my wife and I would bring our children to look for gators and watch the brilliant sunset over the glades.

But we knew not to be there after dark. There were no streetlights, no close civilization, and the waters were filled with alligators and snakes.

But there was another reason: The road was so long and remote that people would drag race at night. The area was an infamous hangout for teenagers to party and race. Kids would stuff their cars with friends, drive to the end to drink for hours, then race home. For decades, the road didn't have guardrails between it and the canal, just feet to the side. Dreadful car crashes were frequent.

The most horrifying incident that rocked our community was when a two-door Pontiac filled with eight teenagers lost control and swerved into the canal. Five of the teens died.

The kids had been on the way to a "swamp party" in the early hours of Sunday, September 27, 1992. The driver of the Pontiac had been trying to pass a friend's car when she lost control, launching the car into the canal. When they submerged, teens in the other car stopped to flag down locals who had been filming alligators. Two men jumped into the murky water in an attempt to rescue the passengers.

One of the rescuers, Tracy Valentine, described the grim conditions. He said, "It was pitch black. We couldn't see; we just had to feel." [93] The car's doors were wedged shut by muck. They finally got one door open far enough to pull the victims through. Valentine and his friends immediately attempted CPR. Three teens died at the scene, and two more within days.

For years thereafter, when my family and I would venture to the end of Lox Road, it was a sobering reminder to see faded tributes spray-painted on the street and plastic flowers where they had entered the water. Over time, there were many more crashes with young victims. Everyone suspected there were other cars in those waters that no one was aware of.

Hillsboro Canal, December 4, 2008

The absence of any guardrails, lights, and witnesses also made it a frequent dumping area for criminals. For our canal dive, local sheriffs workcd with our SIU teams for the fraud aspect. Doug, one of our experienced SIU investigators, had his laptop so we could check the VINs of any recovered vehicles to see who owned them.

Police used sonar to create a map of the canal floor to pinpoint any cars. Divers would swim down into the murk to locate the vehicle and attach chains for the tow trucks. Other officers stood at the water's edge with rifles for any meddling gators or snakes.

When they hoisted a car onto the bank, we would rush in to inspect it. With water gushing out of the doors, we'd see the interior carpeted with algae, sometimes with catfish flopping on the floors. Many cars were so fresh they appeared new. When we searched the trunks, my crime-writing brain hoped to find a duffel bag of cash from some forgotten heist (no such luck).

For our enthralled *Claims Video News* film crew, we demonstrated signs of fraud. Almost every recovered car had a factory key still in the ignition. People who commit fraud also clean out their cars of all personal items. All belongings removed, including baby seats, toys, items in the trunk, even coins in the ashtray. Why would a thief do that? More importantly, why would a thief go through the risk of stealing a valuable car to then just sink it?

Factory key in the ignition of a car recovered from Hillsboro Canal

One recovered leased car had excessive mileage that would've resulted in a steep penalty. The film crew asked us how we could possibly know the mileage since the odometer on the dashboard was dead. We showed them our classic technique: the little oil change sticker on the windshield. It revealed its last mileage and the date. Fraudsters always forgot to peel that off.

When Doug checked his laptop, some of the cars hadn't been reported stolen yet. People were under the belief there should be some "waiting period" before they reported it stolen. We had already contacted their insurance agents, and we would be waiting until they finally reported the car stolen. We couldn't wait to ask them if they still had all the factory keys.

We bought a stack of pizzas for everyone for lunch. We shared information with the officers about the vehicle owners, and they initiated criminal investigations for many of the cars.

But after our lunch, as the sun crept toward the horizon, the unimaginable happened. It was the single threat I had dreaded at every canal dive. Considering we were in South Florida, I knew it would only be a matter of time. In one of the cars was a decomposed corpse.

As much as I consider myself a hardened investigator who loved gory thrillers, I never wanted to see a dead body. I knew the scene in the movie *Goodfellas* where Henry Hill was trying to clean the undying stench from his trunk. Cops and war veterans will tell you it's a smell and sight you will never forget.

By pure chance, the team found the body in a car resting upside down on the bottom of the canal, far from where I was standing. Otherwise, I would have rushed in like usual to inspect the interior. I was wise enough to remain on the sidelines as authorities converged onto the scene.

On that humid December afternoon, the intact skeleton was buckled in the driver's seat of a 1986 Mercedes-Benz coupe. The man was later identified by the car's registration and dental records as Barry Fish from Boca Raton. His body had been hidden in twelve feet of water for over fifteen years.

It appeared to have been an accidental crash. Barry had his seatbelt on, and there was no trauma to his bones. Homicide Detective Michael Bianchi later emphasized to the *Sun Sentinel* that the death could have been prevented if the road had installed guardrails.[94]

When Barry's parents were informed, they said he had often used Lox Road to travel between their house in Parkland and his home in Boca Raton. It was unnerving to envision how his body had been lying at rest in between the two homes for all those years.

"There are hundreds and hundreds of cars in these canals," said Detective Bianchi. "I wouldn't doubt there are some people out there.... The problem is, after you hit the water and the weeds, people don't see you." [95]

Even more unsettling, over fifty sets of unidentified remains rest in boxes in a police evidence room. Tony Mead with the Palm Beach County Medical Examiner's Office told the *Sun Sentinel* that the remains range from whole skeletons to a single tooth, some from as far back as the 1960s.[96]

For our fateful canal dive, our film crew had witnessed an arduous day. Their completed production delved more into the fraud side than our morbid discovery. At the end of the operation, police had recovered 110 vehicles. The divers had started at one end of the canal and worked their way west to recover as many cars as they could over a two-day period. It wasn't even a third of the seven-mile stretch, leaving it to our imaginations how many more mysteries loomed in those bleak waters.

Today, the canal is still a dumping ground. Law enforcement budgets can only do so much. Guardrails were finally installed, and more visible communities have been built in the area—the irony of creating a safer environment at the expense of Florida's natural beauty.

There were also positive developments on the fraud side. Most auto policies no longer protect lienholders if the insured commits fraud. So, for any aspiring fraudsters: Making your car "vanish" will no longer relieve you of your debt—no more summer party cars.

Chapter Twenty-Two
Other Vanishing Acts

Since the motive for fraud is usually financial gain, the scams require the complete destruction or disappearance of a vehicle in order to be paid. If the car is recovered or considered repairable, it defeats the purpose. Aside from submerging them, the best way to ensure a car cannot be fixed is by torching or dismantling it.

Those same desolate backroads and the Everglades provided perfect space, away from any prying eyes, for a car fire. And there are shops whose sole existence was to dismantle and resell parts on the black market. As I said previously, the sum of the parts is greater than the whole.

With owner give-ups, we knew there were many places to make a car vanish and no shortage of criminals who could promise they would never see their vehicle again—at least in one piece.

Charred Cars

Old-school investigators taught me the simplest tool criminals use to start a car fire: a bag of potato chips. It's small, made of paper, blotted with oils, and available anywhere. The firebug places it in the interior, usually under a seat, lights the bag, and flees. The bag continues to burn, fueled by the oils and chips, eventually spreading to the seats, carpeting, and the polymers of the car. The fire proceeds to consume the vehicle, growing larger as it ignites the motor oil and fuel. The 99-cent paper bag leaves no forensic evidence behind.

The owner then reports their car stolen. Eventually someone stumbles across its charred remains. The car is then considered a total loss, and the owner (or lienholder) is paid.

Simple, right? Not so fast. Further illustrating my "fraudsters aren't geniuses" principle, there were plenty of mistakes the insureds made in the execution of the above scenario.

In smaller cars that pride themselves on being airtight, the fires would go out if they didn't crack a window. We learned as kids three things are required for a fire to take place: heat, fuel, and oxygen. Remove one and the fire will extinguish itself.

The skittish fraudster would light the fire, close the door, and exit the scene. He assumed the car would burst into a spectacular fireball, just like in the movies. But after he would report his car stolen, he would receive a call from the insurance company saying something like, "Good news, Mr. Smith: Your car has been found. There's only a little fire damage on the seat and floor—but completely repairable. So just pay your $500 deductible, and we can begin repairs."

Not only would the ambitious fraudster not get his car paid off, he would now have to pay $500 to have a car that he would forever think still smells like smoke—all because he didn't crack a window.

Firebugs also didn't realize actual investigations would take place. Whether it's the fire department or our SIU—or both—it'd be hard to conceal a glaring motive. We'd ascertain immediately if they were behind on their payments. We would request credit reports and ask where they service their vehicles. Did it recently have mechanical problems?

We'd conduct detailed statements from everyone they said they were with at the time of the theft. "What are their names and contact information? Which mall? Which store did you go to? Do you have receipts?" An honest insured would sail through these questions without pause.

And the most vital tool: forensic analysis. We employed experts just as we did with large fires. Arsonists assume everything will go up in flames in the vehicle. In reality, there are layers of evidence left after a fire. Even with the most scorched remains, experts can usually pinpoint where the fire began.

According to the National Fire Protection Association (NFPA), 69 percent of legitimate car fires begin in the engine, running gear, or wheel area.[97] Conversely, most of the cases our team investigated had fires that started in the passenger area, especially under seats. Our experts would rule out if the owner was a smoker or if the car had any wiring problems in those areas.

A rookie arsonist might add fuel such as gasoline. For most blazes, our experts could still find positive traces from carpets and seat cushions. It'd be tough for the owner to explain how gasoline got *inside* the car. They could allege the fire was vandalism, and that might be the case. But we'd weigh the other facts, such as the *coincidence* that the car was on the verge of repossession.

I was amazed to observe how our experts could recover the ignition. If a fire starts in the interior, the heat causes the windshield to fall inward. Anything on the floor is covered with windshield glass. The steel ignition switch drops straight down, so we know exactly where to rake though the debris for it. When located, our forensic locksmiths can determine if the ignition was damaged by a thief or if a key was used. The holy grail was when we'd find the factory key still in the ignition.

In these cases, the owner has to explain how a thief had a key, especially if they already told us that all keys were in their possession when the car was "stolen." If the car was stolen, there would be significant damage to the ignition switch.

Another motive for arson was when the vehicle had a costly mechanical problem. We investigated blown engines all the time. One young man had no idea the oil had to be changed. In that case, our mechanical expert was able to retrieve oil from the engine. He described it as "sludge" with evidence the engine was blown. It would've been impossible for the car to drive. In those cases, the inoperative vehicles were usually towed to the isolated area to burn (or sink).

In another scenario I called the "courteous thief," the owner would claim the car had upgrades such as expensive wheels and rims or a premium stereo system. But when the car was recovered, it would have bald factory tires and a basic radio. To believe the owner's story would mean the thief took the time—after the effort to steal the car—to remove all the tires and gear then reinstall factory tires and equipment before torching (or sinking) it.

I wish we had interviewed convicted car thieves to ask if they or any of their buddies had ever changed the tires or reinstalled a factory radio before burning a car.

Opa-locka Chops

Opa-locka is a unique urban city in northeastern Miami-Dade County. We had an inordinate number of stolen vehicles recovered during chop shop busts in that area.

For whatever reason, the city was developed in 1926 with "Arabian Nights" architecture, and streets named things like Sultan Avenue and Ali Baba Avenue. After countless storms without repairs, portions of the city looked like an abandoned amusement park.

I'm not suggesting the city was entirely crime-ridden during my time in office. I know there are many honest merchants and hardworking residents who live there. But during my tenure, in 2003, the city of Opa-locka had the highest rate of violent crimes of any city in the United States.[98] In 2008, the *Miami New Times* described the city as "mired in crime and sinking fast." [99] The FBI investigated the city's mayor for corruption when Governor Rick Scott issued an executive order declaring the city to be in a state of financial emergency.[100] In 2012, Opa-locka Police Captain Arthur Balom was charged with trafficking ecstasy, cocaine, and oxycodone. He was sentenced to 87 months in prison. Prosecutors said he had protected a violent drug gang by tipping them off about police raids.[101] In 2018, crime in Opa-locka had increased 403 percent from the previous year.[102]

You get the picture. Our team had frequent visits to that fair city as part of our investigations. Instead of dumping the cars, thieves took them to chop shops where mechanics dismantled the cars to sell the parts. As described before, chop shops are often operated by organized crime syndicates.[103] Smaller shops may be part of a larger network of thieves. Some cars are stolen from theft lists provided by the shops. Many vehicles were owner give-ups, as some of our policyholders wanted them to disappear.

Chop shop mechanics can disassemble a car into its components in just hours. A majority of the parts are sold on the black market, others laundered through legitimate channels. They might be sold to salvage yards who resell them to the public or sold to body shops as legitimate. Any parts without identifying numbers are almost impossible to trace. Parts tagged with a VIN, which have been assigned to every vehicle since 1981, are often destroyed or dumped.

Chop shops have been raided to discover motorcycles, boats, Jet Skis, and tractor trailer parts, which have fewer identifying numbers. Fortunately, our local NICB agents knew where to find the hidden VINs stamped onto the frame.

Our team would receive calls from police, informing us they had found parts of cars we insured. We would then investigate any owner give-up scenarios. How long had the parts been at the shop? Was the owner behind on their payments? Or perhaps it was just a garden-variety Miami theft.

During my time, there was also a spike in rental car thefts. Criminals would rent cars for the sole purpose of selling them to chop shops. Criminals used fake or stolen IDs to rent the cars. In some cases, they would first use the cars to commit other crimes (such as staged accidents) then sell them to the chop shop for cash.[104]

In 2014, Miami-Dade County Inspector Jorge Herrera was inspecting a shop in Opa-locka. He fortuitously stumbled upon a rented BMW while it was being dismantled. After Herrera called for backup, police discovered the car had been rented from Avis just a few hours earlier. The rental company didn't even realize their car had been stolen yet.[105]

Tony Fernandez, an NICB agent we enjoyed working with for years, stated, "I've had cases where the same individual has rented six to seven cars from the rental car company." Many of the parts were found in international shipping containers bound for Russia or Latin America.[106] Things had come full circle from my chapter on illegally exported vehicles.

Tears of a Supermodel

Chris, a tireless SIU rep who I'm still friends with to this day, investigated one particularly memorable case. Our young customer, who professed to be a supermodel (a common career aspiration in Miami), reported her new Camaro convertible stolen. She provided receipts for a premium sound system, a nitrous oxide engine for boosted speed, and the inevitable wheels and rims.

Chris tried his best to be impervious to her charms. The young lady cried when she described the harrowing account of discovering her car was missing. But things changed when Chris discovered all of her receipts were bogus. He tried to visit each merchant and discovered that the invoices were either forged or for shops that never existed.

Chris admitted to me that he had almost choked up when he met with the young lady and her father to tell her the receipts were fake. She instantly began crying and offered no explanation.

Then we were notified that her Camaro had been recovered, or at least its skeleton. It had been completely stripped—including seats, doors, and airbags—then dumped. Curiously, the car had factory wheels and a basic stereo (the "courteous thief" strikes again).

The steering column was still intact. We hired a forensic locksmith, who discovered the ignition had not been defeated. A thief could not have stolen it without a key.

We asked the young lady to explain the inconsistencies. Her father immediately hired an attorney, and they dodged any questions surrounding the theft. They then filed a lawsuit against our company for denying her claim.

I previously explained how police can conduct concurrent investigations separate from ours. We had the duty to report our findings to the Division of Insurance Fraud (DIF), who took an immediate interest in the case. A DIF agent then visited the young lady for her statement.

I'm guessing it's more daunting to be questioned by a DIF agent than by an SIU employee. After all, most agents are veteran law enforcement officers. When the DIF agent met with the young lady, she immediately burst into tears and confessed to the entire scheme. She could no longer afford her car, and she had asked her dad to help make it vanish.

The police then arrested her father for his involvement. He struck a deal to give up the chop shop where he had delivered the car. Police obtained warrants and raided the Opa-locka shop. It was a case we all remember because when the shop owner vigorously resisted arrest, his arm was accidentally broken.

It's no surprise the aspiring supermodel and her father dropped their lawsuit and withdrew their claim. As part of their restitution, she was ordered to pay for all investigative costs.

Chapter Twenty-Three
Lambo for a Day? Exotic Car Rental Schemes

Have you driven by a showroom flaunting Ferraris, Lamborghinis, and Porsches with a sign declaring "Exotic Car Rentals?" Maybe you then imagined how fun it would be to cruise around in a Rolls-Royce Ghost for a weekend.

Please fight your impulse and don't do it. The exotic car rental business is rife with deception, both against the shops and you, the customer.

In our area, luxury car rental businesses were on every corner, from Miami Beach to Fort Lauderdale and the Palm Beaches. People want to appear successful. Some renters admitted their goal was to impress their dates. Aspiring singers wanted to post photos on social media seated in their "Lambo." One ambitious young musician told us, "Money attracts money."

But most renters didn't know two things. One: Many of the rental agencies didn't even own their cars, so liability could fall onto the renter. And two: Many of the agencies didn't carry insurance, so again the renter may be culpable for any losses. And the real car owners weren't Boy Scouts; some were implicated in organized crime and murder.

Whose car are you really driving?

The exotic car rental business was an unregulated, unlicensed, and underinsured industry. Brokers borrowed high-end cars, sometimes from unreputable sources, then rented them to third parties, including unsuspecting tourists and weekend attention seekers. South Florida crime rings had begun using the agencies as fronts.

Some brokers filled their showrooms with exotic cars that belonged to owners who couldn't afford their payments. Or worse, they borrowed cars from criminals who expected huge returns. They then opened storefronts to rent the cars to customers, sometimes for $1,000 to $5,000 per day. For a startup broker, a showroom of such cars was almost uninsurable, nor would commercial policies cover a fleet of cars they didn't own.

So, many brokers made the conscious decision to operate uninsured. Similar to a Ponzi scheme, they prayed there would be no losses while they pocketed the exorbitant rental fees. In the event an accident did occur, they would tell the renter they had to submit the claim to their own insurance company. In some of our cases, the brokers had coached the drivers on what to say, such as they had "borrowed the car from a friend."

In more unsettling scenarios, organized crime members would steal the cars back from the unwary renters. In one case, our young customer had rented a Lamborghini for his weekend DJ job at a gentlemen's club. He admitted to us he wanted to pull up to the club and impress the ladies. But within hours, while the DJ was working inside, the Lamborghini was stolen without a trace. He was then coerced to report the theft to our company for over $250,000.

Our investigation discovered the rental agency had experienced numerous similar thefts. We deduced they had spare keys to the cars and must've followed the renters. Their business model was to rent the cars, then track the drivers to easily steal them back. When we accessed corporate records to reveal the agency's ownership, its parent company was owned by a man with a Slavic name and a lengthy criminal record. Law enforcement later confirmed the business was operated by Eurasian organized crime.

Ultimately, we did not pay that claim since the rental agency could never prove ownership of the car. No one could determine the car's origin, so there was literally no one to pay.

Exotic Cars for Money Laundering

One exotic car broker, Mani Chulpayev, allegedly profited from years of organized fraud by renting exotic vehicles to drug traffickers, which also served as a method to launder their illicit cash. Chulpayev allegedly obtained cars through fraudulent means to then lease them to drug dealers. Similar to the boat schemes, he accumulated an inventory of vehicles by recruiting straw buyers to purchase the cars in their names. The buyers would then give the cars to Chulpayev to be leased to criminals who paid using cash from their illegal activities.

The straw buyers rushed to finance multiple vehicles within a brief period to secure loans before the new financial commitments appeared on their credit reports. Chulpayev provided the buyers with forged documents, including fake paychecks, to facilitate the loans.

According to the DEA, Chulpayev initially made some of the loan payments, but he eventually stopped. When the buyers defaulted, the banks were saddled with repossessing cars from drug dealers or locating vehicles that had been exported to foreign nations.

In October 2020, he was arrested and extradited from Ukraine, and charged with money laundering and bank fraud, according to the U.S. Drug Enforcement Administration.[107] A federal grand jury indicted Chulpayev and two of his associates on counts of conspiracy to commit bank and mail fraud and one count of conspiracy to commit money laundering.[108]

From Laundering to Murder

In a more foreboding case, an ambitious Miami broker named Raimundo Modia had the idea of borrowing exotic cars from wealthy owners to then rent to customers. He chose to never insure the cars, creating a virtual time bomb. He rented a Lamborghini Murciélago and a new Audi R8 to two customers who never returned. Just days later, a third renter stole a Porsche Panamera that an NFL football player had loaned to the agency.[109]

A desperate Modia had spent the last week of his life tracking the three cars, according to the *Palm Beach Post*. The real owner of the Lamborghini, a New Jersey collector, had demanded his car back, which was worth over $250,000. Modia was deep in debt; his home was on the verge of foreclosure, and he was now accountable for a half a million dollars worth of cars he didn't own.[110]

He struggled to conduct his own investigation to unravel the scheme and find the cars. One source told him Korean millionaires who owned a hip-hop label had taken one car. Another told him two dangerous pimps had taken the cars to Las Vegas. He attempted to follow every lead.

After spending weeks trying to track down the cars, Modia was found dead. He had been shot several times in a Fort Lauderdale warehouse. No one knows why he had gone to the warehouse, but friends speculated the killers could have thought he was an informant. The murder left our exotic car rental community in a panic. It seemed to be proof Eastern European car thieves were targeting their agencies, and they had finally claimed their first victim.[111]

The scheme involved a web of Eastern European criminals who used locals with false identification as renters. The ring rented luxury vehicles with the purpose of shipping them to Eastern Europe. Some of the cars rented in Miami were also tracked to California chop shops.[112]

In a related case, American Luxury Auto Rental in Miami had the novel idea to use GPS to locate their missing Mercedes-Benz 550. A man with a driver's license from a former Soviet Republic had rented it. When police tracked the car to a Hialeah warehouse, they found the Mercedes and a stolen Audi being shrink-wrapped and loaded into a shipping container by eight Russian criminals.[113]

My ongoing disclaimer: There are many legitimate agencies that rent exotic vehicles. Their cars are obtained ethically, and they are properly insured. But the next time you desire to pull up to your class reunion in a red Ferrari, please thoroughly read your rental contract and ask the agency to verify their insurance.

Chapter Twenty-Four
This Again? Repeated Schemes

I always wondered if fraudsters met at a certain bar to trade the latest schemes and tricks. Someone would invent an ingenious ploy and then tell all their colleagues. In reality, it was probably done in chatrooms or through word of mouth, but we encountered some very distinct schemes that would recur over and over again.

I recall walking in Las Vegas once and seeing a panhandler with a sign that read "Need cash for ninja lessons." It actually made me chuckle, and I gave the guy a buck. Then I began to see different versions of the same sign in California, Chicago, and Key West. I imagined that one guy had conceived the phrase, and others thought, "Good one! Now I'll try it!" Was there a national consortium of panhandlers who trade best practices? Evidently, the same thing happened in the world of insurance fraud.

Attack of the Bees

We received a case for an auto crash with several injured passengers. The driver said he had been driving along when a bee suddenly flew into his car. He began to swat at the insect, which caused him to lose control and hit a tree. All the passengers then made claims for liability, injuries, and so on.

Fair enough. That was a very specific and unique story—the first time we heard it. Soon thereafter, we received another claim: "A bee flew into the car and I lost control." Then a third claim, and then a fourth.

Miami may be known for a lot of things but never as a haven for bees. Were all these drivers passing through floral gardens or honey orchards? No, it was just the latest ploy.

Psychologists and sociologists have studied why people tend to believe complex and far-fetched "big lies" over small white lies. According to Matthew Rozsa in a *Salon* magazine article, a story can be "so grandiose as to make it hard to believe that someone would fabricate it."[114] What were the odds a bee could fly into a car in Miami? It had to be true, right?

Every six months or so, the fraudsters figured it was time to amend their tale. We then received accident cases where drivers said they'd been holding cups of hot coffee in their laps while driving. They hit a bump and it spilled, causing them to lose control and hit a tree.

Some drivers would slightly alter their stories. It could be a cup of hot tea, even a scalding Cup-a-Soup. The accidents always happened away from any possible cameras. They opted to crash into trees or poles to avoid involving a second vehicle. How could we investigate and prove such fortuitous events never happened? It was easier than you would think.

You know the "black boxes" found on planes, ships, and trains that record data to reconstruct the moments leading up to a catastrophic event? Most of our vehicles have them as well.

Since 2014, over 96 percent of new cars have a built-in Event Data Recorder (EDR). An EDR can provide valuable data from seconds before, during, and after an accident. In 2010, the National Highway Traffic Safety Administration required EDRs to collect multiple data elements including changes in speed, which pedals were pressed, if the brakes were applied, if seatbelts were used, and if the airbag had deployed.

Our team was able to request the vehicle's EDR data. The "brains" of the EDR units are located in a protected area of the car, usually under a seat. We had to ask permission from the vehicle's owner, and they had a duty to cooperate with our investigation. Data vendors could download the data for our review for around $500 per vehicle. We would then compare the data to the versions of the tale given by the driver and passengers. Rarely did they match.

In one memorable "bee" case, the EDR had recorded the brakes, accelerator, turns, and seatbelts. The data revealed the car had slowly idled off the road. It continued at two miles per hour toward the tree. It then stopped for a couple of minutes—as if deliberating—and then the driver accelerated to about five miles per hour straight into the tree. None of the passengers had been wearing seatbelts, even though they had stated they were.

In a "hot coffee" case, the driver told us he had lost control at over fifty miles per hour before plunging into a canal. The driver swam to safety, lucky to be alive. However, the EDR data disclosed the car had stopped for an extended period at the canal's edge before slowly idling into the water.

In these cases, the drivers' lawyers had difficulty refuting the EDR findings. Similar to DNA evidence, the data is almost infallible. Most of the people withdrew their cases when we kept pushing for information. If not, their attorneys dropped them as clients.

After the tenth bee or hot coffee story, we felt like exclaiming, "At least come up with some new material."

The Triple Pay

Around 2020, a racket passed through our area with the traits of a gypsy scheme. A traveling group of people made repeated claims to carriers for the exact same damage. Until we exposed the fraud, they received numerous payments. And due to a small technical oversight that we uncovered, they swindled some carriers into paying each individual case up to *three* times.

With heavy competition, many insurers pride themselves on how fast they can pay a claim. To simplify the process, some carriers didn't scrutinize identification from the drivers who weren't their customers. Example: our driver hits a car in a parking lot. With clear liability, the second driver makes an appointment to have an estimate written for their damage, at which time a check would be issued for the repairs. Confirming ownership of their car and analyzing their ID would be beside the point and inefficient. Just pay and close the file.

Preying on this process, the fraudsters would obtain two vehicles that already had damage. They either bought the cars with damage or created their own. They purchased insurance on just one of the cars, then pretended to hit the other car in a minor accident. The driver would admit fault, so the second car could make a claim for repairs. They would pocket the money and then make another claim for the same damage with another company, and so on.

To compound the fraud, this roving gang had discovered a genius way to get paid twice by the *same* company. With the growth of electronic payments, many companies offer customers a choice between a paper check or a direct deposit to their bank. When the adjuster asked the fraudster if they wanted a check or an "e-payment," they requested a paper check. When they received the check, the culprits would race to a nearby check cashing store. A check from a reputable insurance company could be cashed within minutes.

But mere seconds after collecting their cash—perhaps even in the check store parking lot—the culprit would call the insurance company to say they had changed their mind: "I want an e-payment instead." The check disbursement wouldn't show up on the system yet, so the adjuster would stop-pay the check and reissue an e-payment. The company would then wire that money to the criminal's fraudulent account, and they would either withdraw it or wire it elsewhere. Thus, the driver would collect twice from the same company for the same damage.

But it wasn't over. A few weeks later, the check cashing store would inevitably call the insurance company, stating the check they had honored was rejected. In the state of Florida, check cashing stores have protections against fraud, and since an insurance employee had stop-paid the check, the carrier was responsible for reimbursing the check store.

At that point, the same parking lot accident had been paid three times: once in cash, again as an e-payment, and a third time to reimburse the check store.

In the cases we investigated, the group had been using stolen identities to execute their scams. No one, including the check cashing store, had gone to any lengths to verify their IDs. When our team analyzed photos taken at the body shops, the offenders had made sure their faces weren't photographed. In a few photos, we saw their hands holding disposable cups of coffee from nearby cheap hotels, the type given out free in lobbies. This seemed to corroborate the theory they traveled from town to town to commit their crimes.

When the same group began to show up in other parts of the U.S., federal authorities that investigated identity theft opened a project.

Ultimately, as automation progressed with insurers, they designed better systems to verify identification, as well as faster notification when payments were made from banks and check cashing businesses. No more double—or triple—paydays.

How Not to Be a Target

Insurance agents used to give out bumper stickers to customers touting the company's name. Some were just a logo to serve as advertising. But in the fraud business, we called those stickers "targets." When a customer placed the company's sticker on their rear bumper, it announced to potential fraudsters, "I have good insurance!"

If a looming bad guy wanted to find a car on the road to cause a collision with, he might see a 1978 Camaro with a Van Halen sticker and a new Lexus with a sticker from a major carrier. Which car are they going to prey on?

Many accidents that involved an innocent party were known as the "swoop-and-squat." Imagine a culprit driver has targeted your car because you appear to have good insurance. They then pass you just far enough to pull in front of you. Seconds later, they slam on their brakes, causing you to rear-end them. You would typically be found at fault.

Some swoop-and-squats involve a second car that drives beside the victim to box them in their lane, while their partner abruptly stops in front of them. The "swoop" car is usually driven by a senior ring member, while the "squat" car is full of accomplices who will all make injury claims.

Most states have laws stating drivers must maintain a safe distance from vehicles in front of them to avoid a rear-end collision. If you are following too closely and the car in front of you suddenly stops, you will be found at fault in a rear-end collision. The fraudsters know this.

If you tried to argue fault with the police, all the rear-ended driver has to say is, "A squirrel ran out in front of me, and I braked." The victim driver (you) would be found entirely at fault.

Planned Injuries

As with other types of fraud, the ringleaders have no concern for the safety of their participants. Similar to the human trafficking cases, the fraudsters will fill their cars with people who may get seriously injured. In our cases, many were immigrants, probably paid small kickbacks for their involvement. In fact, it would benefit the criminals' schemes if the passengers were severely injured. The worse the injury, the more valuable the lawsuit.

There have been cases where the culprit drivers misjudged the severity of a collision. They have targeted commercial trucks because they have higher liability limits. A freight truck will carry over $300,000 in limits, an oil truck $1 million, and a truck carrying hazardous materials $5 million in coverage. The fraudsters who target the higher limits risk their associates' lives.

One driver, Jose Luis Lopez Perez, was killed after a swoop-and-squat accident, leading to an investigation of a personal injury attorney and a murder charge. According to Ken Dornstein's article, "Accidentally, on Purpose: The Making of a Personal Injury Underworld in America,"[115] poor immigrants are often recruited to drive the swoop cars, some paid only $100.

When Perez intentionally swerved in front of an eighteen-wheeler, the truck lost control and flipped onto Perez's vehicle, crushing him to death. A personal injury attorney, Gary P. Miller, went to trial for Perez's murder, testing the theory that criminal responsibility could extend to accomplices.[116]

Miller had allegedly been part of the ring by paying "cappers" who worked for him to stage the cases for his law firm. His business cards were found in the possession of an arrested capper, a passenger, and the owner of a crashed car.[117] Miller had was linked to eight suspected staged accidents before the one that killed Perez.

After a highly publicized trial, Miller was sentenced to six years for vehicular manslaughter, fraud, and conspiracy. He is believed to be the first attorney ever charged with murder for his role in an insurance fraud ring involving staged crashes.

Moral of the story: Don't be a target or a victim. The next time you're driving in the fast lane and some shabby car pulls in front of you and drives slowly, ignore the temptation to accelerate onto their rear. That might be precisely what they want. They could slam on their brakes, exposing you and your passengers to serious injuries, as well as an onslaught of insurance claims and relentless litigation.

And don't put your insurance company's sticker on your bumper. Stick with Van Halen.

PART SEVEN –
INJURY CRIMES

Chapter Twenty-Five
Lessons in La La Land

After my first work of fiction in 2014, I continued to write articles within the industry. After the Russian Mafia article for *SIU Today*—with my many loyal readers in the Russian Federation—my next articles were less inflammatory. My article, "High-Performance Boats and the Rise of Human Smuggling" for *National Underwriter*, became a popular topic for lectures at fraud conferences, as well as a presentation for the U.S. Coast Guard in Miami Beach.

The fiction-writing side of my brain plodded forward as well. After Hurricane Charley tore through Southwest Florida, I was inspired after hearing a shocking news report on the radio. The bridge that linked the mainland to the island of Sanibel had been disabled. The news declared, "Please don't attempt to return to your homes. There is no power, and police will not respond."

I was stunned at the message. They had just announced a huge opportunity for thieves. The island off the coast of Southwest Florida was a mecca for wealthy seasonal homeowners. Thieves would now know there's no electricity or alarms and police would not respond.

I envisioned burglars boating up to the docks, going house to house, and looting mansions at their leisure like the Grinch. Then to fictionalize my story, I imagined a team of thieves preying on homes in evacuation zones, having to race the clock with impending storms. They'd have high-tech gear, night-vision, and body armor, allowing them to narrowly escape as the storms come ashore.

While researching my plot, I discovered actual spikes in burglaries during storm evacuations. When Hurricane Matthew raged into South Carolina, thieves stole 230 semi-automatic rifles and handguns. Thieves robbed a Palm Beach art gallery during a hurricane, and other criminals broke into Sanibel pharmacies, stealing prescription narcotics. This was a plausible threat.

And so, *Storm Crashers* was born, published in 2016, about high-tech thieves who target wealthy areas evacuated due to hurricanes. The novel went on to win Best Popular Fiction at the Florida Book Awards. For an action-thriller, the honor meant a lot to me because the judges included authors and literature professors. As part of the award ceremony, my wife and I were invited to the Florida Governor's Mansion for a luncheon. It was a fun, proud moment, and the entire event seemed surreal.

My concept of burglars striking during hurricanes also captured the imagination of Hollywood. As a film buff, I knew that in over a hundred years of cinema, no movie had been made with my exact idea. After many queries, producers at Union Entertainment in Los Angeles loved the script

version I had written from the book. They also saw its potential as a video game, with its "race against nature" plot. I signed to have Union represent *Storm Crashers,* and they shopped the project to the major film studios. Thanks to producers Dan Jevons and Richard Liebowitz, an option for my story was sold within days to 20th Century Fox.

An "option" meant the studio paid for the rights to create a movie for a specified amount of time. While I continued my day job in Miami, producers on the West Coast worked hard to pitch a version that would get a green light for a movie. Though Fox did also pay me to extend the option for another year, ultimately a film never came to fruition. Our theory, based on the scale of the story, is that it would've been a very expensive film: cities destroyed, air battles, flooding, wrath-of-God stuff.

That was okay; it was a fun ride. I got to take many trips to L.A. and had a distinguished Beverly Hills attorney (thank you, Tom Collier). I recall during a tour of Paramount Studios, our escort shushed us as we passed a door with a red light above it. He whispered, "Be quiet, Tom Hanks and Julia Roberts are filming in there" (evidently the movie *Larry Crowne*). Although no film was made based on my story, I made cherished contacts, memories, and friends that I still have to this day.

However, a suspiciously short amount of time later, studios greenlit at least three movies about "high-tech thieves planning a heist during a storm." Only a couple made it to completion, including *Force of Nature* and the cornily titled *Hurricane Heist.* The low-budget movies went straight to video or were fleetingly released without fanfare. These B-level studios had completely devalued my entire concept.

"Sue them!" my beautiful wife and mother shouted. But I learned you can't copyright an idea alone. Remember when two movies came out during the same summer about an asteroid headed toward earth? But I did find it highly coincidental—after a century of no such plot—that the other movies were created within months after my story had been presented to every major studio in the city.

It was fun working my job in Miami one day, then hopping on a plane to L.A. the next. I'd throw on a blazer and attend meetings and lunches around Hollywood for a day or so, then take a red-eye back home. Most of this was unknown to my coworkers; I preferred to keep the two worlds separate. A workmate would stroll by my desk and ask, confused, "Didn't you post on Instagram from lunch in Malibu yesterday?" I'd squint as if to recall, "Yeah, maybe…"

It was a learning experience about the nature of the industry. I just figured my same brain would concoct something else inspired by the cases we investigated every day.

Real Fake Accidents

In the early 2010s, a shift in fraud abruptly altered our focus. SIUs had originated to tackle property crimes, but as time progressed, more money went out the door for injury cases. I understood the rationale: Taking down one fraudulent medical clinic would stop countless claims, saving millions in benefits versus investigating property cases one at a time.

One holiday season, my boss informed us that starting on January 2, our team would exclusively focus on investigating injury cases. We had to be quick studies on staged accidents and fraudulent medical clinics. We agreed that fraud was fraud, and many of the same players were implicated in all forms of organized insurance crimes.

Groups were orchestrating accidents for the sole purpose of creating patients for sham clinics. To illustrate—and this still goes on today—they staged vehicle accidents just severe enough to claim all occupants were injured. Many passengers were needy locals who the ringleaders had approached, offering financial incentives such as cash kickbacks.

It was not uncommon to have drivers report six to eight grown adults stuffed into a car. I recall a driver who told us eight grown men, all over six feet tall, were crammed into his Toyota Corolla. More ruthless perpetrators would bring a child or toddler to gain credibility or sympathy. A two-car accident could total twelve to sixteen people, who would all make injury claims and initiate a dozen lawsuits, cross-suing each other for liability.

Many accidents happened at night or in remote areas to decrease the likelihood of witnesses or cameras. In Miami, you'd have to drive pretty far west to find a rural area. We would ask, "Why were you, six friends, and your baby driving toward the Everglades at 2 a.m.?" The participants already had attorneys to thwart our attempts to interview the occupants until they could get their stories straight.

There were law firms that specialized in representing these types of cases. One indicator might be when multiple passengers hire the same attorney—even more so if people from *unrelated* accidents keep hiring the same law firm. We could use analytics to review all claims associated with that firm and see if those cases had similar patterns: minor collisions, known participants, no witnesses, or late at night.

There were also staged injuries that didn't involve vehicles, such as the classic slip-and-fall. Those incidents were faked to pursue benefits from a business or homeowner. We had a woman who sued her best friend, claiming she had fallen in her home at a New Year's party. It was never personal; she knew her friend's insurance would pay. In grocery stores, a common ploy was to drop a grape or an egg on the floor to make it slippery. After a dramatic fall, the alleged victim would insist that the manager complete an incident report or call for an ambulance. And so, the treatments would commence.

Our beloved Miami had earned the honor of being the nation's capital for medical fraud.[118] Over time, we realized that an inordinate number of suspicious accidents and clinics were in specific areas of South Florida. It seemed as if certain municipalities were more business-friendly to these criminal enterprises. How could we possibly go up against crooked cities?

My boss would ask, "How can you describe a 'city' as crooked?"

I would then explain using facts and analytics.

Chapter Twenty-Six
Fighting Crime in Gotham City

To establish context, it would be unfair to depict the city of Hialeah as entirely corrupt during my decades of fraud investigation. There are thousands of hardworking, honest residents in this western suburb of Miami, many of whom are long-time friends. Many of my coworkers and fellow SIU investigators also grew up in the city. However, a disproportionate number of fraudulent medical clinics were also in Hialeah.

Our police partners jokingly called the area Gotham City, comparing it to Batman's crime-ridden hometown, where even some city officials and police officers were corrupt. I learned Hialeah's dodgy reputation had begun years before with its highest-ranking officials: its mayors.

At the launch of my career, Hialeah kept reelecting a convicted felon as its mayor. In the early '90s, a grand jury indicted Hialeah Mayor Raul Martinez for eight charges of extortion and racketeering.[119] He was sentenced to ten years in prison but appealed, citing flawed jury instructions. His second trial ended in a hung jury. After a third trial, he was acquitted on one count of extortion and the jury deadlocked on the remaining counts. Ultimately, the remaining charges were dropped. Even the *Los Angeles Times* chimed in: "When Raul Martinez was reelected to his third term as Hialeah mayor in 1989, he had just been indicted on federal charges of racketeering and extortion. He still won 53% of the vote." [120] Martinez was reelected as mayor through 2005. The fine folks of Hialeah elected him a total of nine times.

Next in line, Hialeah Mayor Carlos Hernandez got caught loansharking by providing high-interest loans to a convicted Ponzi schemer in 2014. He admitted under oath he had loaned $180,000 to a conman at an interest rate of 36 percent.[121] He never reported any of the earned interest, which totaled over $100,000, on his tax returns filed in his public disclosures. The mayor paid a $4,000 ethics penalty using 145 boxes of pennies and nickels.[122]

That same mayor bought a trip to Las Vegas using $7,621 from a grant created to feed poor children, according to the *Miami Herald*.[123] He purchased airfare and rooms at the MGM Grand for himself, his chief of staff, a detective, and four employees to attend a parks and recreation conference in Las Vegas. In a curious twist, Hernandez never arrived in Vegas for the conference. His whereabouts for seven days remain a mystery, according to the Miami-Dade Commission on Ethics Report.[124] Despite his crimes, Hialeah residents reelected Hernandez through 2021.

Even more unimaginable, the mayor of adjacent Hialeah Gardens was arrested for trying to hire a contract killer to murder her husband. Mayor Gilda Oliveros was charged and sentenced to almost five years in prison for solicitation to commit murder, insurance fraud, and voter fraud.

According to the *Washington Times*, police had opened a fraud investigation against Oliveros, which uncovered the alleged plot to kill her spouse.[125] They had been involved in a bitter divorce and, according to the *Sun Sentinel*, she had obtained a $1 million life policy in her husband's name. During the trial, handwriting experts testified she had forged her husband's signature on the application.[126] One of the men she had allegedly approached to murder her husband became a star witness for the prosecution. However, three years later, her conviction was overturned, ruling that the $1 million policy should not have been admitted as evidence because it wrongly suggested a financial motive for the alleged scheme.

It wasn't just a revolving door of dubious mayors. Some of its police officers were "creating" patients for medical clinics. During the era we were in our Little Havana office, the owners of a Hialeah medical clinic were arrested and charged with racketeering, insurance fraud, and grand theft. The clinic had billed thousands of dollars in phony services for accident victims. As part of the investigation, a Hialeah Gardens police officer was charged with creating a false accident report for a staged accident to generate patients for the clinic.[127]

That same year, a Hialeah Police detective was arrested for filing a phony accident report to create patients for his friend's medical clinic. After a joint investigation with Hialeah's Internal Affairs and the Division of Insurance Fraud, the detective was arrested for submitting a false report naming his father and friend as passengers to "help out a friend who owns a clinic."[128] The clinic had billed insurers over $125,000 based on the fake accident.

I'm happy to write that today's Hialeah is a much better place. It is a city where multi-generational families embrace their cultural identity and entrepreneurial spirit driven by small businesses. The real estate values are experiencing a significant increase, with an influx of young professionals choosing to relocate to the city.

Regrettably, during my time, many believed that a group of unscrupulous city officials held sway over the world in which the majority of our medical fraud occurred. We wondered if we could trust officials or authorities with our cases.

For the bad guys, it was easy to see why it was an ideal environment to commit fraud. Medical clinics were popping up in every strip mall, and some of them were never really there, as if they were invisible. But that didn't stop them from relentlessly billing our company.

Chapter Twenty-Seven
Runners of the Mill

Presuming a *real* car accident occurred, the schemes would begin with the runners. These are the individuals who would show up at the scenes of accidents and hand out cards to the vehicles' occupants to persuade them to use a specific medical clinic or attorney.

No, these practices are not legal or ethical. And how did they just "show up" at an accident scene?

According to Florida Statute 817.234, a lawyer, healthcare practitioner, or owner of a clinic may not solicit accident victims or their families within sixty days of an accident to be new patients or clients except through general advertising.[129] The Florida Bar also prohibits solicitation, including face to face, by cold calls or through a third party of a client who is not a family member or someone with whom the lawyer already had a prior relationship.

But runners still existed on every proverbial corner. To find their prey, they'd monitor police scanners or offer kickbacks to tow truck drivers who were called to the scenes. They would sometimes pay cash bribes to accident victims to use a specific attorney or clinic. Then they'd coach victims on what to say and which parts of their bodies were hurting for when the EMTs arrived.

Some runners offered rides to victims to specific medical clinics, where the runner would earn a handsome referral fee. Even more repugnant, runners would offer cash to hospital workers, ambulance drivers, or even police to sell victims' contact information.

These crimes always struck a chord when they touched our personal lives. My wife was once involved in a minor fender bender. Her vehicle was drivable, but the other car had to be towed, so the police called the tow company with which the city had a contract. The next morning, my wife received calls from a medical clinic and two body shops, who promised to "waive the deductible." The callers claimed they had our information because they were "partners" with our insurance company.

I knew that was a lie because we hadn't reported the claim yet. Using the process of elimination, since there was no police report yet either, the only party that had our names and phone numbers was the tow truck driver. He had evidently sold our information to the clinic and body shops. It was disturbing to know people were selling our private information to, ostensibly, criminals. I was already aware of the scam, but it's easy to see how people would fall for these calls.

Unfortunately, arresting runners was not a top priority for authorities. They offered some of them leniency to provide information about who had hired them, to go after the bigger fish. Few talked, which was understandable if the larger fish had anything to do with organized crime.

The above scenarios were for the real accidents. Add to that the plethora of staged and intentionally caused accidents. Imagine all those passengers—men, women, old, young, and even infants—all funneled to specific clinics and attorneys. They were practically printing cash.

Build Them and They Will Come

A federal agent jokingly offered a reporter a dollar for every strip mall in Hialeah that didn't contain a medical business. The reporter claims he's still broke, in a city where "strip malls line the boulevard like concrete."[130]

When I write "clinic," it could mean a doctor's office, medical supply business, physical therapy, or diagnostics such as an MRI facility. Many

strip malls could have two or more of these services next to each other. Some were next door to the offices of the attorneys who had referred people to the clinic. We even observed some separate businesses, such as a law office and a clinic, that connected through secret back doors.

Why the proliferation of clinics and medical fraud? Criminals discovered they could make more money this way than they could selling narcotics, without using weapons or risking long prison sentences. Our company was billed for medical equipment and treatment the alleged victims never received or required.

From my experience, an alarming number of our insureds were complicit in the scams. They knew they weren't getting all the treatment we had been billed for. Some accepted cash kickbacks at the clinics just to show up.

As an example of how we investigated, if a person is prescribed treatment three times per week, it might seem excessive if it was from a minor accident. (The clinics' own gluttony was usually their downfall.) We would hire surveillance to monitor the patient on one of those days. Video might show the person staying at home, going to the gym, or commuting to work. But, during that day, they never visited the clinic. Yet we would still receive bills from the clinic for that same day.

We would ask the insured to attend an examination under oath to clarify the facts. We'd ask if they had visited the clinic on that day. Many would staunchly insist they had, and even give details about where they had parked and how long they'd been there. At that point, we could either show the video proving they had never gone, or save it as part of a larger investigation.

Fortunately, we also had honest customers who admitted they had never visited the clinic for the days we had been billed for. Some grew upset, realizing they were victims of fraud as well. Some asked, "Why is my $10,000 in coverage already gone? I only went twice." We'd show them the billing for twenty visits. Those honest customers could become our best witnesses.

Almost all the credit for investigating these businesses goes to our organized activity teams. They used advanced analytics, assessing data from mountains of fraudulent billing. I won't profess to have the expertise those teams used every day. There was still a place for our field teams. We needed people to do in-person investigation such as visiting clinics, meeting various players, and knocking on doors in Hialeah back alleys. And together, our efforts paid off.

Imaginary Clinics

What if a clinic was never real? We had to verify if some clinics even existed. We were never shocked to discover a vacant storefront at the clinic's address. We would take photos of the abandoned offices. Some had a few toppled chairs and electrical cords snaked across ripped carpet. Though the offices had been gone for a while, our company would still receive daily billing.

We would try to question the building's landlord: "Did the clinic really have a lease? When did they leave?" We'd knock on the doors of the neighboring tenants. Few people talked; I guess there was some code of *omertà* among the conspirators. Many times the buildings were owned by the ringleaders.

For offices that billed us for MRIs and X-rays, our investigators would make impromptu visits to confirm they had the equipment. MRI machines are massive, extremely expensive, and need additional voltage. An MRI scanner also requires calibration and regular maintenance. We could ask for those records.

How did clinic employees react to our surprise visits? Recall our investigator Chris who was chased out of an office by two perturbed Russian gentlemen. Others were friendly and happy to help, allowing us inside for a tour of their facility.

What's the smallest clinic in the world? In a common ploy, a clinic might have a prominent address such as Biscayne Boulevard, specifying "Suite 402." But when we drove to the address, we discovered it was a Mail Boxes Etc. or other mailing service instead of a clinic. "Suite 402" really meant "P.O. Box 402." The entire medical office never existed except in a mailbox. So that clinic was about four-by-four inches. We called that a "paper office."

We had amusing questions for our insureds in those cases. We'd ask them to confirm the clinic's address and "suite number." They'd explain how they drove there and where they parked. We'd ask them to describe the inside of the clinic. One woman was specific, describing beige couches,

a magazine rack, and potted palms. Our attorney would just let them drone on. The woman added details about a reception window and a pot of free coffee. The whole time she kept rambling, we knew that was a lot of furniture to fit inside a four-by-four-inch mailbox.

For clinics that did exist, there was no guarantee they performed the services we had been billed for. Many clinics would require patients to sign a stack of blank forms. The victims had no idea what they were signing. A receptionist handed them a bundle of forms and told them they had to sign every page. Keep in mind many of these patients were either elderly or didn't speak English as a first language. If an authority figure told them to sign all the forms, they did so.

The blank forms were used to falsify multiple treatments or as sign-in sheets to misrepresent how many times they had visited the facility. A few sloppy clinics went as far as forging our insureds' signatures, which our handwriting experts could attempt to refute.

More brazen clinics would pay people cash bribes to visit clinics or sign blank forms. According to a police detective who visited clinics undercover as a patient, they would pay varying amounts depending on which insurance company the patient had. If it was a larger carrier that prided itself on how fast it paid claims, the patient would get a larger reward. If it was a smaller company that scrutinized its bills, they'd offer less.

Our company had begun to earn a reputation for being tough with fraudulent clinics. Our SIU teams asked a lot of questions, made unannounced visits, and had the resources to pursue broad investigations. The ultimate compliment was when an illicit clinic would no longer accept accident victims insured with our company. Some had signs on their doors: "No customers from ABC Insurance!"—not exactly the essence of the physicians' Hippocratic oath.

No Good Deed

Regarding the dubious nature of some local police, I was alerted to an event that seemed inconceivable. We had hired a surveillance firm to monitor a Hialeah clinic. They were watching the only door to the clinic to record how long certain patients stayed. Most medical procedures require specific amounts of time to perform, in addition to the wait times, yet patients were walking in and out of the office within minutes (probably just for the sign-in sheet).

One day, our surveillance van was discreetly parked to watch the office. A Hialeah police officer approached the van and tapped on the driver's window. When the investigator rolled down the window, he showed his credentials and explained he was a licensed P.I. conducting surveillance. The officer just nodded. He then proceeded to the clinic to warn them they were being watched.

That's the world in which we labored. Note, these were certainly rare occurrences. We worked hand in hand with all law enforcement, including Hialeah P.D., who were usually very helpful and supportive of our investigations. They also wanted a positive reputation for their city, and we knew all professions can have bad apples.

What happened when a clinic did close shop? When the fraudulent clinic owners knew they were being watched, they would abandon shop, sometimes overnight, just to reopen down the street under a new name.

It was like a game of "Whack-a-Mole." As described by Hank Walther, a federal prosecutor who led a medical fraud task force, "You knock one down, but now there's a bigger one somewhere else."[131]

Our pursuits may have seemed futile, but we couldn't just remain idle. And *just maybe* we could be so relentless and inquisitive that a bad clinic might refuse to submit fraudulent billing to our company. We had to change the behavior and push back at the thug in the schoolyard.

I always kept a suit jacket on the back of my office door for any unplanned meetings. I figured a classic blue blazer would go with anything I'd be wearing—a dress shirt, a polo, or Tommy Bahama. Occasionally, we would get a last-minute call from the NICB to attend a press conference. They'd give us a heads-up about major arrests and invite us to attend the big announcement for the local news. The Miami-Dade Justice Building was less than twenty minutes away, and it was always exciting.

On Thursday, May 16, 2013, we got a call about one of the largest clinic and staged accident stings in Florida's history, and evidence from our SIU teams had played a large part.

"Operation Sledgehammer" would require me to dust off the jacket.

Chapter Twenty-Eight
Bringing Down the Hammer

As a result of a three-year federal and state investigation, charges were announced against medical clinics involved in staging accidents and filing false insurance claims. As part of "Operation Sledgehammer," thirty-three defendants were charged, which included South Florida doctors and clinic owners. At the time of the arrests, four of the defendants had already fled to Cuba, with an additional three missing and considered fugitives.

The operation got its name when undercover police observed suspects using actual sledgehammers to make vehicles look like they had been in accidents. By the time Operation Sledgehammer concluded in 2013, a total of ninety-two defendants had been charged for their participation in the vast ring.

The accidents were staged by people who had been trained to defraud insurers to earn money for the organized group of medical professionals, clinic owners, and recruiters. They also enlisted area chiropractors and others to serve as registered owners of the sham clinics.[132]

The suspects had recruited people they referred to as "*perro*" and "*perra*" to act as drivers and passengers in the accidents. They hired complicit chiropractors and therapists who billed for services that were never performed. The clinics submitted the claims to insurers, charging over $20 million in fraudulent billing.

The reason we were invited to the press conference was because our teams, along with SIU teams from other carriers, had provided a substantial part of the evidence against the clinics. For all the empty storefronts, fake sign-in sheets, and cooperative witnesses we had uncovered, our findings had been referred to the Division of Insurance Fraud. Imagine authorities receiving identical findings from multiple insurers all saying the same thing.

We stood alongside the authorities wearing our blue blazers and fine apparel as they announced the arrests to every local news outlet. The magnitude of the arrests made national news as well.

FBI Special Agent William J. Maddalena said to the press, "If you get upset about your car insurance premiums going up, this crime is one of the reasons why. Every time an insurance payout is made for a staged accident in Florida, we all feel the pain in the pocketbook."[133]

An Invasive Species

What did clinic criminals do when there was more heat in South Florida? They crept north. Like a spreading infection, the ringleaders set up shops in Orlando and Tampa.

The NICB had concentrated its resources almost entirely in Miami, which had been "ground zero nationwide" for fraud.[134] NICB President Joe Wehrle said, "Our partnership with law enforcement and member company investigators has shut down a number of fraud rings in that area and, as a result, some of the criminals have moved further north."[135]

Tampa had become Florida's new number one city for accident fraud by 2010, with a 290 percent jump from the prior year, second only to New York City.[136]

Criminals prayed the adjusters were working from cubicles four states away rather than trained investigators visiting their clinics in person and demanding answers under oath. SIU teams in those areas tackled the crisis with the same tactics we used in Miami, including using analytics to identify patterns within thousands of submitted bills.

Time marched on, and in 2019, a $42.7 million fraud ring was exposed with ten arrests. One of the ringleaders, a former Miami doctor, is still at large. His associates stole the identities of twenty physicians and filed 23,708 claims for fraudulent services totaling over $42,742,000. The claims were submitted by fifteen "phantom clinics" across Florida, with physical addresses that functioned solely as drop boxes for insurance payments.[137]

I'm compelled to include one amusing story. A Hialeah man tried to flee the U.S. on a Jet Ski after he was charged in a $4.2 million medical equipment scheme. In 2022, the man's fictional company had filed claims for medical equipment that were never provided to anyone. The U.S. Coast Guard found the man aboard a broken Jet Ski south of Key West, headed toward Cuba. For his planned 90-mile trek, the suspect was on the Jet Ski with a known migrant smuggler. The watercraft had been outfitted with extra fuel, food, and water bottles. Is there a sense of *déjà vu* with other schemes previously described?

This illustrates the interconnection within organized fraud, whether it's clinics, stolen boats, or human smuggling. Robert Trigaux of the *Tampa Bay Times* concluded how Florida had become the epicenter for medical fraud, "It gained traction in South Florida when illegal immigrants were told they could pay off the price of being smuggled into the country by faking injuries in staged accidents."[138]

The significance of understanding one type of fraud, no matter how seemingly unrelated, helped us recognize other crimes.

We were soon bewildered to learn the U.S. federal government wanted to meet with us. They had become interested in our unique investigative niche.

Chapter Twenty-Nine
New Colleagues: The Feds

One quiet afternoon in 2018 while probably sipping a *café Cubano,* I was puzzled to receive an invitation to attend a meeting with the United States Secret Service. It was to be at their Miami office, and the tone of the invitation did not invite debate.

The Secret Service? I sat upright. Had we done something horribly wrong? Maybe we had targeted one of their deep-cover agents?

I had to admit I didn't understand all of the Secret Service's duties. I thought the agency primarily existed to protect the president, the White House, and other lofty officials from threats. So what did they want with a bunch of insurance investigators?

I was fascinated to learn they also investigate economic crimes, specifically against the U.S. financial system committed by criminals around the world.[139] Fraudulent insurance claims were certainly generating millions of dollars of monetary crimes in the United States.

Evidently the Secret Service had been informed about how our SIU teams were investigating certain parties concurrently with their cases. Their invitation was a gesture of cooperation.

Coincidentally, the Secret Service's Miami headquarters was two blocks from our office. With its security gates and armed guards, it appeared ominous every time I drove by. So it was exciting to be welcomed into the building along with members of our organized activity teams. After a security check as thorough as at an airport, I couldn't resist sending my wife a photo of me standing on the immense seal for the U.S. Secret Service on the polished marble foyer.

The meeting was remarkably not intimidating. The agents were friendly and gave us their business cards—and yes, the cliché is true: All the agents were impeccably dressed in suits and ties. They offered trays of bagels and coffee, and it became clear why we had been invited. Their presentation revealed the names of clinics and suspects we had been investigating for years.

A collaboration with our teams could save months of research for pieces of the puzzle we already had. SIU teams from multiple companies would have depositions, payment amounts, surveillance footage, and analytics charting the players.

The Secret Service was especially interested in the money laundering aspect. To simplify, money laundering is the method used to make illegally earned money appear legitimate. Fans of *Breaking Bad* already know Mr. and Mrs. White used a carwash to launder their money. Al Capone used laundromats to "clean" his cash, and it's believed that's where the term "laundering" originated.

In our world, we knew money laundering was tied to fraudulent medical clinics. I imagine to a criminal, nothing would appear cleaner than checks issued by prominent insurance companies. Collectively, dirty clinics were generating tens of millions of dollars through fraudulent billing to insurers and Medicare.

Why did criminals begin using clinics to launder cash versus laundromats or that mattress store in your community that no one visits? Medical clinics give the impression of a respectable health-related business.

Suspicion would be lower than for a sketchy check cashing store, and it's not unusual for medical businesses to transfer large amounts of cash for equipment and salaries. Financial transactions, perhaps even offshore, might appear routine.

The U.S. Secret Service was asking for our help. Through statutes that allowed us to share certain file material, we were able to show them how much we had paid and to whom, providing fresh blueprints for their investigations. It was a win-win for all investigating parties.

I was fascinated to learn this wasn't the first time a government agency had reached out to the private sector for fresh and creative ideas.

The Pursuit of Imagination

After the 9/11 attacks on the World Trade Center, American Airlines Flight 93, and the Pentagon, someone in the U.S. government had the novel idea of meeting with creative civilians to brainstorm future threats.

Fans of author Tom Clancy were horrified to realize a plot in his thriller *Debt of Honor* was grimly similar to the 9/11 attacks, yet the book was published seven years before the tragedy. In his 1994 novel, a suicidal terrorist uses a 747 airliner to crash into the U.S. Capitol. The man wields a crude knife to kill a pilot and made sure the plane had a "full load of fuel." [140]

No one in 1994 believed such a concept was plausible. In a 2004 report from the Committee on Government Reform, Commissioner Bob Kerrey admitted, "Had more of us read Tom Clancy, we might have been able to figure this out… when we say failure of imagination, that is what happened to all of us." [141]

Federal authorities had begun to wonder if the public, including creative thinkers, could assist with their efforts. Defense experts decided to solicit terrorist scenarios from authors and filmmakers. Less than one month after 9/11, the U.S. Army met with artists at its ROTC office at the University of Southern California. The goal was to conceive possible terror plots and offer solutions to those threats. Though the meetings were secret at the time, they included writers for *Die Hard* and *MacGyver,* and director David Fincher. [142]

The Department of Homeland Security recruited best-selling author Brad Meltzer for its "Red Cell" program in 2004. To anticipate potential threats, the government brought together what it called "out-of-the-box thinkers." Meltzer, a writer of acclaimed crime thrillers, had been identified as one of those thinkers.

Meltzer stated what inspired him most in the program was the other people who had also been chosen for the group. In addition to members of the FBI and CIA, there were college professors, transportation employees, and software programmers.[143] People from a variety of trades were chosen to offer creative investigative avenues.

Envious of such an opportunity, I wondered how I could be part of a similar group. Imagine that same tactic for critical thinking applied in the business-risk world. We had already proven how teams like ours were creative and had a lot to contribute.

Then I was excited to discover the FBI had already devised such a forum for innovative ideas—and I could be part of it.

InfraGard

The Federal Bureau of Investigation created InfraGard, a partnership between the FBI and the business sector. Its mission was to share intelligence between businesses, academic institutions, and law enforcement to prevent hostile acts against the United States.

It's easy to imagine industries that could be vulnerable to terrorism, such as power plants, chemical factories, banks, and IT firms. Leaders from those industries were invited to join InfraGard to attend meetings with the FBI to share knowledge and discuss safeguards.

When I discovered InfraGard, I was curious if my profession would be of interest. I completed an application, asserting how insurance fraud had proven links to organized crime, sham businesses that launder millions, and boat theft tied to trafficking. Someone at the FBI evidently agreed with my proposal. In 2011, after a thorough background check, I was thrilled to receive a binder and ID card welcoming me aboard as a member.

I was eager to attend my first meeting. InfraGard meetings were hosted by the FBI and held quarterly in private auditoriums. Considering my fascination with creative crimes—for my job and for my writing—my first meeting was everything I hoped for. Speakers included a security expert from a national bank who described how criminals hide money offshore. An IT specialist discussed malware that could cripple entire economies.

When I heard an upcoming speaker was a forensic botanist, I was puzzled, *a botanist? How could a scientist of plants offer anything relevant?* However, the scholarly woman explained that certain plants could be used to create toxins deadly to humans yet mimic a heart attack and not show on routine toxicology tests. As a crime writer in the investigative world, I was in heaven. I couldn't believe there were meetings with well-dressed professionals talking about stuff like this.

The presiding FBI agent, the tenured and friendly Agent Nelson Barbosa, called for future presenters. My hand darted in the air without any forethought. Barbosa accepted my offer, stating they were always seeking fresh perspectives. They had never heard from anyone about insurance crimes.

What have I done!? I asked myself as I drove home. I had joined the group as a lark and now was on the hook to speak to an auditorium full of FBI agents, experts, and law enforcement about… something. How was I going to pull that off? I had to conceive an angle to plausibly tie my job to some facet of terrorism.

Borrowing the adage "write what you know," I decided to keep it simple with an overview of fraud including theft rings, exports to South America, and organized crime with medical clinics. For my finishing touch, I would float an idea to get their attention: Could terrorists enter the U.S. through Cuba? Smugglers were bringing undocumented people to our shores almost daily, and our Coast Guard admitted it didn't have the resources to catch but a few.

While researching for my presentation, I was startled to learn it was a credible threat. The U.S. had labeled Cuba a state sponsor of terrorism (made official in 2021). According to a hearing before the Committee on Homeland Security, "Some people believe that terrorists will use Cuba as a gateway to gain entry into the United States."[144] But at that time, the U.S. was solely focused on airlines, with no attention given to nonstop smuggling boats. Terrorists could easily enter Cuba or Bimini, and then get to the U.S. by sea. I would discuss red flags with boat theft and the smugglers' schemes. I'd leave them with a taste of how all of our interests intersect.

The InfraGard conference was held at Nova Southeastern University in December 2011. I put on a suit and tie to match my hosts. I was younger than much of my audience and had zero law enforcement experience, but I knew my material. My hour-long presentation included stats, photos, and video. The time sailed by and members of the audience raised their hands with astute questions. They seemed astonished by the material, and a few proceeded to chat with me during lunch. It was fun, and I enjoyed every minute of it.

The next year I spoke again, focused entirely on Eastern European organized crime, including the "B-Girl" scheme and the Russian mob's involvement with theft, staged accidents, and clinics. While the FBI agents in attendance were certainly more experienced than I was in dealing with Russian crimes, others in the audience came from unrelated fields, such as IT and banking.

At the conclusion of my second InfraGard presentation, I was honored when Agent Barbosa presented me with the FBI's Exceptional Service in the Public Interest Award. It was a nice photo opportunity, and the award binder with the FBI seal is something I treasure to this day.

Today, I'm still a member of InfraGard, and I continue to attend meetings with stimulating guests. It's where I first learned how cryptocurrency was used on the dark web for very bad things. I met the agent responsible for arresting Jordan Belfort, the subject of the film and book *The Wolf of Wall Street*. In the wake of grisly mass shootings across the nation, there was a poignant-but-necessary training for active-shooter threats. InfraGard has been extremely worthwhile.

My company also benefited from my inclusion in InfraGard. Aside from gaining a profusion of local crime data, I received bulletins from the FBI's Cyber Division with the latest warnings on computer threats. I shared the (shareable) reports with our IT department. Our company's director of information security distributed the memos to his teams and told me to keep them coming.

I developed relationships with local FBI agents and other branches of law enforcement. A key part of any SIU's success comes from having valuable contacts. I could call or text a cop or federal agent any time with questions—which also came in handy with fiction writing. "Hi Nadine, do FBI recruits really have to endure tear gas at Quantico?"

A Constructive Conclusion

From working with the U.S. Secret Service and FBI, I made one significant discovery: neither knew of our legal ability to share information with them.

In SIU we called it "immunity" or "626 statutes." Applying Florida Statute 626.989, our SIU investigators could provide information and file material to any "local, state, or federal enforcement officials or their agents or employees."[145] We used the statute to exchange information with other carriers, and this provision also allowed us to share our findings with law enforcement about any fraudulent acts.

"So you're saying," a stunned FBI agent asked during an InfraGard meeting, "we don't need a subpoena to see your file material?"

"Nope. If you formally ask for it, per the statute, we can hand it to you."

"So that's basically free discovery," a Secret Service agent mused during our meeting. "And you have years' worth of investigation on these parties?"

"You are correct," we responded.

Using the above statute, a carrier would not be subject to civil liability for furnishing the information, as long as it was done without malice, bad faith, or reckless disregard for any party. As a practical matter, with any civil or criminal case, law enforcement might use the statute first to see if any information was pertinent to their case. If it was, they could then follow up with a formal subpoena, and the company would have to comply.

The agencies were not aware of this "free" tool for their cases—more proof that our world of insurance fraud investigation has been an invisible domain.

Every U.S. state and the District of Columbia have enacted similar statutes for reporting insurance fraud and sharing information.

I recall an amusing example of how these relationships were mutually beneficial—and a big lesson about swallowing my pride.

"Timmy" submitted a suspicious claim for his stolen Ferrari. Timmy was about twenty-three, and would routinely call to shout at my entire staff. He was the kind of guy who would say things like, "I can buy and sell all of you!"

When Timmy thought our investigation was taking too long, his father started to call me to scream condescending threats. He actually said, "You brown-bag-lunch adjuster, get out your little checkbook and pay my son!" One false move and Timmy's daddy had me on speed dial. Timmy and his dad belittled my staff daily to get the claim paid.

As we examined any financial motive to fake the theft, we requested Timmy's credit statements. I couldn't fathom him spending $300 per month on dry cleaning. His charges at South Beach clubs were over $600 per night. Evidently, he was the guy who would buy everyone's drinks. Yet he could never clearly explain what he did for a living.

After his dad went above my head to complain, my boss and I reviewed the case. I had to admit, despite the peculiarities, we had no solid evidence of fraud. We decided to pay for the theft. Timmy demanded that he pick up the check in person—from me. He arrived at our office, and I had to deliver the check with a smile. Wearing his white-framed sunglasses, he took the six-figure check from my hand. His smirk reeked of, "I know that you know what's going on here."

My boss understood my frustration. He suggested I let it go and just move on. He offered, "If he committed fraud once, he'll do something wrong again."

Fast-forward a year. Just when I had forgotten about Timmy, I received a request from the FBI for our file materials about his case. The request gave no indication of what they were investigating. I volunteered to hand-deliver a copy of our material, which included statements and the amount paid, to the FBI office in North Miami Beach. The agents were appreciative, and I understood they couldn't discuss their case. Again, I had to let it go.

About six months later, I saw Timmy's unmistakable name splashed in the news, arrested for Medicare fraud.

Seven people, including Timmy, were indicted for operating a multimillion-dollar fraud involving electric wheelchairs. The ringleader was sentenced to 90 months in prison and ordered to pay $2 million in restitution. His accomplice had fled to Costa Rica after pleading guilty and later surrendered.

The seven were indicted for submitting over $5 million in fraudulent claims for wheelchairs, purportedly supplied by shell companies across South Florida. They had paid people to serve as fictitious wheelchair recipients. They had staged deliveries with photos of the patients in their chairs and documents signed as "delivery confirmation tickets."

What goes around…. There was no mention of whether Timmy's daddy was involved. I presume our file material played some small part in the FBI's indictments, and my boss was right about letting karma play itself out.

Chapter Thirty
Death: The Final Injury

Reports of my death have been greatly exaggerated.
—Attributed to Mark Twain, 1897

Would you be shocked to learn it's not illegal to fake your own death? If you want to pretend you're dead to lounge on a tropical beach all day next to a duffel bag of cash, knock yourself out.

"I am unaware of any federal statute that would apply to an individual who fakes their own death," FBI spokesperson Bill Carter told *Live Science* magazine.[146] However, there's a catch: it would require orchestrating so many separate, interwoven frauds that legally faking your own demise would be virtually impossible.

The problem comes when it's time to check into a hotel, rent or buy a place to live, sign up for utilities, deposit money in a bank, purchase a vehicle, or anything else that would require an identity with or without a passport or social security number, all of which would be fraud.

Or worse, did you have a life insurance policy before you "died"? It would be a felony if you collected the proceeds. If your family received any of the funds with knowledge you weren't dead, they could be charged as accessories. Did you owe any state or federal taxes? Faking your death to avoid those debts would be tax fraud.

"Pseudocide" is the term for when a person stages their own death or leaves behind evidence to suggest they're dead to mislead others. Apparently, the concept is so common someone invented a word for it.

Our SIU team did not regularly investigate death claims, which were handled out of the ironically named "life" department. However, we were called upon to do tasks for their cases. We would conduct activity checks to see if there was any evidence a person was still alive, speak to potential witnesses or neighbors, or investigate any suspicious death records.

In movies and mystery novels, a death could be faked by a swimmer or hiker who never returns, or by a raging fire with a vagrant's corpse. But in the modern world, it's almost impossible. The primary reason: 99 percent of all deaths leave behind a body, or at least part of one. The remains of drowning victims and lost hikers are usually found. That creates an obstacle for any aspiring death fraudsters. No matter how bold the culprits might pride themselves as being capable, few are committed enough to resort to grave digging to supply a corpse. Even if they did, DNA tests and dental records would refute its identity.

To sidestep these hurdles, fraudsters began using a repeated scheme: the report of a sudden death while visiting a developing nation (formerly known as a "third-world" nation).

South Florida is a melting pot with a spectrum of nationalities. It was common for people to visit family in those developing areas. But if we received a death case without a body or with a suspicious death certificate from such countries, it could require further investigation.

As insurers began to increase their global market, they began selling policies in countries with less stringent data collection. The schemes we saw involved a death, such as a drowning, while visiting a nation in turmoil from political unrest or a national tragedy. The nation might have sloppy records or civil servants who could be bribed to fake reports. We observed purported deaths from people while visiting Haiti, Cuba, and Eastern European nations.

The fraudster is hoping the adjuster, seated in their cubicle in the middle of the U.S., doesn't have the skills or resources to confirm a death thousands of miles away. However, our team could.

Mr. Smith and the Zombies of Haiti

One memorable death case we received was for a man who had reportedly drowned while swimming off a beach in Haiti. Red flags included the man had crushing debt and a vague death certificate. More significantly: Why had Mr. and Mrs. Insured chosen to vacation in Haiti?

We had many wonderful policyholders who hailed from Haiti who would visit their families in the beautiful country. However, Mr. and Mrs. Insured had no ties to Haiti.

Though the geography of the Caribbean island of Hispaniola is gorgeous, Haiti was going through heavy political crises at the time. During that period, gangs had overtaken Port-au-Prince. Electricity, drinking water, and food were in short supply. On top of that, Haiti suffered a series of earthquakes and hurricanes between 2010 and 2021. The 2010 earthquake alone killed over 220,000 people. It was an area ripe for deception and missing people.

More troubling, according to Ron Poindexter, the then-director of Florida's Division of Insurance Fraud, medical examiners in Haiti were not required to view a body before issuing a death certificate, provided three people would swear a death had occurred.[147]

When Mrs. Insured reported her husband's drowning, she told us his body had been recovered and already buried in Port-au-Prince, even though they had no other family in the nation. She presumed that would be the end of our investigation and we would hand her the $1 million life insurance check.

We soon discovered Mr. Insured's construction business had gone bankrupt, and he was facing lawsuits from several builders. His $700,000 home was in the process of foreclosure. Combined with his claim of drowning while holidaying in Haiti, the case demanded a closer look.

Our company had never paid for an SIU employee to fly to Haiti, but we did hire private investigators for international work. I'll call our international P.I. "Jim Smith" because the nondescript man had an equally generic name. He was thin, fiftyish, always had a cigarette, and wore ironed khakis and a dress shirt with the sleeves rolled up. He was a licensed private investigator and worked with no advertising. Rumor had it he was a former CIA agent, and he certainly had a knack for obtaining information from authorities in any country.

We had success using Mr. Smith on a variety of cases. When a man claimed he had purchased diamonds from a jeweler in Bogotá, Colombia, Smith discovered the store never existed and the appraisals were phony. When a woman reported she had been robbed in a hotel in Havana, Smith learned she had never been a guest and the police report was forged. The culprits always presumed we wouldn't have the ability to verify their stories.

For our drowning case, we hired Mr. Smith to confirm Mr. Insured's death and burial in Haiti. Right away he knew death certificates from

Haiti were virtually worthless, so he turned his attention to the burial. We learned autopsies were rarely done and, absent any special circumstance (such as a death during a crime), Haitian law allowed the remains to be cremated or embalmed immediately. Drowning was not considered a unique circumstance.

Mr. Smith had contacts in Haiti's Department of Interior and Public Health. Considering the dubious death certificate, the local police also became curious. Authorities offered to have the body exhumed for a $1,000 fee. Considering our set of facts, it was a reasonable investment.

Upon Smith's return to the U.S., over coffee (a cigarette for Smith), he told me a horrifying account of the cemetery. He had seen skeletons on the ground wearing suits and ties. Most Haitians were opposed to cremation due to their religious beliefs. As a result, undertakers were charging predatory rates to bury the dead when 60 percent of Haitians earned less than $2 per day.[148] So, bodies were cast aside as they decayed. Families would rent mausoleums for a few years, enough time for a body to erode to a skeleton. When the money ran out, workers would dump the unclaimed bones in a vault or leave them scattered. Few families returned to collect the remains.[149]

Smith depicted an unsettling scene before even discussing digging for the casket.

Mrs. Insured said she had paid for her husband's burial with cash. Since it was recent, the alleged grave was easy to locate among thousands. Smith told me that the superstitious police officers wanted to hurry with their task to avoid being in the cemetery after sundown. The men had to dig with shovels to locate the plywood casket, a rather crude shipping crate. Once they had pried it open, their flashlights revealed no corpse, only three sandbags. Smith and the cops dropped it back into its hole and got out of there.

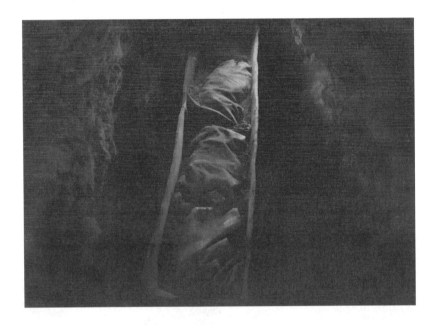

Local authorities opened an investigation into the parties that had issued the death certificate and the morticians who had agreed to bury the "casket." Florida authorities arrested Mr. and Mrs. Insured after the wife confessed to the entire scheme. A $1,000 investment (plus Mr. Smith's fees) allowed our company to avoid issuing the million-dollar check.

The Secret Twin

Now for some levity—I can say that because no one truly died again. We had an amusing case investigated by Sonia, the same talented rep who was caught in gunfire behind our Little Havana office.

We received a death case for a young woman, "Nelly," just months after she had purchased a life insurance policy. She had reportedly died suddenly of "natural causes" while visiting the Dominican Republic. We were alerted to the case because our company had received billing from a doctor's office for visits dated *after* her death.

We predicted several possible scenarios. We didn't necessarily suspect Nelly wasn't dead. It could've been a case of identity theft, or the clinic might've been issuing fraudulent billing. As discussed, our local clinics didn't have stellar reputations. Sonia's first stop was the medical clinic that had submitted the bills.

The doctor wasn't present, so Sonia showed a photograph of our insured to a nurse and receptionist. Due to HIPAA privacy rules, Sonia knew they couldn't reveal any names or treatments, but the ladies did confirm the woman in the photo had visited their office—after the date of her supposed death.

Sonia then visited Nelly's former neighborhood in Opa-locka. She conducted an old-school neighborhood canvass, knocking door to door, an investigative tool often ignored as too time-consuming. We always found canvasses to be productive. We knew that every neighborhood had a nosy neighbor who saw everything that was going on. Even in your own neighborhoods, you know a person who seems to sit at their window all day, watching everything. The key was to find that neighbor because they usually loved to talk.

Sonia spoke to the deceased's neighbors. Things became more curious when several said they had recently seen Nelly at her home. In fact, she'd been with her son and boyfriend.

Sonia knew the boyfriend and son were both beneficiaries on Nelly's six-figure life policy. When Sonia pursued the boyfriend for a statement, he reluctantly agreed. His story about the death seemed blurred, and he had no excuse as to why he hadn't attended her funeral.

We agreed to conduct surveillance on the boyfriend's home. If Nelly *was* alive, would she be foolish enough to be seen outside? Within hours of the stakeout, Sonia received a call from our P.I. from his surveillance van. He had sighted a female who matched Nelly's description. From photographs, it was evident it was her.

It was time to hire international P.I. Mr. Smith to try to verify the death in the Dominican Republic. He confirmed with the country's *Oficialía del Registro Civil* (Registration Office) there was no record of Nelly's death. Smith discovered there was no marked grave for our insured—thankfully, no digging required.

Sonia called Nelly's mother in the Dominican Republic. If she wasn't truly dead, could a mother keep such a secret about her own child? Sonia, who speaks Spanish, convinced the older woman to give us a statement. The woman remained vague about her daughter's death, insisting it had been due to natural causes, despite the fact that Nelly was in her early 40s. She also reiterated that Nelly's son and boyfriend were devastated.

Sonia decided to disclose her findings to the woman, including the absence of any death records, multiple sightings, and a fresh photograph of Nelly from our surveillance.

Nelly's mother gave a long, tongue-tied pause. Then, with theatrical emotion, she said she had a confession: When she had given birth to her daughter, she had really delivered identical twins. So the neighbors must have seen the *twin*.

Skeptical—and probably trying to maintain a straight face—Sonia asked why there were no records of a twin sibling.

After a beat, the mother replied that one twin had never been registered. "Nelly's twin was very ill at birth and not expected to live, so she was never documented." She shrugged, "But then she never died."

On top of that, she told us she had named both of them Nelly.

Fueled by this absurd story, Sonia decided to review Nelly's social media. Her profile image depicted her face on a cloud as if gazing down from heaven. As Sonia scrolled down the page, she saw a comment written in Spanish by her niece that read, "Run, run Aunt Nelly or they will catch you!"

Sonia was never able to locate the niece, but our findings were reported to the Division of Insurance Fraud, which opened an investigation. When agents visited the "twin" sister in Opa-locka, her fingerprints confirmed she was our very-much-alive insured. She and her boyfriend were arrested and charged with insurance fraud, and they "withdrew" their death claim.

Are criminal entrepreneurs now making the death fraud trade even easier? In countries such as Haiti, Nigeria, and other developing nations, you can purchase what's known in the pseudocide world as a "death kit," according to *Playing Dead: A Journey Through the World of Death Fraud* by Elizabeth Greenwood.[150] For several hundred dollars, the death kit includes a fake death certificate, burial permit, and photographs of a burial plot. For extra money, the sellers can add a video of the alleged funeral, complete with people crying, and even a funeral procession ambling down the road.

With people hoping to escape debts by vanishing with new lives, death fraud operations have been described as "a shell corporation for fraud."[151]

Considering the pitfalls, consequences, and lifelong paranoia of constantly looking over your shoulder, faking your own death appears worse than facing any burdens in the real world.

Neighbor must pay for damage caused by an "exploding corpse" (cont. Pg 6.)

Chapter Thirty-One
The Exploding Corpse

If this title seems over the top, it's the precise headline that went viral in 2014. I declared to my boss that we had officially made "international news" when an Australian news site and the UK's *Daily Mail* reported, "Home Damaged by 'Exploding Corpse.'"[152] Our investigation also resulted in important case law that is used in Florida to this day.

From the onset, the case was horribly bizarre. Our insured, "Ms. Rollins," had noticed a foul smell emanating from her next-door neighbor's condominium unit. The condo association called the Palm Beach Sheriffs, who discovered a dead body next door. The deceased woman had been there for some time, causing bodily fluids to seep into Ms. Rollins's unit.

The body belonged to her elderly neighbor who had been deceased for over two weeks. Due to the unconscionable circumstances, Ms. Rollins temporarily moved out of her apartment. The condo association allowed her to stay in a vacant unit free for twenty days. She then moved in with a friend for a month, then with her sister in Texas.

Our company was sympathetic to Ms. Rollins' plight. A biohazard company worked on her unit for two weeks after a crime-scene cleanup. Our company then worked with the condo association to remediate the unit. We replaced drywall between the units, then sealed the blocks with cement, painted the walls, and replaced some flooring.

Despite our efforts, Ms. Rollins complained the stench was still in her unit. She made a claim with our company for new furniture, replacement of all personal belongings, and even new appliances, arguing everything still smelled.

As a "named risk" policy, Ms. Rollins's condominium policy listed the types of losses covered, such as damage from fire, theft, or vandalism. No condo policy lists "smell from decomposing corpse." Our company had performed a cleanup, but there was no coverage to buy her new furniture, appliances, or personal items.

Ms. Rollins was not pleased with our explanation. She hired an attorney and sued our company for replacement of all property and additional living expenses, though she hadn't incurred any of those costs. We had compassion for everything Ms. Rollins had endured, but our company had to defend the lawsuit based on our policy.

I admit the attorney's tactic was creative. Since "decomposing corpse" was not listed in our policy, her attorney asserted it qualified as an "explosion," which was a named hazard. He alleged the body was so decayed that gases had caused the abdomen to bloat and eventually burst—i.e., explode—releasing fluids. The lawsuit stated, "Another unit owner's body exploded, thereby causing blood and bodily fluids to go into the adjoining condominium owned by (his client)."

We did not agree a rupturing corpse qualified as an explosion. As our SIU investigator Judy continued to investigate other aspects of the case, Rollins's attorney increased their demand to nearly $300,000, though the condo was valued at less than half that.

We filed a motion for summary judgment, which is a decision a judge can make without having to go to trial, based on the evidence. With Florida's congested dockets, summary judgments are often used to resolve cases more quickly when there's no dispute about the facts. We asserted the corpse did not explode, as defined in the policy.

The Circuit Court of Palm Beach County agreed with our argument. We essentially won the case without the need for a lengthy trial. The facts were clearcut: Damage from the corpse had not come from any explosion.

Rollins's attorney wasn't about to give up. He filed a Notice of Appeal, which progressed to the District Court of Appeal. When that court affirmed the ruling, the attorney didn't pause before threatening to march straight to Florida's Supreme Court.

At that critical juncture, we had to make a recommendation whether to continue to defend the case or not. Our corporate legal department would ultimately decide, but I had to submit a sound written proposal. Defending a case in any Supreme Court was never to be taken lightly. If you choose the wrong case, you risk making bad case law or "bad law." A legal adage from 1837 states, "Hard cases make bad law." An unfavorable verdict could negatively affect future cases for decades. Other carriers would be uneasily watching from the sidelines to see what we did.

Hypothetically, we could have negotiated a settlement to quietly make the entire case go away. But I remained adamant that a bloating corpse was not anyone's version of an explosion. My management and our legal department agreed. We continued to defend our position.

The Court affirmed the ruling, declaring, "The plain meaning of the term 'explosion' does not include a decomposing body's cells explosively expanding, causing leakage of bodily fluids."

Though imaginative in their attempt, the insured's attorney could not convince anyone of their premise.

The "exploding corpse" tagline created fodder for online and printed news, a talk show monologue, and international papers: "The big insurance company won't pay for damage from an exploding corpse." But as with many cases, the news didn't always report the entire story.

Why was SIU involved? We didn't dispute the death, and it was certainly not a staged loss. I mentioned that SIU rep Judy had continued to investigate. She was a shrewd researcher I had worked with for over a decade. We became curious during Ms. Rollins's deposition when her attorney kept interrupting to tell her not to answer any financial questions.

We uncovered evidence that she had allegedly filed other claims against the condo association and the restoration company, which were never disclosed to us. She had reportedly claimed the same damage as with us, which would mean collecting multiple times for the same damage.

The Court's decision also strengthened case law regarding the requirement of a policyholder to submit a sworn proof of loss. A *proof of loss* is a form completed by an insured to provide information under oath about their claimed damage. Most policies require insureds to complete a proof of loss form shortly after the loss, usually within sixty days.

Ms. Rollins never submitted a sworn proof of loss despite our many requests. That, in addition to the unparalleled facts, helped create one of the more interesting cases in my SIU career. And the verdict would be useful to the industry for years to come.

Chapter Thirty-Two
Pain & Gain – Our Most Horrific Case

I presided over many, many bizarre cases and homicides. This case is by far the strangest and most impactful case on everybody that I've ever been involved with.[153]
—Alex Ferrer, Florida Circuit Court Judge (ret.)

If you recall during our Little Havana era, we were startled by a blast behind our office to learn director Michael Bay was filming a movie. None of us knew the director of *Armageddon* and *Transformers* would be back in a few years to film a movie about one of our cases.

The facts are so extraordinary that deciding which chapter to include them in was difficult, as they encompass almost every topic I've described: death; stolen vehicles; one dumped in the Everglades; a staged accident; a home burglary; and organized criminals. Then add to that kidnapping, extortion, and dismemberment.

Many cases came into SIU simply because they contained outlandish facts. We once received a burglary case because the man claimed, "I hired a prostitute who tied me up. Then she called her pimp, who came over and robbed my house."

In that case, when Steve took the statement of the man—who was a married professional—he said, "If I was going to lie, why would I admit to hiring a hooker who tied me up and her pimp robbed me?" He was right. Despite the man's proclivities, he had been robbed, and we paid the claim.

But when we received a claim that would later be known as the "Pain & Gain" case, we had no idea the bizarre facts would be profiled in a slew of news reports, at least two books, and a movie starring Mark Wahlberg and Dwayne "The Rock" Johnson.

All of the following details were confirmed as true.

Imagine our reaction when a new claim involving auto theft and a home robbery was reported as follows: "These men kidnapped me, tied me up, drugged and tortured me for days. Then they moved into my house and stole everything I own. Then the men put me in my car and crashed it into a pole. Then they set the car on fire and tried to run me over."

Needless to say, that case came straight to our SIU team. It was assigned to our seasoned investigator Chris (the guy chased out of a clinic by Russian gentlemen) with the help of Steve (our uncontested boat expert). The rest of us followed the story from the edges of our seats as the case unfolded. The culprits and the entire scheme were ultimately exposed by Miami police, the FBI, a private investigator, and Chris's investigation.

Our Insured's Story

The saga began when one of our insured's employees at his accounting firm discovered he was worth over $1.2 million. Later, while the employee was visiting a gym in Miami Lakes, he began discussing our insured's wealth with the Hulk-sized Daniel Lugo. They wondered if our insured would be easy to rob. Lugo, along with another giant thug named

Doorbal and the insured's employee—later collectively referred to as the "Sun Gym gang"—planned to kidnap our policyholder. They snatched him as he exited a Schlotzsky's deli he owned. They zapped him with a Taser, wrapped his head in duct tape, and then drove him to a warehouse in Hialeah.

Our insured told us he called Doorbal "Mr. Torture" because he loved inflicting pain. Lugo and Doorbal bound and tortured our insured with fire, beatings, and games of Russian roulette to force him to sign over his assets. The gang even had their own notary to help process the ownership documents. Our insured was forced to sign over $1.2 million in cash, vehicles, assets, and a $2 million life insurance policy.[154]

With our insured restrained in the warehouse, the Sun Gym gang moved into his home. Our policyholder lived in a two-story house with a pool (that we also insured) with his wife and two children. To explain his absence, the gang forced him to call his friends, claiming he had fled town with a young mistress. He instructed his family to hide in Colombia for their safety.

With the family gone, the gang partied in the home and even placed the pool cleaning contract in their name. According to a CBS News report, the gang stole his furniture, wore his jewelry, and drove his Dodge Viper and Mercedes.[155] When they had exhausted our insured's cash, the gang realized they didn't need him anymore.

At that point, according to our insured, they forced him to drink a mixture of tequila, vodka, and sleeping pills. When he passed out, they loaded him into his SUV, and Doorbal crashed it into a pole. With our insured still in the truck, they doused it with gasoline and set it on fire.

But they had forgotten to buckle in our insured. As the Sun Gym gang watched the SUV burn, our insured had revived enough to stumble out of the flaming vehicle.

That's when the gang tried to run him over—twice. But they fled the scene when another car happened to drive by. "Divine intervention," is what our insured called it. "There's no explanation," he later told the *Sun Sentinel*.[156]

Our insured's Toyota SUV that he'd been placed in before it was crashed into a pole and set on fire

Courtesy Miami-Dade Police Department

When our insured woke up in the ICU of Jackson Memorial Hospital, the staff didn't believe his bizarre story. In a desperate attempt to verify the events, he retained a lawyer, who hired a private investigator. When the P.I. shared the allegations with Miami Police, they were also skeptical.

But as the P.I. and law enforcement kept digging, they discovered something even more sinister. Our insured was not the only victim. The Sun Gym gang had an appetite for kidnapping the wealthy to drain their accounts—and then dispose of their bodies.

Our policyholder had been the only one to escape alive, and the tale didn't end there.

Frank and Krisztina

Shifting the story a few miles west, a state trooper came upon a yellow Lamborghini abandoned in the Everglades. He traced the registration to Frank Griga, a wealthy Hungarian immigrant living in Miami. When the police tried to contact Griga, they discovered he and his 23-year-old girlfriend, Krisztina Furton, had been reported missing three days earlier by their housekeeper. The housekeeper noticed their dog had been left

behind, something the couple would never do. They were last seen going to dinner with two men described as "large."

Witnesses and an inspection of Griga's home yielded few clues. With just a vague description of two "muscular men" the couple had gone out with, it seemed like a dead end.

However, those details rekindled a memory in Miami Homicide Captain Al Harper. He recalled the chat with the private investigator about the strange man who insisted he had been kidnapped and tortured. Miami Homicide and the P.I. met again with our insured to recount his ordeal. Captain Harper was so startled by his story that he called the elite SID Division, which handled conspiracy, money laundering, murder for hire, and organized crime.[157]

The Sun Gym gang's first dumb mistake was with their notary. The man who had helped transfer their victims' assets was also the owner of Sun Gym. Our SIU investigation contained the transfer documents displaying the notary's name. The police's investigation of that man led to multiple suspects tied to the abductions, most of them gym members, including Lugo and Doorbal. They discovered Lugo had a criminal record as a felon for defrauding the elderly out of millions in insurance schemes.

When police questioned Doorbal's girlfriend, she admitted she had introduced him to the young Hungarian couple, Frank Griga and Krisztina. When police searched Doorbal's townhouse, they found a mountain of evidence connected to the missing couple and our insured's abduction, including bloodstains, Griga's business card, the red outfit Krisztina had worn, and a "kidnap kit" of duct tape, Tasers, and handcuffs.

When police interrogated Doorbal, he finally cracked, confessing to the entire thing—kidnapping our insured and murdering the couple. He described the grisly massacre; he and Lugo had lured the couple to his home with a fake business pitch. In a scuffle, Doorbal had strangled Griga and accidentally killed him. When Krisztina had become hysterical, they had tried to subdue her by injecting her with horse tranquilizer. But the gang didn't realize they had given her too much. They desperately needed her alive to provide bank account information and passwords.

"They gave her enough horse tranquilizers to kill four 1,000-pound horses," according to retired Miami Judge Alex Ferrer, who presided over the trial.[158] Krisztina Furton died, and the gang was unable to pillage any of their assets. They had botched their own plan.

If the story could get any more dreadful, Lugo and Doorbal called additional associates (one was a Miami-Dade corrections officer) to help dismember the bodies and put them in fifty-five-gallon drums. They dumped the couple's remains in a remote area on the fringe of the

Everglades, not far from the couple's Lamborghini (an area coincidentally known for Santería rituals).

The barrels were eventually found containing the severed corpses, but without heads or hands, police were unable to confirm if it was the missing couple.

Nearly a month later, an anonymous caller led police to buckets containing the couple's heads off I-75, "Alligator Alley." Through a forensic miracle, authorities were able to identify Frank from a tooth and Krisztina from a breast implant's serial number.[159]

Lugo's girlfriend was granted immunity in exchange for her testimony. She knew all the specifics about the gang and the abductions. The naïve girl hadn't reported anything to the police earlier because Lugo had told her he was an undercover CIA agent, and she had believed him.[160] When all the facts were assembled, eleven people were arrested and charged in connection with the horrendous crimes.

For our SIU case, Chris was among the first to learn our insured's story directly from the man himself. After his first recorded statement, before the tale had been made public, Chris rushed back to the office. He wanted to notify management of the shocking, perhaps dangerous, allegations. Similar to the police's reaction when they first heard the story, our manager didn't believe it—yet.

We were notified the insured's stolen vehicles had been recovered. When Chris inspected them, he discovered the gang was so advanced that they had altered the VINs and retitled the cars to themselves. It was a time-consuming struggle to unravel the documentation to prove the cars belonged to our customer, but Chris succeeded.

We also insured the victim's posh Miami home. He filed a claim with us for vandalism, stolen furnishings, jewelry, and cash. Chris learned the Sun Gym gang had even forged a quit-claim deed to transfer the home's ownership to them.

Based on the insured's frightening story, Chris asked Steve to ride along to inspect our insured's home. Chris described the house as eerie and

Fraudulent deed the Sun Gym Gang forced
Marc Schiller to sign (with the gang's notary)

Courtesy Miami-Dade Police Department

completely vacant, with nothing left behind. They anxiously inspected attic spaces and closets to confirm that nothing—and no one—had been hidden.

When our customer reviewed the bloody crime scene photos from Doorbal's townhouse, he was astonished. He saw his own furniture, which they had stolen. The couch the gang used to move the corpses had been our insured's couch, taken from his home.

Thanks to our insured's help, we confirmed the theft of his vehicles and the entire robbery from his home. They were covered losses, and we paid the claims in full.

The Verdict

Chris was questioned by Miami-Dade Homicide and deposed by Lugo's attorney for the criminal case. Chris was rarely intimidated, and no one knew the case better than him. He was represented by an attorney from our company, and a state prosecutor was there to supervise. During the four-hour deposition, Lugo's attorney vigorously tried to paint our insured as a liar, asserting he was also a member of the Sun Gym gang. Chris remained cool and stuck to the facts.

The criminal trial lasted nearly ten weeks, overseen by Miami State Attorney Katherine Fernandez Rundle. It was the longest and most expensive trial in Miami-Dade history, with over 1,200 pieces of evidence and 98 witnesses.[161]

Our insured, Mr. Marc Schiller, was the prosecution's star witness. He later told CBS News, "Walking in and seeing Lugo and Doorbal, I realized that I was in the driver's seat because they never imagined that I'd be sitting there accusing them."[162]

Lugo and Doorbal were convicted for double murder, as well as attempted murder of our insured, along with racketeering, money laundering, fraudulent notary, and forgery. For their heinous crimes, both men were sentenced to death. Their notary was sentenced to 56 years in

Daniel Lugo (left) and Noel Doorbal (right)
Courtesy Miami-Dade Corrections

prison, and the other gang members received a variety of prison sentences.

The Aftershock

As improbable as it may seem, the above account is heavily abridged. The unthinkable case had so many jarring twists that it had to be reported as a ten-part story in the *Miami New Times*. I recommend anyone interested to read that full riveting story by Pete Collins.

The story also caught the attention of Hollywood, with Michael Bay onboard to direct the movie. However, the film took vast liberties with the facts. They changed Marc Schiller's name so they could fictionalize his character. The screenwriters oddly chose to go with a dark-comic tone. Anyone connected to the brutal case found it impossible to see it as any sort of comedy.

And our team was disappointed there were no characters in the film called "insurance investigator." Again, we toil in an invisible world.

I contacted our former insured and victim, Mr. Marcelo "Marc" Schiller, who now leads a quiet life with his accounting practice in Boca Raton, Florida, just a few miles from my house. I was shocked to learn his ordeal wasn't over. Marc said the case may go to trial again due to the death penalty appeals, and the state will need him to testify. He will have to relive the entire horror for which he still bears physical scars.

"It seems I will never be able to put this behind me," Marc said, "This is truly the never-ending story that has consumed my life."

I asked Marc if he was unhappy with the film's depiction of the ordeal.

Victim, Marcelo "Marc" Schiller, today
Photo courtesy of Mr. Schiller

"Unhappy does not begin to describe my view of the movie," Marc scoffed. "It was a joke of a movie." He said he was never consulted, even though he was the sole survivor and locally available.

In an effort to set the record straight, Marc Schiller authored his own book describing his torment, *Pain and Gain – The Untold True Story*. It's available everywhere, and I recommend reading his perspective. Judge Alex Ferrer wrote in his review of the book, "I still find myself cringing at Marc Schiller's description of his captivity, torture and attempted murder."[163]

Marc shared with me a flicker of his eternal optimism: "I'm very fortunate to be alive. I keep pushing forward because that's all I have ever known."

Several years later, I received a random call from a claim manager in Texas. He was interviewing candidates for a job and wanted to ask me about an applicant named Chris who had used me as a reference. He told me Chris had mentioned during his interview that he had worked on high-profile cases including two projects for *Claims Video News* and the infamous "Pain & Gain" case. The manager said, "Like that movie starring The Rock. Is any of that true?"

"Yep," I had to reply. "He did all that. Everything Chris told you is 100 percent true."

Chris was hired for the job the next day.

Chapter Thirty-Three
In the Wake of Injury Fraud

During my decade-plus managing injury investigations, I was amazed by the creativity. And I had a renewed appreciation for how many crimes, no matter the type, were interconnected. In fact, I had enough inspiration for a new crime thriller.

My third novel, *Eyes of Poseidon,* was inspired by an oft-told tale among injury investigators. The myth involves a struggling strip-mall chiropractor (or any doctor) who is approached by Russian mafia offering their services: "Work for us and you will be wealthy." The mob promises thousands of patients from fake accidents so the clinics can generate millions of dollars.

At that juncture, the strip-mall chiropractor has a choice: say yes to the mob and get rich or refuse and suffer the consequences.

In my novel, the well-intentioned chiropractor gets in over his head. When he realizes who he *really* works for, he desperately searches for a way out for him and his family.

Did my day job inspire my story? Almost all of it. My book includes bogus Miami clinics, staged accidents, the infamous B-Girls, and even an SIU investigator hot on their trail. My protagonist visits the same Russian dinner club I visited, depicted in all its gaudy, creepy glory. I also detailed how someone could fake their own death without leaving a body behind.

(Spoiler alert) In my book, the doctor leaps from a ship in the dead of night to fake his demise to escape his crimes. Through meticulous planning, there is a search at sea, his body is never recovered, and he is presumed dead.

Was my plot even remotely plausible? It appears so. On December 22, 2022, the *New York Times* reported a doctor wanted for medical fraud had gone missing at sea, but prosecutors believed he had faked his own death.[164]

The Manhattan man, Dr. Marvin Moy, had been accused of paying first responders to solicit victims for his medical practice as part of a $100 million insurance fraud. Before he could be arrested, he had allegedly gone boating with a friend. The next day, rescuers responded to the boat's emergency beacon. After they pulled the doctor's friend from the water, he claimed they had hit a larger vessel and Moy had been thrown overboard. A Coast Guard search commenced, and they never found Dr. Moy's body.

Prosecutors didn't buy the story. They believed Moy staged his disappearance to avoid arrest. A judge found the notion plausible enough to issue a bench warrant. The doctor is still missing.

If only I could prove Dr. Moy had read a copy of my book. Just like Hollywood, my plot had been ripped off again.

From lessons I had learned from my SIU peers, the FBI, and Secret Service, I could see signs of medical fraud and money laundering everywhere. In my own community, every strip mall had a nondescript "injury clinic," sometimes next door to a personal injury attorney.

Near our home, a non-branded "pharmacy" had opened almost overnight. I couldn't help but go inside (career curiosity). The shelves were virtually empty with only a few products on display. There was no one behind the desk, nor any customers. A man finally appeared from a back room, still chewing a hot dog. He seemed puzzled as to why I was there and asked if I needed help. I pretended I had made a wrong turn and exited, praying I hadn't been caught on some sting operation video. I knew the pharmacy was committing some variety of fraud.

Subsequently, in 2022, two men were found guilty of using twenty-one fake pharmacies across South Florida in a $9 million scheme. The storefronts only existed to transmit fraudulent claims to insurers and drug companies. According to the DOJ, "The pharmacies did not have real customers or prescriptions and did not dispense medications."[165]

Even driving around with my children, my daughter would point and say, "That mattress store is laundering money, right Daddy? There's never anyone inside."

"Good job, Honey."

"That fancy restaurant has been there for years with no customers. Why is it cash only?"

"Exactly, Junior." It was like playing travel bingo.

As upper management shifted over the years, the clever and genial Russell from Colorado preferred the idea of specialization: "You should do what you do best." Since my expertise was with property fraud (theft, burglaries, autos, fires), he put me in charge of the entire state.

Florida was so large and diverse that it seemed to represent a microcosm of the U.S. South Florida was ground zero for large thefts, exporting, and injury fraud. The West Coast had fake sinkhole cases. The Northeast had fraudulent contractors preying on the less informed. The expanse of the panhandle had more home arsons (due to fewer potential witnesses). Eventually, my territory spread north to include states up the Eastern

Seaboard. I had enjoyed injury cases but was thrilled to get back to claims I considered tangible and not investigated through spreadsheets.

In 2013, I was flattered to receive an invitation to speak at a national CPCU conference in New Orleans. I guess word of my fraud presentations had made the rounds. Amy, a wonderful senior manager, agreed to fund it, seeing the value in having me represent the expertise of our company. CPCU (Chartered Property Casualty Underwriter) is a premier designation for the industry, like a CPA of insurance. Being in the French Quarter was just icing on the cake.

When I told my wife I had to speak for 90 minutes, she remarked, "That's as long as a comedy movie!" It was true, but I had plenty of material (many of the cases in this text). The presentation "The Invisible World of Insurance Fraud" went without a hitch. It was a lot of fun, and the crowd seemed engaged, despite Bourbon Street being three blocks away.

Having covered many varieties of fraud, I shifted my article writing to focus on future risks. Bad guys always seemed to be one step ahead of us. By the time our industry became aware of a new scheme, it had already been in use for a year or more, milking the system. The culprits just move on to the next scheme. It was all about predicting and being prepared for the *next thing*.

To foresee and investigate crimes that had never existed before, we almost had to have the imagination of a crime fiction writer.

PART EIGHT –
FUTURE FRAUD, TODAY

Chapter Thirty-Four
The Dawn of Cyber Fraud

The world was changing with risks that hadn't existed a decade earlier. Fraud could be committed entirely online. Policies were sold virtually without ever meeting a human. Considering the prevalence of identity theft, were the customers or victims even real people? The concept of rideshare companies like Uber and Lyft created potential for new accident schemes. Unanticipated events such as a pandemic created opportunities for fraud our industry had never envisioned.

With the press of a button, cybercriminals could rob people and businesses from thousands of miles away. Crooks were stealing millions of dollars without weapons or the need for contrived insurance stories. The new exposures were so real, the term "cyber insurance" had to be invented.

Toward the dusk of my tenure, cybercrimes were just emerging. None of us were IT experts, nor did we know anything about tracking malicious code. But investigations were still needed on a street level.

In an early example, we were tracking an organized group that was staging losses—multiple cars crashing over and over again, stuffed with strangers, being treated at the same clinics, suing for injuries. We noticed all their policies with our company were new and had been purchased online. None of our insurance agents had ever met any of the people. Of course, now most carriers sell policies virtually, but we exposed an early pitfall.

Every computer has a unique Internet Protocol (IP) address, a virtual address that identifies a device on the internet or local network. You don't receive a new IP address for every device in your home, otherwise it would mean a new address every time you buy a new cellphone, computer, or tablet. In short, your dedicated IP address can be tracked to the geographic location of your network, such as your home.

In our investigation of the crime ring, all participants, from all vehicles, had policies purchased through our company's website. We asked our IT department to give us the specific IP address from where each policy had been purchased. To our astonishment, they had all come from one single IP address. That meant all the policies—from people who supposedly didn't know each other—had been bought from inside the same house. It was like that horror movie where police track a stalker's calls to discover they came from inside the home.

Geolocation tools can derive a latitude and longitude from an IP address. They all pointed to a building in nearby Opa-locka. We could envision the ringleaders hovering over the same home computer, pretending to be multiple people as they applied for coverage.

The perpetrators' foolish mistake in the infancy of cyber fraud had helped make a dozen lawsuits vanish overnight. They had obtained policies with other companies as well. They had only paid the first month's premiums for their scheme using stolen credit cards. The alleged passenger names had come from identity theft, taken from stolen driver's licenses. It was an expansive case and the closest thing to a slam dunk for law enforcement.

It was also a sobering indicator that our old workflows to investigate fraud were out the window. There were no paint-by-number methods to identify the new crimes. Culprits could be thousands of miles away, far from the reach (or jurisdiction) of local law enforcement and prosecutors.

Our core organization was under attack—as are all of yours. Who among you have not had mandatory training about "phishing?" We receive repeated warnings about malicious emails designed to fool us into scams. The attackers' intent is to get you to unwittingly reveal financial data, passwords, or other confidential information. This applies in our private lives as well.

Phishing is a form of "social engineering," techniques cyber thieves use to manipulate your psychology. Attackers prey on your emotions, wanting you to act quickly without thinking. Your job, finances, or family may seem to be in jeopardy. Emails appear urgent—maybe an emergency banking situation or a message from your company's superiors. Social engineering can include misdirection, lying, and falsifying emails from a known business, complete with realistic logos.

Examples include emails purportedly from your bank stating, "URGENT, your account has been compromised. Click this link to confirm your identity." (Yes, a fraud about an alleged fraud.) Or "Attention (you, a new employee) must process this invoice immediately to avoid penalty. Click here to access. Signed, (your company's vice president)."

If your company is like mine, you may wonder why we receive so many warnings and have to attend constant training sessions. Then I learned how cyber thieves have stolen hundreds of millions from companies, sometimes to the point of bankruptcy. Private individuals have lost fortunes, depleting their savings or retirement funds.

There's another less-publicized reason cyber fraud training is relentless: A company's executives can lose their jobs if there's an attack and they did *not* provide training and proper safeguards.

And there were new forms of cyber fraud directly targeting those executives.

Chapter Thirty-Five
Whaling from Afar: Executive Fraud

A young man is seated at a café overlooking the grassy banks of the Uzh River in western Ukraine. He sips his espresso and closes his laptop. The man stands and smiles at fellow patrons as he strolls away.

He's smiling because he just robbed your U.S. company of $11 million. Your company's CEO will ultimately be fired because of the theft. And the young man used one of your employees as his unwitting accomplice.

A new cyber fraud had emerged known as "CEO fraud" or "BEC" (business email compromise). Fraudsters were impersonating company executives to deceive employees into enabling the thefts. Even worse, this created an exclusion under many cyber insurance policies.

Cyber fraud insurance, also known as cyber liability insurance, was created in the 1990s. The first policies covered data processing errors but excluded "rogue employees," fines, and penalties. As cyber policies progressed into the 2000s, they began to cover network security, data breaches, and virus-related cases.

In the ensuing decades, there was a sharp rise in cyberattacks due to ransomware, malware, and social engineering. As we became reliant on technology—with actual minicomputers in our pockets every day—these attacks evolved. Early cyber policies were like the Wild West. Carriers had to revise their products to cover a growing list of attacks, but the policies could be daunting with ambiguous language and exclusions.

A theft might be excluded if you failed to maintain basic security, hence the constant training we all endure. Losses from social engineering attacks could be denied if your employee was involved, even unknowingly. If your well-intentioned employee inadvertently clicked a malicious link, thus transferring money on behalf of the company, the losses could be excluded.

Fortunately, as cyber insurance progressed, policies now offer social engineering endorsements, which would be wise as deceptive emails become increasingly convincing.

Despite all the training, CEO fraud has grown. The scams seem to target businesses that work with foreign suppliers or regularly perform wire transfer payments. According to a 2022 FBI Congressional Report, losses from CEO-related fraud totaled over $2.4 billion. There was a 65 percent increase between July 2019 and December 2021.[166]

The scams have been reported in all 50 U.S. states and 177 countries. Interestingly, the primary international destinations for the fraudulent funds are banks in Thailand and Hong Kong. China ranked third, followed by Mexico and Singapore.[167]

How Can CEO Fraud Happen?

Phishing for specific high-profile individuals has been called "whaling." The attacks cleverly mimic an email from someone within management, demanding financial transfers. The prey (an employee) receives an email from an ostensibly authentic source that contains a malicious link. Junior employees are less likely to question requests that appear authorized by senior leadership. The scams can occur at the end of the day or workweek to add a sense of urgency, in hopes the employee is pressed for time.

Cybercriminals conduct extensive research for their attacks, including on open sources. Imagine your LinkedIn profile or anywhere an executive's business title or email can be found (many corporate websites). They will learn industry jargon and send "feeler" emails to get in the door. Some have created bogus company websites to lend credibility to their emails.

A common scheme is to imitate a company's email address. If your company's legitimate email is "@abc-company.com," the criminals will create a counterfeit email address that closely mimics the address such as "@abc_company.com." Someone new or in a rush might not notice.

Businesses should be suspicious of any financial transfer requests made by email or alleged to be high priority. Employees who receive such requests should always confirm the credentials of the sender. Companies should also utilize multi-level verification for large transfers.

Cautionary Cases

Imagine you're a stockholder of Ubiquiti Networks, reading their fourth quarter Fiscal Earnings Report in 2015. It revealed that cyber thieves stole $46.7 million through fake emails purportedly from executives of their company, which initiated the fraudulent transfers.

The San Jose-based company admitted that "fraudulent requests from an outside entity" had targeted its finance department. The funds were transferred to "overseas accounts held by third parties."[168] Even worse, the company had to admit to its shareholders it may not be successful in obtaining insurance coverage for the loss.

The social media app Snapchat was a victim of a similar scheme. An email intruder pretended to be CEO Evan Spiegel and asked for employees' payroll information. The employee who received the email didn't realize it was a con and responded with the information. The hacker then exposed the data to the outside world. To date, Snapchat has not disclosed what information was compromised or how many employees were impacted.[169]

To heighten the crisis, executives could lose their jobs. The CEO of Austrian aerospace company FACC was fired by its board after a hacker sent a fraudulent email pretending to be the CEO, stealing approximately

$47 million. An employee had inadvertently helped wire the funds offshore for a fictitious project. The board decided the CEO had "severely violated his duties, in particular in relation to the 'fake president incident.'"[170] Although an employee had been deceived by a fake email, the board believed it should not have been that easy.

Retailer Target suffered one of the largest and earliest cyber breaches in 2013. Following the $40 million loss, its CEO lost his job after 35 years with the company. Gregg Steinhafel, Target's chairman and chief executive, resigned after the massive breach had exposed personal details for over 110 million shoppers.

In a more public case, when Sony Pictures was hacked in December 2014, it disclosed employee information, celebrity contact information, and private emails from Sony Pictures. As a result of the breach, Co-Chairman Amy Pascal resigned within two months. It didn't help that her own leaked emails criticized then-President Barack Obama and popular actors.

Organizations are taking tougher action in response to errors that compromise data security. Up to 25 percent of workers lost their jobs in 2021 after making cybersecurity errors, according to a 2022 report by security company Tessian.[171] With schemes becoming more elaborate, one in four employees made mistakes that compromised their company's security.[172]

To add insult to injury, imagine explaining to shareholders that the losses might not be covered by insurance. With phishing and CEO fraud, employees are almost always implicated, whether they realize it or not, which can trigger the exclusions.

Today, carriers offer special endorsements to cover fraudulent wire transfer. Beazley Group, a syndicate of Lloyd's of London, was among the first to offer "fraudulent instruction insurance" to cover financial losses due to "fraudulent instructions from a person purporting to be a vendor, client, or authorized employee."

Another Eastern European Connection?

Russian cybersecurity firm Kaspersky Lab reported a hacker gang called *Carbanak* had stolen over $1 billion since 2015 from over 100 financial institutions in over 30 countries. The multinational gang included cybercriminals from Russia, Ukraine, China, and parts of Europe.

According to Kaspersky, authorities from numerous countries, including Interpol and Europol, worked together to investigate these unparalleled cyber robberies.[173]

The Carbanak thieves sent phishing emails to their victims' employees. The emails were infected with malware that allowed them to navigate into the companies' internal networks, mimicking legitimate transactions. Victims included companies in Russia, the U.S., Germany, China, Ukraine, Canada, Hong Kong, and eighteen other countries.

Europol announced it had arrested Carbanak's mastermind in 2018. Law enforcement raided a house in the coastal town of Alicante, Spain. They detained a man from Ukraine who was the head of the Carbanak gang. According to Europol's statement, the group's criminal profits had been laundered via prepaid cards linked to cryptocurrency wallets which were used to buy goods such as luxury cars and houses.[174]

How to Combat Phishing & CEO Fraud

What entices an employee to click on a link? Companies can reduce the number of these incidents by understanding the employee behaviors that lead to wire fraud.

Have you received an email "phishing test?" This training measure includes a deceptive email sent by a company to its own employees to monitor their response and help spot training deficiencies. The phony emails usually prey on emotions. They might infer threats about your job, financial warnings, or even financial incentives to click.

In an almost farcical example, the web hosting company GoDaddy sent its employees an email offering a holiday bonus of $650 before Christmas in 2021. Regrettably, it was a phishing test. Those who clicked the link were indeed rewarded, not with money, but with additional cybersecurity training.[175]

An organization should have rules for financial requests over a specified amount, with multiple employees required to approve the transfers. In conjunction with ongoing training, companies should continue with random phishing tests, praising employees who report phony emails. Most importantly, IT departments must ensure all security software remains up to date to minimize vulnerabilities for criminals to exploit.

The above cyber frauds all stem from voiceless emails from fake managers. So, imagine hearing the unmistakable human voice of your CEO—or a family member—asking you to do something deceptive. That inconceivable form of fraud didn't surface until 2019.

Chapter Thirty-Six
AI Deepfakes: That's Not Your Boss on the Phone

AI: It is hard to see how you can prevent the bad actors
from using it for bad things. [176]
—Geoffrey Hinton, "The Godfather of AI"
and former Google Vice President

As technology advances, so do opportunities for fraud. You've seen those "deepfake" videos, where images of politicians or celebrities are manipulated to say or do things they never said or did. A deepfake is a technique for human image synthesis based on artificial intelligence (AI). Initially considered an "image" application, deepfakes have now been used for voice mimicry. In 2019 was the first report of an AI-generated voice used to commit a major heist.

A CEO was conned into transferring $243,000 to cyber thieves who had used a voice deepfake, according to *The Wall Street Journal*. The CEO of the undisclosed company believed he was on the phone with his boss, the chief executive of their parent company. After speaking to an actual voice, he followed its orders to immediately transfer approximately $243,000 to a bogus bank account.[177]

The voice belonged to a criminal who was using AI voice technology to mimic the firm's CEO. This radical new fraud was insured by Euler Hermes Group SA, a subsidiary of Allianz SE. According to Rüdiger Kirsch of Euler Hermes, the victim said he had recognized his boss's German accent, and it even carried his specific vocal "melody."[178] By the time they caught the fraud, the funds had already been routed to a second account in Mexico, and then disbursed to multiple international accounts.

Since the COVID-19 pandemic, with a rise of people working virtually from home, more voice schemes have surfaced. According to the FBI's *2022 Internet Crime Report*, criminals have exploited our reliance on virtual meetings to fool victims into sending fraudulent transfers.

How it works: The culprit's first step is to compromise an executive's email to invite employees to a virtual meeting. During the bogus meeting, the fraudster might insert a still photo of the executive accompanied by a deep fake of the person's voice to instruct employees to initiate financial transfers.[179] In one case, the criminals even told the viewers the audio wasn't working perfectly to account for any voice glitches or sound flaws.

Joe Rogan Said What?

Who would invent voice deepfake technology, and why? Not only did one company claim to have conceived the technology, but it also boasted about it.

In the summer of 2019, researchers from Dessa, a Toronto-based AI firm, announced they had produced a perfect voice simulation of popular podcaster and comedian Joe Rogan. For nearly two minutes, Rogan's voice casually discusses a hockey team of chimpanzees and other odd stories. However, Rogan had never said any of it.

Dessa had obtained voice samples from Joe Rogan himself—without his knowledge. Rogan is one of the most popular podcast hosts in the world. With over 2,000 episodes to date, his shows supplied thousands of hours of voice samples for the technology to absorb.

The researchers created the imitation of Rogan's voice using a text-to-speech program called RealTalk, which generates lifelike speech using only text inputs. The user only had to type the words—no speaking required. The final result even included nuances such as breathing and the "ums" and "ahs." If sufficient data is available, the program can mimic anyone's voice. (I recommend listening to the deepfake of Rogan's voice on Dessa's own YouTube channel.)

Fortunately, with the expertise required, the general public can't use RealTalk technology—yet. What about in the near future? Apps already exist on our phones for easy deepfake videos. Will AI technology progress to the point that only a few seconds of a target's voice will be required to create a perfect voice deepfake?

If your company's executives aren't famous orators like Joe Rogan, how would cyber thieves get their voice samples to mimic? Easy, considering the corporate videos and interviews available online. Imagine earnings videos created for shareholders, published on company websites, in addition to interviews done for the news, available on YouTube, LinkedIn, and so on.

Here's a twist: that first reported voice deepfake heist was committed two months *before* Dessa unveiled RealTalk. The $243,000 heist described above had used a technology similar to RealTalk, but it occurred in March 2019. To date, no suspects have been identified. Nothing is known about the software they used or how they gathered voice samples.

In 2020, a $35 million heist occurred when a United Arab Emirates bank was deceived by criminals using AI voice cloning. Imposters had used a deepfake voice of an executive to fool a bank manager into wiring the money.[180] The phony voice stated the firm was planning an acquisition and needed the funds. The bank manager said he recognized the executive's voice, so he authorized the transfer, which was funneled straight into the criminals' accounts.

The Emirates asked the U.S. for help since nearly $400,000 went into American banks. Investigators believed the operation involved at least 17 people using deepfake voice technology, with the funds routed to banks around the world. To date, no suspects have been caught.

It's regrettable that we can no longer trust the voice of someone who introduces themselves or gives commands. With a merger of video and voice deepfakes, confidence in calls and videos could decline.

What's the Exposure?

Voice deepfake fraud is now so widespread it's been dubbed "vishing" (voice phishing). The use of vishing to manipulate companies has increased since the COVID-19 pandemic due to more business being conducted virtually. The frequency of voice fraud increased over 10 percent in financial institutions in 2020 compared to pre-pandemic times. Financial losses due to voice fraud increased 42 percent between 2019 and 2020.[181]

Why was voice AI invented in the first place? Believe it or not, it was created for noble purposes. There are valuable needs for speech synthesis. Imagine improved communication for people with speech disabilities or who speak through text devices, such as patients with Parkinson's or cerebral palsy, or stroke victims.

From a commercial aspect, synthesized voices can serve as voice aides for customers that sound as natural as talking to a friend. Consider customized applications for devices using a voice that's comforting to the listener, or apps endorsed by celebrities.

For the 2022 hit movie *Top Gun: Maverick*, an AI-powered voice was created for actor Val Kilmer, who had lost his ability to speak after enduring throat cancer treatment. The AI voice company Sonantic recreated Kilmer's voice using hours of recordings of his natural speaking voice. As many of you have seen in the movie, the results are seamless. Viewers had no idea Mr. Kilmer had not actually spoken the dialogue.

However, with any technological advance, nefarious uses can emerge. Risks might include the use of a synthesized voice to gain access to secured systems or locations by mimicking officials. Using the crime fiction side of my brain, imagine a foreign enemy using voice AI to enter a military or government facility, or a deepfake of a politician or world leader used to manipulate election results or incite disorder.

I predict we will see an increase in cybercrimes involving artificial intelligence in the near future. We've already seen video deepfakes to imitate celebrities and public figures, and voice deepfakes have been used to steal substantial funds.

Will forms of AI or deepfakes be the next frontier for insurance fraud? Creating "homemade" deepfakes will become easier. A deepfake of a CEO reporting negative financial results could instantly sink a company's value. Imagine deepfakes of people doing or saying things they never did or said for the purpose of blackmail or harassment.

Consider routine insurance fraud, such as deepfake videos of accidents or people getting injured. At this moment, there are phone apps that create fake images of damage to your car. The user can upload an image of their vehicle to the app, which then adds collision damage, dents, or even fire damage. It is a disconcerting tool, considering more insurers now estimate damage virtually using photographs. Of course, the apps all declare, "For amusement purposes only!"

What Can We Do?

It's imperative to educate our peers, families, and employees about security risks. It has to be an ongoing effort, as the perpetrators are constantly modifying their tactics.

For financial risks, verification techniques should be employed before funds are transferred. Two-factor authentication is a common and effective technique to add extra security. Consumers should understand any insurance policies they have to cover cyber fraud, as well as the exclusions. Carriers and agents can work with you to assess your fraud risks to cover any exposures for financial loss.

There are valuable applications for artificial intelligence. But anyone who recalls the AI of Skynet in *The Terminator* movies (maybe an extreme example) knows we need to prepare defenses to ensure our networks and communications are genuine and secure.

Chapter Thirty-Seven
Let's Rideshare the Risk

You're going to put me in a car with a stranger? What's wrong with you?
—Actor Mila Kunis to husband/investor Ashton Kutcher when he
pitched Uber [182]

What could possibly go wrong with a business model that recruits amateurs and students to drive other people? But as most of you know, it has worked out exceedingly well. Being a rideshare driver is the "perfect part-time solution" for college students, according to a post on Uber's Newsroom blog.[183] Compared to working in retail or in a restaurant, Uber touts the freedom and flexibility of being one of its esteemed drivers.

However, some drivers are not being honest with their insurance companies. They're using their personal auto policies to fraudulently insure their commercial activities. Most auto policies exclude injuries as a result of using your vehicle to carry people or property for a fee. If your teenage daughter uses your personal car to deliver pizzas and hits a pedestrian, your personal auto insurance may not protect you for the accident.

A higher risk is created for everyone when rideshare drivers are deliberately dishonest with insurers about their side gig, and the rogue drivers are openly sharing advice with each other online on how to get away with it.

Thank You, Mr. Bond

Who knew James Bond helped invent Uber? In 2008, the company's founder, Garrett Camp, was not a fan of San Francisco's taxi cabs. When he finally got home one evening, he decided to relax by watching one of his favorite James Bond movies, *Casino Royale.* On this particular evening, one of 007's nifty gizmos grabbed his attention. In the film, Bond is driving a silver Mondeo in Nassau, Bahamas. As he pursues his nemesis, *Le Chiffre,* Bond monitors his cellphone to see a real-time graphic of his vehicle moving on a map toward his destination.

Camp must've sat upright with a gleam in his eyes. He imagined a phone app that would allow you to track your ride through your cellphone.[184] After Uber's co-founder Travis Kalanick had trouble hailing a taxi in Paris, the duo put their minds together. The Uber app was launched in March of 2009.

However, Camp's original plan had been a fleet of black Mercedes vehicles to pick up riders. Kalanick convinced him to consider a plan in which drivers used their *own* vehicles. With a business model that didn't require any investment in vehicle inventory, Uber quickly expanded. Lyft followed in its trail, and Uber has since grown with services in 70 countries and 10,500 cities, according to its 2023 SEC filing.[185]

The rideshare concept has skyrocketed since its inception. The companies can offer lower rates than taxis through the use of personal vehicles that evade commercial regulation. However, with most personal auto policies, ridesharing can trigger an exclusion since there are higher risks. The cars drive many more miles, including in unfamiliar and unsafe areas. There's an increased exposure due to multiple unknown—perhaps dangerous—passengers.

Drivers who have chosen to not disclose their rideshare employment to their insurance company have warned their peers through chatrooms and social media.

"Don't let your insurance company know that you're driving for Uber," according to a post on Reddit. "They did not underwrite the policy for that, and they'll want you to pay for extra coverage…"[186]

In a 2022 Reddit post, a driver offered this advice about insurance companies: "Don't tell them you'll be using it for rideshare it's not their business."[187] A more responsible contributor described the don't-tell tactic as having "a whistling-past-the-graveyard attitude."[188]

Drivers also share advice on how to get claims paid after an accident. According to a post on rideshare forum UberPeople.net, "Next time, if you are empty and have an accident, remove all your Lyft/Uber signs, and don't tell your insurance you were doing this if you don't have full coverage…"[189]

Many rideshare drivers worry about being canceled by their insurer as a result of their dishonesty. A contributor on the same site warned, "If you never mentioned you were doing rideshare in the police report, you may want to go with your personal insurance.… Whatever you do, don't tell your insurance you were doing rideshare. They will drop you and your insurance will go up."[190]

One driver admitted, "I drove for Uber for 3 days (12 hours) without rideshare insurance. I wanted to make sure it was something I was going to continue with before I purchased rideshare insurance."[191] Imagine if you were the unlucky passenger in that guy's three-day "tryout" period and got into an accident.

Thankfully, based in part on these concerns, rideshare companies began to offer liability insurance with up to $1 million in coverage for injuries. Coverage is available under certain conditions based on what "period" the driver was in when the accident occurred. Periods are verified based on the pick-up and drop-off times on the rideshare app.

Here are examples of certain "periods" for a rideshare driver.

- Offline – When the driver's app is off, the driver's personal auto policy would insure them. Fraudulent exposures occur when drivers work "off the books," taking rides for cash, or they believe their personal insurance is preferable (e.g., lower deductible).
- Period 1 – The driver is online and available for hire. They're waiting for ride requests but haven't received any yet. This could involve heavy driving, such as circling high-traffic or high-exposure areas they don't usually travel in.
- Periods 2 and 3 – The driver has received a ride request and is en route "on trip." This would initiate additional coverage from the rideshare's carrier during these periods.

The rideshare companies' insurance coverage comes with strict guidelines. The smallest detail can jeopardize coverage. This could tempt drivers to misrepresent the facts. Drivers might report accidents to their own insurance if they fear losing their permit to drive for the rideshare or due to higher deductibles. Uber reportedly has a $1,000 deductible; Lyft's is $2,500.

One chatroom driver offered, "I don't recommend calling Lyft in case of an accident.… I have a police report stating it was the other driver's fault. But Lyft doesn't care, deactivated my account…. They will deactivate you and you can't drive for Lyft anymore. Beware!"[192]

Some rideshare drivers have charged fares with their app turned off, doing jobs off the record for cash or through the use of money transfer apps such as Zelle or Venmo. The driver might offer a discount because they don't have to share a commission with the rideshare company. In these situations, the rideshare's coverage would not exist. In an offline status, the driver's personal insurance would come into play, creating serious exposure for any injured parties.

Staged Accidents in Rideshares

If a criminal wanted to stage an accident to commit fraud, what better target than a vehicle with a $1 million policy? Even more disconcerting, by using the rideshare app, they would know the car's location and destination in advance. The offender could plan the pick-up and drop-off points in an unsavory area far from potential witnesses or cameras.

Another form of staged loss could occur if the driver reports a fictitious hit-and-run accident. Passengers might even participate as false witnesses or profess to have injuries.

To adjust to our modern world, insurers have chosen to protect rideshare drivers if they disclose their activity during the application or renewal process. "Do you drive for a rideshare company?" is now a standard question when obtaining coverage with most auto insurers. The policy could then be priced appropriately.

The rideshare industry is not a fleeting concept. The companies are recruiting new drivers every day. Those same drivers have online forums to communicate insurance "hacks" and schemes. As consumers and passengers, we need to remain aware of the risks and adjust our practices to be protected from any potential hazards.

Chapter Thirty-Eight
Fraudsters Even Profited from COVID?

Could people sink so low as to commit fraud to cash in on the COVID-19 pandemic?

Consider the facts: Fraudsters have put infants and migrants in cars before intentionally crashing them. They have torched their property without any concern for people or pets. Temptresses have drugged and robbed naïve tourists. Fraudsters have created countless fake medical clinics. So yes, the same insidious minds found a way to bilk money allocated for victims of the pandemic.

One of my annual duties as a manager was to create a "business continuity plan." The report contained strategies for how to remain operational in the event of a catastrophe, such as a hurricane disabling our office. On the report, there was always a heading for "pandemic." We would shrug, not fully sure what that meant, and the likelihood seemed trivial. It sounded like something from *The Walking Dead*. Then came 2020; we learned very quickly what a pandemic was.

As if by some criminal reflex, con artists instantly shifted their efforts to exploit the COVID epidemic—including the ensuing vaccines, variants, and stimulus funds—to commit a spectrum of frauds.

Do you recall the shortage of COVID testing kits? I would've purchased one from anywhere at any cost. Leveraging that demand, fraudsters began to administer fraudulent COVID antibody tests for the sole purpose of gaining your personal information. According to the FBI, there were fraudsters collecting personal data (name, date of birth, Social Security number) and insurance information at the exam, to be used for ID theft and insurance-related fraud.[193]

There was also fraudulent advertising through texts, social media, and robocalls for high demand supplies such as facemasks, testing kits, and cleansers. With new variant strains and renewed mandates for masks, the scams continued. The Federal Communications Commission issued ongoing alerts about COVID-related fraud through a website that was updated with an ever-growing list of schemes.[194]

The pandemic also generated fraud within the stock market. The U.S. Securities and Exchange Commission issued warnings to investors about fraudulent companies touting products alleged to prevent, detect, or cure COVID-19. The warning stated, "We urge investors to be wary of these promotions, and to be aware of the substantial potential for fraud at this time."[195]

In a July 2021 SEC alert, a company called "Earn Cash Quarantine Lending Consultancy Services" promised up to 300 percent profit within 75 days.[196] The company was not registered with the commission and lacked the license to collect investments from the public.

Unscrupulous brokers suggested that their clients "buy now" before prices skyrocket. With the manipulative "pump and dump" scheme, the fraudsters accumulated the firms' stock, at times for cents on the dollar. The hype then escalated the stock's value, so the perpetrators could dump their stock, burdening the remaining investors with substantial losses.

Cyber Fraud + COVID = Even More Fraud

Even cybercriminals cashed in on pandemic fraud. They registered tens of thousands of COVID-related web domains to use in spoof ads and phishing attacks. The domain names contained key words such as "pandemic," "coronavirus," and "COVID-19," according to cybersecurity firm Palo Alto Networks.[197] The Justice Department shut down hundreds of the sites, which had promised relief benefits and vaccines, often masquerading as federal agencies or charitable groups.

On Twitter, a virtuous data contributor using the handle "Dustyfresh" updated a list of fraudulent pandemic-related domains, such as "CoronaVirusUpdate.com."[198] If an unsuspecting victim were to visit one of the sites, they would receive phishing emails to plant malware on their systems, to access passwords and personal information for purposes of identity theft. Fake sites have mimicked ads from Pfizer and Moderna, promising "free" rewards if the person submitted their bank or credit information to cover their small "handling fee."

Pandemic-related fraud was so easy to commit that it was even done from jail. In July 2021, a grand jury arrested three men for a scheme designed to steal $1.4 million, though two were already behind bars, operating the scam from prison. They had submitted fraudulent unemployment claims in other inmates' names to the California Employment Development Department. The applications claimed the men had worked as retailers and handymen before pandemic-related layoffs and had been available to work (despite being in prison). The men were charged with conspiracy to commit mail fraud and aggravated identity theft.[199]

To avoid detection, the prisoners had created fake email accounts and used their friends' mailing addresses scattered throughout the state. Some had paid family and friends up to $1,000 each to use their home addresses.

In our own illustrious Miami, a manager for a top national bank committed pandemic fraud using his own employer as well as other banks. He was sentenced to ten years in prison for leading a conspiracy to defraud the Paycheck Protection Program (PPP), which provided loans for emergency financial assistance to millions of people suffering economic hardships caused by the COVID-19 pandemic.

The bank manager allegedly conspired with friends to submit over 90 fraudulent loan applications to two banks: his own company and his previous employer, another national bank. They attempted to defraud the programs of nearly $25 million. They had succeeded in collecting about $15 million, and the investigation recovered about $800,000.[200]

The manager pleaded guilty to one count of conspiracy to commit wire fraud. His accomplices also pleaded guilty for their roles in the conspiracy and were also sentenced to prison.

The case was investigated by the Attorney General's COVID-19 Fraud Enforcement Task Force. According to the Federal Trade Commission, it had received over 910,400 consumer complaints as of September 2023. Over 71 percent involved fraud or identity theft. The total fraud loss amounted to $1.1 billion, with a median fraud loss of $465.[201]

Though COVID-19 may be considered over, pandemic-related fraud will be investigated for years. The Office of the Attorney General created the National Rapid Response Strike Force, which includes prosecutors dedicated to large-scale pandemic fraud. In 2021, they filed 281 indictments against 444 defendants who jointly billed insurers over $1.7 billion. They obtained 288 guilty pleas and litigated 23 jury trials, resulting in guilty verdicts against 21 defendants. They imprisoned 175 defendants, with an average sentence of over 49 months.[202]

Like chameleons that change colors to acclimate to their environments, criminals' tactics to commit fraud will always adapt to the headlines. They modify their practices as new economic and health issues arise worldwide. They will be better prepared for the next crisis—as will investigators.

Chapter Thirty-Nine
And in the End...

It is good to have an end to journey towards;
but it is the journey that matters, in the end.
—Ernest Hemingway

Around 2021, just as the pandemic was considering the notion of winding down, it was time to move on from my career at one of the largest insurance carriers in the U.S.

Thirty years had passed in the blink of an eye. Twenty-five of those years had been in the Special Investigation Unit, and over twenty of them spent leading many wonderful and diverse SIU teams. I began my odyssey as a wide-eyed young man, then met the love of my life (at a law office on the job), which resulted in three children who have sprouted into amazing adults.

To paint a visual of my career's span, on day one I was given a pager for my belt. If my boss beeped me, I'd have to find a safe, functional pay phone in the middle of Opa-locka to call him back. We progressed to giant brick phones that looked cool on my Fort Lauderdale happy hour table. Then we graduated to the flip phone, which made it easier to do my classic Captain Kirk impressions: "Beam me up, Scotty." Then on to smartphones, where we could research our targets, access records, and take photos from anywhere in the field at any time.

As the preceding chapters have illustrated, there was never a boring day, and my collaboration in the world of insurance crimes was far from over.

It seemed I had collected a few amusing stories. I discovered insurance crimes were considered interesting to the masses. I had no idea; it was just part of the job. As my magazine articles and word of mouth spread, I was invited to speak about creative insurance crimes at conferences in Los Angeles, Las Vegas, Atlanta, Palm Beach, and the University of Missouri.

The public appreciates the stories because all of them are consumers, and it's their money going out the door. Insurance professionals enjoy the cases because they enhance their awareness and strategies. Law enforcement is always intrigued by how our interests overlap and the fact that we could be resources for each other's investigations. As the cliché goes, knowledge is power. Understanding the schemes is truly the first step in identifying and avoiding them.

I discovered a group that miraculously combined fiction writing with my day job. The Public Safety Writers Association (PSWA) is a group of law enforcement and first responders who are also authors. Its mission is accuracy in crime fiction—and who would know better than them? Members also include former FBI and CIA agents. It was like a dream organization; I could actually discuss terrorist plot ideas with former FBI and CIA agents? The answer was yes, and I did. It helped with the accuracy of my fifth thriller, *Don't Be Home for Christmas*, where (spoiler alert) a terrorist hides a dirty bomb inside the New Year's ball in Times Square.

Mike Black—a PSWA board member, author, and former Chicago cop—told me they had never had anyone talk about insurance crimes: "It would be new territory." I was invited to speak on panels for four years at PSWA's annual conferences in Las Vegas, with a full lecture, "Creative Crimes," in 2022. I got to discuss my favorite topics in my favorite conference city. I've met many friendly authors in the group, and we've helped each other with plot ideas and accuracy.

In 2023, I released an action-thriller inspired by stories I'd heard from Coast Guard officers. Drug cartels had begun to use homemade submarines, known as "narco subs," to smuggle narcotics. In 2020, authorities seized the largest one to date—a hundred feet long with twin electric engines. The U.S.'s fear was cartels acquiring a Russian submarine from the black market.

My research discovered there was a thriving black market for Russian vehicles and hardware. The DEA's "Operation Odessa" exposed a close attempt to sell a Russian submarine, complete with a captain and crew, to the Cali Cartel. Expanding on this, I created a modern-day remake of Jules Verne's classic, titled *20,000 Kilos Under the Sea*, published by Fireship Press. The book received five-star reviews and won gold for Best Suspense/Thriller at the 2023 President's Book Awards from the Florida Authors & Publisher's Association.

Back on the insurance side, I was fortunate to be invited by the editor of *Claims Magazine* to be a keynote speaker at its litigation conference in Las Vegas. She asked if I would discuss my top "believe it or not" cases. My response was a resounding yes. As you might predict, the lecture included one "exploding corpse," the infamous B-Girls, Santería rituals gone wrong, and pulling cars from canals with at least one skeleton. The crowd approached me afterward with questions and tales of their own. With my wife along for the ride, it was as fun as it gets. I was invited back in 2024 to discuss AI and cyber threats, such as the phishing heists. It seems we'll never run out of new topics.

As for the SIU industry, new schemes and strategies have forged on. The pandemic accelerated a shift that was already occurring in the industry: working from centralized locations versus being "on the road." We had already seen SIU teams morph from field investigators to desk investigators, and now they were virtual investigators.

The notion of *not* working in the field to investigate was originally viewed as detrimental, especially by old-schoolers such as myself. For decades we had touted the need to "knock on doors" and "look people in the eye," and all those private eye clichés.

But the SIU industry realized it could be more productive. Utilizing advanced analytics, we could cross-reference millions of past and present cases for suspicious indicators. For SIU teams, it's about how many claims you touch, and we could indeed touch many more claims.

Before any fraudsters get any ideas: Yes, investigators still work in the field. They still check records for accuracy, visit addresses to see if they exist, inspect medical clinics, and hire forensic experts. Many carriers have investigators in different geographic areas just for field work. Others contract with vendors that specialize in SIU services. Their employees may be former law enforcement or have P.I. licenses, offering even greater expertise.

Virtual work has also enhanced investigations. Statements, examinations under oath, and proceedings such as depositions can be done virtually through video. Back in the day, asking someone to attend an EUO might consume an entire day. People had to drive downtown, pay to park, walk to whatever building, and then sit for hours. Video meetings can be done in a fraction of the time. Better yet, any deceitful parties have no excuse for *not* appearing. Judges have little tolerance for people not attending something if it's offered virtually.

Why should you care about any of this? Aside from these cases being interesting, horrifying, or comical, it's your cash that's burned every time a fraudulent claim is paid. What would you do if you had an extra $932.63 in your wallet? As stated earlier, that's how much we are all paying annually in increased premiums to offset the cost of fraud. For a family of four, that's almost $3,800.[203] With that much cash, you could go on a cruise (but think twice before buying any art).

If you're reading this as a consumer (that's all of you), I hope this material can help you avoid being a target. Don't buy things that seem too good to be true. You can research the legitimacy of people and property from your phone in minutes. Beware of strangers knocking on your door to do repairs or making other odd offers. Don't accelerate to drive onto someone's tail when they're going slow in the fast lane. If you do get into an accident, ask if anyone is hurt. Today, everyone has cameras on them, so take photos of both cars to document any damage. Don't accept business cards from strangers at accident scenes, and only visit medical offices you can research. If you require the services of an attorney, check their references and don't be persuaded to go to *their* clinic. And gentlemen: If an exotic younger woman approaches you at a bar, please use sound judgment.

If you're a business owner, be cautious of claims made against you. Do you have sufficient security cameras without blind spots? Did anyone witness the person who claimed they slipped and fell? Did they insist that you make an incident report with no witnesses? Have you received a letter from an attorney for an incident you were unaware of? Has a customer asked you to falsify purchase documents? With any of the above, contact your insurance carrier or agent immediately. You don't want someone else's scheme affecting your good reputation or hard-earned dollars.

If you're an insurance professional, I hope this material will help you identify potential schemes so they can be avoided or investigated in a timely manner. Agents should ask questions; fraudsters hate questions. Why are they insuring a $100,000 boat in Georgia if they live in Miami? Does it make sense? A fast-food cook wanting to insure their Rolex. A grandmother insuring a go-fast who has never owned a boat. If they're insuring any property (auto, vessel, art, jewelry), ask to see it with your own eyes. Beware of unknown applicants who push for service right before lunch or at 4:55 p.m. Check the validity of appraisals or other documents. If a stranger is answering their questions for them, ask who that person is.

If you're a company employee, perhaps in claims or underwriting, fraudsters are hoping you're too busy to check basic information. Even if you are four states away, they presume you won't have the ability to confirm their statements. With today's technology, you can easily check the validity of appraisals, receipts, and purchase documents. Corporate checks can confirm businesses. Databases such as Verisk's ISO can confirm if someone has had prior losses. Today, all of the above searches can be done in minutes. Make friends with your company's SIU department and know their referral process. SIU employees love to help with training.

As for law enforcement or any investigating agency including police, fire marshals, state fraud bureaus, Coast Guard, or FBI, please know that insurance companies' SIU departments are there to help. As described, all states have statutes that allow carriers to share information with law enforcement for any suspected fraud. We're all on the same team, many times investigating the same offenders.

If any of the cases described in this text were paid, they were funded in part by you. Whether the fraudsters preyed upon private insurers or the government, e.g. Medicare or loan assistance subsidies, *you* paid through increased premiums or taxes.

My favorite analogy about SIU investigators: The IRS conquered Al Capone when law enforcement couldn't. After years of futile police investigations, the mobster made the mistake of boasting, "They can't collect legal taxes from illegal money." With those words, Al Capone was investigated by the IRS and found guilty of tax evasion and sentenced to eleven years in prison for failing to file his tax returns.

Do you think IRS investigators ever felt cool before that? The unsung investigators of our Special Investigation Units may feel the same way. They are there to help identify and stop fraud before the money is disbursed. Their sole mission is to preserve your precious premium dollars.

And I'd wager they have more than a few good stories to tell.

Author's Acknowledgments

A special thanks to the dedicated SIU investigators who were vital to our teams. The recollections in this text would not have been possible without the help of Steve Andris, Chris Hunter, Sonia Florez, Doug Goldman, Efrain Ventura, Albert Negrin, and Kim Lawrance. Many cases involved countless other SIU investigators who were on my teams or our partner SIUs within the industry.

I'd also like to thank the many NICB Special Agents I've worked with for decades, including Senior Special Agent Fred Burkhardt and Special Agents Ralph Garcia, Herb Price, and Tony Fernandez. Thanks to Commander Nancy Alvarez with Monroe County Sheriffs in the Florida Keys for always including and educating us, and to FBI Special Agent Nelson Barbosa for the incredible opportunities with InfraGard.

I must express my gratitude to some of my favorite bosses who were mentors, supported my far-fetched projects, and allowed my participation in exclusive events: Tom Waggoner, Gerry Farina, Don Johnson, Todd McGrath, Russ Kyle, Gregory Law, and Maureen Hasselmann.

And a final thanks to Mr. Marc Schiller, who was kind enough to chat and answer questions that must have evoked horrific memories. Considering what you have endured, your resilience is inspiring.

Richard Wickliffe, January 26, 2024 – Somewhere over Chicago

References

1   "Scott Says PIP Program 'Has to be Fixed'" Deslatte, Aaron. Jan. 26, 2012, *Orlando Sentinel.*

2   "Private Security: Implications for Social Control, Social Problems", Volume 30, Issue 5, 1 June 1983, Pages 493–506. Clifford D. Shearing, Philip C. Stenning.

3   2021 Florida Statutes. http://www.leg.state.fl.us/statutes/index.cfm?App_mode=Display_Statute&URL=0600-0699/0626/Sections/0626.9891.html

4   "Background on: Insurance fraud," Aug 1, 2022. *Insurance Information Institute.* https://www.iii.org/article/background-on-insurance-fraud

5   Insurance Fraud Detection Market Size; 2019-2025, *Grand View Research.* https://www.grandviewresearch.com/industry-analysis/insurance-fraud-detection-market#:~:text=The%20global%20insurance%20fraud%20detection%20market%20is%20expected%20to%20grow,USD%209.7%20billion%20by%202025

6   "Insurance fraud costs $309 billion a year — nearly $1,000 for every American", Dr. Michael Skiba, Nov 13, 2022. *Bristol Herald Courier.* https://heraldcourier.com/business/article_4fb8ab1c-98e2-5f8c-ac1e-6a023105f2b8.html

7   "Fraud Stats - Impact", Coalition Against Insurance Fraud. https://insurancefraud.org/fraud-stats/

8   "The Impact of Insurance Fraud in the Economy 2022," Coalition Against Insurance Fraud, https://insurancefraud.org/

wp-content/uploads/The-Impact-of-Insurance-Fraud-on-the-U.S.-Economy-Report-2022-8.26.2022.pdf

9   Background on: Insurance Fraud, Nov. 18, 2021. *Insurance Information Institute.* https://www.iii.org/article/background-on-insurance-fraud

10   ISO ClaimSearch: Fast-track claims and detect fraud. *Verisk.* https://www.verisk.com/insurance/products/claimsearch/

11   Definition of "theft", *Merriam-Webster Dictionary.* https://www.merriam-webster.com/dictionary/theft

12   "Protecting Cultural Heritage from Art Theft: International Challenge, Local Opportunity", *FBI Law Enforcement Bulletin*, Noah Charney, M.A., M.A., Paul Denton, M.B.A., M.S.C.J., and John Kleberg, M.Ed. https://leb.fbi.gov/articles/featured-articles/protecting-cultural-heritage-from-art-theft-international-challenge-local-opportunity

13   "After Drugs and Guns, Art Theft Is the Biggest Criminal Enterprise in the World," Kris Hollington, 7/22/14. *Newsweek.* https://www.newsweek.com/2014/07/18/after-drugs-and-guns-art-theft-biggest-criminal-enterprise-world-260386.html

14   "Spielberg Collection is Found to Contain Stolen Rockwell Art," Mar. 4, 2007. The Associate Press. https://www.nytimes.com/2007/03/04/us/04rockwell.html

15   "Ever Bought Art on a Cruise? Prepare to Be Seasick," Vernon Silver, Dec. 14, 2016. *Bloomberg Businessweek.* https://www.bloomberg.com/news/features/2016-12-14/ever-bought-artwork-on-a-cruise-prepare-to-be-seasick

16   "Art Auctions on Cruise Ships Lead to Anger, Accusations and Lawsuits," Jori Finkle, July 16, 2008, *New York Times*, https://www.nytimes.com/2008/07/16/arts/design/16crui.html

17   Ibid

18   "Lawsuit against Park West over Dali art moves forward," Zlati Meyer, Dec. 3, 2014. *The Detroit Free Press*. https://www.freep.com/story/money/business/michigan/2014/12/03/salvador-dali-lawuit/19861427/

19   "Cruise passenger told to leave in art auction row," Calhal Milmo, July 31, 2009. *The Independent*. https://www.independent.co.uk/arts-entertainment/art/news/cruise-passenger-told-to-leave-in-art-auction-row-1765688.html

20   Ibid

21   "Park West, the Gallery Best Known for Selling Art on Cruise Ships, Wants to Turn the Tide After Years of Legal Battles. Will a New York Outpost Help?" Eileen Kinsella, Jan. 31, 2023. *Artnet News*, https://news.artnet.com/market/park-west-cruise-seller-new-york-gallery-2246377

22   "Ever Bought Art on a Cruise? Prepare to Be Seasick," Vernon Silver, Dec. 14, 2016. *Bloomberg Businessweek*. https://www.bloomberg.com/news/features/2016-12-14/ever-bought-artwork-on-a-cruise-prepare-to-be-seasick

23   "Park West, the Gallery Best Known for Selling Art on Cruise Ships, Wants to Turn the Tide After Years of Legal Battles. Will a New York Outpost Help?" Eileen Kinsella, Jan. 31, 2023. *Artnet News*, https://news.artnet.com/market/park-west-cruise-seller-new-york-gallery-2246377

24   "FTC Shuts Down Purveyors of Fake Documents Used for Fraud, Identity Theft," Press Release, Sept. 18, 2018. Federal Trade Commission. https://www.ftc.gov/news-events/press-releases/2018/09/ftc-shuts-down-purveyors-fake-documents-used-fraud-identity-theft

25   Ibid

26   U.S. Patent US5723391A, Charles Eric Hunter, Dirk Verbiest. https://patents.google.com/patent/US5723391

27   "Little Havana Locks Its Doors in Quiet Protest," Juan Forero, Apr. 26, 2000. *The New York Times.* https://www.nytimes.com/2000/04/26/us/the-elian-gonzalez-case-the-city-little-havana-locks-its-doors-in-quiet-protest.html

28   "Criminalistics: Forensic Science, Crime and Terrorism, James E. Gerard," 2011, Jones & Bartlett Learning, LLC.

29   "Motive-Based Offender Profiles of Arson and Fire-Related Crimes," David J. Icove, PhD, P.E. April 1987, *FBI Law Enforcement Bulletin.* https://www.ojp.gov/pdffiles1/Digitization/105100NCJRS.pdf

30   "Prosecutor targeted for hit by suspect in insurance scam," Feb. 9, 2018. *Miami Herald.* https://www.miamiherald.com/news/local/crime/article199272074.html

31   "Public Adjusters—a family affair!" by Scott Johnson, June 28, 2018. JS Johnson Strategies, LLC. https://johnsonstrategiesllc.com/public-adjusters-a-family-affair

32   "First Responder/Fire Chaser," Craigslist ad (undated) http://johnsonstrategiesllc.com/wp-content/uploads/downloads/2016/03/Fire-Chasers-Ad.pdf

33   "Public Adjusters—a family affair!" by Scott Johnson, June 28, 2018. JS Johnson Strategies, LLC. https://johnsonstrategiesllc.com/public-adjusters-a-family-affair

34   "The Propensity of Lit Cigarettes to Ignite Gasoline Vapors," Justin Gelman, January 2013, Fire & Risk Alliance LLC. https://www.researchgate.net/publication/271921785_The_Propensity_of_Lit_Cigarettes_to_Ignite_Gasoline_Vapors

35   "Can A Single Cigarette Set Gasoline (Or Petrol) On Fire?" John Straughton, Nov. 11, 2021. *Science ABC* https://www.scienceabc.com/eyeopeners/can-cigarette-ignite-light-puddle-gasoline-fire.html

36   *Kattoum v. New Hampshire Indemnity Company*, District Court of Appeal of Florida, Sept. 29, 2007. https://scholar. google.com/scholar_case?q=968+So.+2d+602+&hl=en&as_ sdt=40006&case=2402347154337680439&scilh=0

37   "Church of the Lukumi Babalu Aye v. City of Hialeah," William Crawford Green, 1993. *The Free Speech Center*. https://www. mtsu.edu/first-amendment/article/29/church-of-the-lukumi-babalu-aye-v-city-of-hialeah

38   "Santeria or Voodoo, they're used to headless chickens", Paul Guzo, Nov. 27, 2019, *Tampa Times*. https://www.tampabay.com/news/hillsborough/2019/11/27/santeria-or-voodoo-theyre-used-to-headless-chickens-at-tampa-cemetery/

39   "Grave Robbers Remove Bones From Miami's Historic Cemeteries," Linda Robertson, June 9, 2018. *The Miami Herald*. https://www.staugustine.com/story/lifestyle/faith/2018/06/09/grave-robbers-remove-bones-from-miamis-historic-cemeteries/12024073007/

40   "Mysterious, controversial: Santeria sacrifices protected," Mike Clary, July 27, 2008. *Sun Sentinel*. https://www.sun-sentinel.com/news/fl-xpm-2008-07-27-0807260071-story.html

41   "Why Santeria Woman Burned to Death," Jamie Schram, Feb. 26, 2004. *New York Post*. https://nypost.com/2004/02/26/why-santeria-woman-burned-to-death-in-the-bronx/

42   Ibid.

43   Top 10 Busiest U.S. Ports, Susan Piprato, Jan. 27, 2014. WeathManagement.com. https://www.wealthmanagement.com/property-types/top-10-busiest-us-ports

44   "Importing a Car into Colombia: Taxes and Duties." Stuart Oswald. https://www.stuartoswald.com/2018/03/importing-your-car-and-household-goods.html

45   "Changing the Russian Mafia Mystique" James Finchenauer and Elin Waring. *National Institute of Justice Journal*, April 2001. https://www.ojp.gov/pdffiles1/jr000247b.pdf

46   "Miami becomes 'Little Moscow'" *Daily Mail*, June 1, 2011. https://www.dailymail.co.uk/news/article-1393246/Russian-mob-eclipses-Italian-Mafia-South-Florida-FBI-says.html

47   "Viral petition urges Russian club in Hallandale to scratch live tiger from stage act," Jay Weaver, Oct. 29, 2015. *The Miami Herald*. https://www.miamiherald.com/news/local/community/broward/article41732346.html

48   "FBI: Russian mob overshadows Italian Mafia in South Florida," Jay Weaver, June 1, 2011. *The Miami Herald*. https://www.mcclatchydc.com/news/crime/article24645904.html

49   "Miami Under 'Red Threat' from Russian Mob," 5/31/2011, *The Miami Herald*. http://www.miamiherald.com/2011/05/31/v-fullstory/2244321/russian-mob-eclipses-italian-mafia.html#ixzz1O1WhrfDL

50   Florida Statute 509.151. http://www.leg.state.fl.us/statutes/index.cfm?App_mode=Display_Statute&Search_String=&URL=0500-0599/0509/Sections/0509.151.html

51   "Nightmare on South Beach," 2012, Pat Jordan, *Playboy*. https://spjflorida.com/wp-content/uploads/2012/06/16517798974f48162bcfce6_0.pdf

52   "John Bolaris, Former Weatherman, Allegedly Seduced, Conned Out of $43,000." Hilary Hanson, Dec 6, 2012. *Huffington Post*. https://www.huffpost.com/entry/john-bolaris-conned-bar-girls_n_1564954

53   "Real-Life Hangover Weatherman Scammed and Drugged in Miami by Russian B-Girls," Rachell Quigley, June 1, 2012, *Daily Mail*. https://www.dailymail.co.uk/news/article-2153281/Weatherman-

John-Bolaris-scammed-drugged-Miami-Russian-B-Girls-tells-story-months-sacked.html

54   Ibid

55   "Drugged, Scammed by Beautiful Women," Michael Koenigs, Mar. 26, 2012. *ABC News.* https://abcnews.go.com/US/drugged-scammed-beautiful-women-weatherman-tells-story/story?id=16005588&page=2#.T8pJ1uY_p18

56   "From South Beach to Prison" Jan. 20, 2013, *Associated Press.* https://www.tampabay.com/archive/2013/01/20/from-south-beach-to-prison/

57   United States v. Marina Turcina, United States District Court, Southern District of Florida, case no . 11-20279-cr-Martinez. Fe. 27, 2012. https://www.govinfo.gov/content/pkg/USCOURTS-flsd-1_11-cr-20279/pdf/USCOURTS-flsd-1_11-cr-20279-6.pdf

58   Hearing Before the Subcommittee of European Affairs of the Committee on Foreign Relations United States Senate, One Hundred Eighth Congress, First Session, October 30, 2003, https://www.govinfo.gov/content/pkg/CHRG-108shrg92792/html/CHRG-108shrg92792.htm

59   "Thirteen members and Associates of Transnational Organized Crime Groups Charged in South Florida," U.S. Attorney's Office, Feb. 16, 2011, FBI Press Release. https://archives.fbi.gov/archives/miami/press-releases/2011/mm021611.htm

60   Ibid

61   "Mafia, violent criminals turn to Medicare fraud," Oct. 6, 2009. *The Associated Press.* https://www.nbcnews.com/id/wbna33196132

62   "The $272 Billion Swindle," *The Economist*, May 31, 2014. https://www.economist.com/united-states/2014/05/31/the-272-billion-swindle

63   "Clinic Manager Pleads Guilty In $70 Million Scheme To Defraud Medicare And Medicaid," Dept. of Justice Press Release, Feb. 6, 2017. *Healthcare Finance.* https://www.justice.gov/usao-sdny/pr/clinic-manager-pleads-guilty-70-million-scheme-defraud-medicare-and-medicaid

64   "New York Doctor Who Performed Unnecessary Back Surgeries Pleads Guilty To Participating In Trip-And-Fall Fraud Scheme," Department of Justice, Southern District of New York, Sept. 29, 2022. https://www.justice.gov/usao-sdny/pr/new-york-doctor-who-performed-unnecessary-back-surgeries-pleads-guilty-participating

65   "Steps Unveiled to Fight Medicare Fraud," Kelli Kennedy, Jan 24, 2011. *The Associated Press.* https://www.heraldtribune.com/story/news/2011/01/25/steps-unveiled-to-fight-medicare-fraud/28992125007/

66   "Mafia, violent criminals turn to Medicare fraud," Kelli Kennedy, Oct 6, 2009. *Associated Press,* https://www.nbcnews.com/id/wbna33196132

67   "Brothers Enter Guilty Plea in Massive Insurance Fraud," Susan Moffat, Mar. 17, 1993. *Los Angeles Times.* https://www.latimes.com/archives/la-xpm-1993-03-16-me-456-story.html

68   "2 Are Ordered to Pay $185 Million in Health Care Fraud," Sep. 25, 1994, *The Associated Press.* https://www.nytimes.com/1994/09/25/us/2-are-ordered-to-pay-185-million-in-health-insurance-fraud.html

69   "Russian Organized Crime," Daniel Lunden, Mar. 1996. California Office of Attorney General. https://irp.fas.org/world/para/docs/rusorg3.htm

70   "Who Are the Irish Travelers in the US?" Casey Egan, Jul. 10, 2020. *Irish Central.* https://www.irishcentral.com/culture/who-are-irish-travellers-us

71   "Irish Traveller rural construction fraudsters plead guilty," Mikkel Pates, Feb. 8, 2021. *AG Week.* https://www.agweek.com/news/crime-and-courts/6878109-%E2%80%98Irish-Traveller%E2%80%99-rural-construction-fraudsters-plead-guilty-to-North-Dakota-cases

72   "ND AG issues cease-and-desist on widespread 'Irish Traveller' construction scams," Mikkel Pates, Jan. 17, 2020. *The Dickenson Press.* https://www.thedickinsonpress.com/news/crime-and-courts/4870450-ND-AG-issues-cease-and-desist-on-widespread-Irish-Traveller-construction-scams

73   Ibid

74   Ibid

75   "Insurance Agent Jailed Over Huge Irish Traveler Insurance Scam," Lyle Adriano, Dec. 10, 2018. *Insurance Business magazine.* https://www.insurancebusinessmag.com/us/news/breaking-news/insurance-agent-jailed-over-huge-irish-traveler-insurance-scam-118350.aspx

76   Ibid

77   "The Most Terrifying Actos of Life Insurance Fraud," Warren Hersch, Nov. 2, 2015. *Think Advisor.* https://www.thinkadvisor.com/2015/11/02/the-most-terrifying-acts-of-life-insurance-fraud/?slreturn=20211127081807

78   "Irish Travellers in Texas charged with murdering elderly woman for life insurance policy," Casey Egan, Mar 24, 2015. *Irish Central.* https://www.irishcentral.com/news/irish-travellers-in-texas-charged-with-murdering-elderly-woman-for-life-insurance-policy

79   "Four Miami-Dade Residents Charged In $1.5 Million Bank Fraud And Money Laundering Scheme In Connection With Fraudulent Boat Loan Applications" United States Attorney's Office for the Southern District of Florida, June 19, 2013. https://www.justice.gov/usao-sdfl/pr/four-miami-dade-residents-charged-15-million-bank-fraud-and-money-laundering-scheme

80   Florida Department of Financial Services, Division of
Insurance Fraud, Annual Report, Fiscal year 2012/2013. https://
www.myfloridacfo.com/docs-sf/investigative-and-forensic-
services-libraries/difs-documents/2012-2013_annualreport.
pdf?sfvrsn=f54ffc71_2

81   "Cubans are Risking Everything to Enter the US," Patrick
Oppmann, June 25, 2021. *CNN.* https://www.cnn.com/2021/06/25/
americas/cuba-migrants-us-sanctions-economy-intl/index.html

82   Florida Statutes 787.06 (1) (a) – Human Trafficking - http://
www.leg.state.fl.us/Statutes/index.cfm?App_mode=Display_
Statute&URL=0700-0799/0787/Sections/0787.06.html

83   "Trafficking in Persons in the United States," Kevin Bales,
Ph.D.; Steven Lize, Ph.D., Nov 5, 2005, U.S. Dept of Justice. https://
www.ojp.gov/pdffiles1/nij/grants/211980.pdf

84   "Plundering America – The Cuban Criminal Pipeline" Sally
Kestin, Megan O'Matz, John Maines, Tracey Eaton, Jan 8, 2015. *Sun
Sentinel.* http://interactive.sun-sentinel.com/plundering-america/

85   "Cuban migrant died of blunt trauma", Marlene Naanes, Jul.
10, 2006. *Sun-Sentinel,* https://www.orlandosentinel.com/news/os-
xpm-2006-07-10-mmigrants10-story.html

86   "Cubans are Risking Everything to Enter the US," Patrick
Oppmann, June 25, 2021. *CNN.* https://www.cnn.com/2021/06/25/
americas/cuba-migrants-us-sanctions-economy-intl/index.html

87   "A Tiny Tourist Island Off the Coast of Florida Is a Human
Smuggling Hub", Maeva Bambuck, Oct. 21, 2022. *Vice World News.*
https://www.vice.com/en/article/qjkx3x/bimini-bahamas-human-
smuggling

88   Ibid

89   "Historic wave of Cuban migrants will have a lasting impact on Florida," Carmen Sesin, Dec. 16, 2022. *NBC News.* " https://www.nbcnews.com/news/latino/historic-wave-cuban-migrants-florida-impact-lasting-rcna61989

90   "2022 Trafficking in Persons Report – Cuba", U.S. Embassy in Cuba, https://cu.usembassy.gov/2022-trafficking-in-persons-report-cuba/

91   "No Money Down," Elise Ackerman, Aug 16, 1996. *Miami New Times.* http://www.miaminewtimes.com/news/no-money-down-6361495

92   "Quick Facts and Figures," South Florida Water Management District. https://www.sfwmd.gov/who-we-are/facts-and-figures

93   "Fifth Teen Dies from Canal Accident." Sept 29, 1992. *UPI Archives.* https://www.upi.com/Archives/1992/09/29/Fifth-teen-dies-from-canal-accident/8523717739200/

94   "Unsolved Mysteries Likely Lie in the Hillsboro Canal," Rachel Joyner, January 4, 2008, *Sun-Sentinel.* https://www.sun-sentinel.com/news/fl-xpm-2008-01-04-0801030552-story.html
95
 Ibid

96   Ibid

97   "Vehicle Fires," Marty Ahrens, March 2020. National Fire Protection Association. https://www.nfpa.org/-/media/Files/News-and-Research/Fire-statistics-and-reports/US-Fire-Problem/osvehiclefires.pdf

98   "Opa-Locka Fl Had Highest City Violent Crime Rate," Oct 26, 2004. *TheCrimeReport.org.* https://thecrimereport.org/2004/10/26/opa-locka-fl-had-highest-city-violent-crime-rate/

99   "Opa-Locka Boots the Boss," Calvin Godfrey, Jan. 31, 2008. *Miami New Times.* https://www.miaminewtimes.com/news/opa-locka-boots-the-boss-6366940

100   "Former Opa-Locka City Manager Charged with Corruption Scheme," Aug. 5, 2016. CBSMiami.com. https://miami.cbslocal.com/2016/08/05/fmr-opa-locka-city-manager-charged-in-corruption-scheme/

101   "Cop Charged with Helping Drug Trafficking." Paula McMahon, Sept 2, 2012. *Sun-Sentinel.* https://www.sun-sentinel.com/news/fl-xpm-2012-09-24-fl-arthur-balom-to-plead-20120924-story.html

102   "Crime in Opa-Locka is Up 403 Percent This Year," Jessica Lipscomb, Nov. 28, 2018. *Miami New Times.* https://www.miaminewtimes.com/news/opa-locka-crime-is-up-403-percent-this-year-report-says-10933611

103   "How Chop Shops Work: Vehicle Theft on the Rise.," K. Dailey, Lojack. https://lojack.com/blog/2017/07/how-chop-shops-work/

104   "Rental Car Thefts on the Rise," Oct 28, 2014. NBC Miami, https://www.nbcmiami.com/news/local/rental-car-thefts-on-the-rise/61401/

105   Ibid

106   Ibid

107   Drug Enforcement Administration Press Release, Oct. 14, 2020. "Luxury car purveyor extradited on fraud and money laundering charges" https://www.dea.gov/press-releases/2020/10/14/luxury-car-purveyor-extradicted-fraud-and-money-laundering-charges

108   Ibid

109   A Miami Story: Flashy Cars, Brazen Thieves and Murder," Frances Robles, March 12, 2012. *The Palm Beach Post.* https://www.palmbeachpost.com/story/news/crime/2012/03/12/a-miami-story-flashy-cars/7266317007/

110   Ibid

111   Ibid

112   Ibid

113   Ibid

114   "The psychological reason that so many fall for the "Big Lie," Matthew Rozsa, Feb 3, 2022, *Salon.* https://www.salon.com/2022/02/03/the-psychological-reason-that-so-many-fall-for-the-big-lie/

115   "Accidentally, on Purpose: The Making of a Personal Injury Underworld in America." Ken Dornstein, 1998. Palgrave Macmillan, p. 3

116   "Lawyer Faces Murder Trial in Staging of Car Accident," Ann O'Neill, May 14, 1996. *Los Angeles Times.* https://www.latimes.com/archives/la-xpm-1996-05-14-me-4095-story.html

117   "Lawyer's Drive for Success is Measured in Fraud Case…" Amy Pyle, Nov 22, 1992. *Los Angeles Times.* https://www.latimes.com/archives/la-xpm-1992-11-22-me-2230-story.html

118   "12 Arrested in Miami-Based Medical Fraud Scheme," Amanda Batchelor. Local 10 News. Aug. 8, 2016. https://www.local10.com/news/2016/08/08/12-arrested-in-miami-based-medical-fraud-scheme/

119   "Florida Mayor, Councilman Indicted in Racketeering Case," April 4, 1990 *Associated Press.* https://apnews.com/article/6d752273d917aa4ca16f681febce61db

120   "Mud is flying in Hialeah's mayoral horse race : Despite the fact that he is a convicted felon, Raul Martinez is favored to win reelection in no-holds-barred contest," Mike Clary, Nov. 1, 1993. *The Los Angeles Times*. https://www.latimes.com/archives/la-xpm-1993-11-01-mn-51999-story.html

121   "Hialeah Mayor Carlos Hernandez fights to silence whistleblower firefighter," Francisco Alvarado, Feb 20, 2019, *Florida Bulldog*. https://www.floridabulldog.org/2019/02/hialeah-mayor-carlos-hernandez-fights-to-silence-whistleblowing-firefighter/

122   Hialeah Mayor Pays $4000 Ethics Fine -In Pennies and Nickels," May 5, 2016, *Miami Herald*. https://www.miamiherald.com/news/local/community/miami-dade/hialeah/article75829512.html

123   "In Hialeah, Money Meant to Feed Hungry Kids Pays for Las Vegas Trip," by Francisco Alavarado, Sept. 21, 2017, *The Miami Herald*. https://www.miamiherald.com/news/local/community/miami-dade/article174610061.html

124   Miami-Dade Commission on Ethics & Public Trust, Investigative Report, Feb. 19, 2016. https://ethics.miamidade.gov/library/closed%20investigations/2016/k_16-13_hernandez_et-al.pdf

125   "Ex-mayor gets 5 years in murder-for-hire plot," August 29, 2000. *The Washington Post*, https://www.washingtontimes.com/news/2000/aug/29/20000829-011855-7309r/

126   "Ex-Mayor Convicted Of Plot To Kill Husband," Jose Dante Parra Herrera, July 1, 2000. *The Sun-Sentinel*, http://www.sun-sentinel.com/news/fl-xpm-2000-07-01-0007010213-story.html

127   "Pair Arrested for PIP Fraud Scheme in Florida," August 26, 2003. *Insurance Journal*. https://www.insurancejournal.com/news/southeast/2003/08/26/31763.htm

128   "Clinic Owner Arrested for PIP Fraud Scheme," My Florida CFO Press Release, 8/22/03. https://www.myfloridacfo.com/sitePages/newsroom/pressRelease.aspx?id=1589

129   Florida Statute Chapter 817, Section 234 – False and fraudulent insurance claims. https://www.flsenate.gov/laws/statutes/2018/817.234

130   "South Florida Is Ground Zero for Medicare Fraud," Chris Parker, May 2, 2013, *Miami New Times*. https://www.miaminewtimes.com/news/south-florida-is-ground-zero-for-medicare-fraud-6391954

131   "How Medicare Fraud Became The Nation's Most Lucrative Crime," Chris Parker, April 25, 2013, *LA Weekly*, https://www.laweekly.com/how-medicare-fraud-became-the-nations-most-lucrative-crime/

132   "Thirty-three Defendants Charged In Staged Automobile Accident Scheme," Dept of Justice Press Release, U.S. Attorney's Office, Southern District of Florida, May 16, 2023. https://www.justice.gov/usao-sdfl/pr/thirty-three-defendants-charged-staged-automobile-accident-scheme

133   Ibid

134   "Tampa Streets Littered With Fake Car Crashes," Jun. 29, 2010, Robert Trigaux. *Tampa Bay Times*. https://www.tampabay.com/archive/2010/06/29/tampa-streets-littered-with-fake-car-crashes/

135   "NICB Opens Central Florida Medical Fraud Task Force," Aug 10, 2010. National Insurance Crime Bureau Press Release. https://www.prnewswire.com/news-releases/nicb-opens-central-florida-medical-fraud-task-force-100338859.html

136   "Tampa Streets Littered With Fake Car Crashes," Jun. 29, 2010, Robert Trigaux. *Tampa Bay Times*. https://www.tampabay.com/archive/2010/06/29/tampa-streets-littered-with-fake-car-crashes/

137   "CFO Jimmy Patronis Announces 10 Arrests in $42.7 Million Insurance Fraud Bust," Feb. 6, 2019 Press Release, MyFloridaCFO.com. https://www.myfloridacfo.com/sitepages/newsroom/pressrelease.aspx?id=5187

138   "Tampa Streets Littered with Fake Car Crashes," Robert Trigaux, June 29, 2010. *Tampa Bay Times*. https://www.tampabay.com/archive/2010/06/29/tampa-streets-littered-with-fake-car-crashes/

139   United States Secret Service, "About Us," https://www.secretservice.gov/about/overview

140   Clancy, Tom, 1947-2013. 1994. *Debt of Honor*. Thorndike, Me., Thorndike Press.

141   Hearing Before The Committee On Government Reform, One Hundred Eighth Congress, Second Session, August 3, 2004. https://www.govinfo.gov/content/pkg/CHRG-108hhrg96537/html/CHRG-108hhrg96537.htm

142   "Feds Seek H'Wood Help," 2001, Claude Brodesser, *Variety*. https://variety.com/2001/biz/news/feds-seek-h-wood-s-help-1117853841/

143   "Author Brad Meltzer was recruited in government agency, 'horrified' at how easy it is to attack U.S." Brad Meltzer, Jan. 13, 2019. *New York Daily News*, https://www.nydailynews.com/2011/01/11/author-brad-meltzer-was-recruited-in-government-agency-horrified-at-how-easy-it-is-to-attack-us/

144   "Shutting Down Terrorist Pathways Into America," Committee on Homeland Security. Sept. 14, 2016. https://www.govinfo.gov/content/pkg/CHRG-114hhrg25268/html/CHRG-114hhrg25268.htm

145   Florida Statute 626.989. http://www.leg.state.fl.us/statutes/index.cfm?App_mode=Display_Statute&URL=0600-0699/0626/Sections/0626.989.html

146   Is Faking Your Own Death a Crime?" Natalie Wolchover, Aug. 17, 2012, *Live Science Magazine*. https://www.livescience.com/22473-faking-death-crime-law.html

147   Fake Deaths Abroad Are a Growing Problem for Insurers," Joseph B. Treaster. July 1, 1997. *The New York Times*. https://www.

nytimes.com/1997/07/01/business/fake-deaths-abroad-are-a-growing-problem-for-insurers.html

148   "Ten Facts About Hunger in Haiti," World Food Programme, https://reliefweb.int/report/haiti/10-facts-about-hunger-haiti

149   "Grieving Haitians Go Into Lifetime of Debt to Fund Funerals" Apr 6, 2017. *The Associated Press.* https://www.voanews.com/a/grieving-hatians-go-into-lifetime-of-debt-to-fund-funerals/3798711.html

150   *Playing Dead: A Journey Through the World of Death Fraud,* by Elizabeth Greenwood. Simon &Schuster, Aug. 15, 2017.

151   Ibid

152   "Florida woman loses battle for insurance coverage after home was damaged by 'exploding' corpse", Alex Greig, Apr. 24, 2014. *The Daily Mail.* https://www.dailymail.co.uk/news/article-2614034/Florida-woman-loses-battle-insurance-coverage-home-damaged-exploding-corpse.html

153   "'Florida Man Murders' star Judge Alex Ferrer details case that inspired Michael Bay's 'Pain & Gain' film", Julia Young, Jan. 9, 2021. *Fox News.* https://www.foxnews.com/entertainment/florida-man-murders-star-judge-alex-ferrer

154   "Pain and Gain," Troy Roberts, Feb. 22, 2014. CBS News, https://www.cbsnews.com/news/pain-and-gain-the-real-life-story-behind-miamis-murderous-sun-gym-gang/

155   Ibid

156   "Real-life 'Pain and Gain' victim tells story of survival," Ben Wolford, May 17, 2013, *Sun Sentinel.* https://www.sun-sentinel.com/news/fl-xpm-2013-05-17-fl-pain-and-gain-20130515-story.html

157   "Pain and Gain," Pete Collins, Jan 6, 2000. *Miami New Times.* https://www.miaminewtimes.com/news/sidebar-6357215

158   "The 'Sun Gym Gang' Of Miami 'Meatheads' Murdered A Wealthy Couple In A Botched Theft," Becca van Sambeck, Jan 9, 2021. *Oxygen True Crime.* https://www.oxygen.com/florida-man-murders/crime-news/how-danny-lugos-sun-gym-gang-killed-frank-griga-and-krisztina-furton

159   Ibid

160   "Muscle and mayhem: The real-life story behind Miami's murderous Sun Gym gang," Apr. 28, 2013. *CBS News.* https://www.cbsnews.com/news/muscle-and-mayhem-the-real-life-story-behind-miamis-murderous-sun-gym-gang/

161   "Pain & Gain, Part 3," Pete Collins, Jan 6, 2000. *Miami New Times.* https://web.archive.org/web/20140226004821/http://www.miaminewtimes.com:80/2000-01-06/news/pain-gain-part-3/10/

162   Ibid

163   Amazon book review of "Pain and Gain-The Untold True Story," Amazon, https://www.amazon.com/Pain-Gain-Untold-True-Story/dp/0615740065

164   "The Mysterious Case of the Doctor Who Disappeared at Sea", Michael Wilson, December 22, 2022, *New York Times.* https://www.nytimes.com/2022/12/22/nyregion/marvin-moy-boat-missing.html

165   "Two Miami Residents Plead Guilty for Their Role in $9 Million Scheme to Defraud Prescription Drug Coupon Programs", Feb. 4, 2022. Dept of Justice, U.S. Attorney's Office, Southern District of Florida. https://www.justice.gov/usao-sdfl/pr/two-miami-residents-plead-guilty-their-role-9-million-scheme-defraud-prescription-drug

166   "Business Email Compromise and Real Estate Wire Fraud", 2022 FBI Congressional Report. https://www.fbi.gov/file-repository/fy-2022-fbi-congressional-report-business-email-compromise-and-real-estate-wire-fraud-111422.pdf

167   Ibid

168   UBIQUITI NETWORKS, INC.", Aug 4, 2015, United States Securities And Exchange Commission, Washington, D.C., https://www.sec.gov/Archives/edgar/data/1511737/000157104915006288/t1501817_8k.htm

169   "Hacker Pretends To Be Evan Spiegel To Steal Snapchat Employee Data", Thomas Brewster, Feb 26, 2016. *Forbes.* https://www.forbes.com/sites/thomasbrewster/2016/02/29/snapchat-data-leak/?sh=48aa26331769

170   "Austria's FACC, Hit by Cyber Fraud, Fires CEO", May 25, 2016. *Reuters.* https://www.reuters.com/article/us-facc-ceo/austrias-facc-hit-by-cyber-fraud-fires-ceo-idUSKCN0YG0ZF

171   "25% Of Workers Lost Their Jobs In The Past 12 Months After Making Cybersecurity Mistakes", Edward Siegel, Mar 29, 2022. *Forbes.* https://www.forbes.com/sites/edwardsegal/2022/03/29/25-of-workers-lost-their-jobs-in-the-past-12-months-after-making-cybersecurity-mistakes-report/?sh=64c8dcdc49b2

172   "Why Do People Make Mistakes That Compromise Cybersecurity?" 2022 Report, Tessian. https://www.tessian.com/blog/new-research-psychology-of-human-error/

173   "The Great Bank Robbery: Carbanak cybergang steals $1bn from 100 financial institutions worldwide", Feb 16, 2015. Kaspersky Press Release. https://www.kaspersky.com/about/press-releases/2015_the-great-bank-robbery-carbanak-cybergang-steals--1bn-from-100-financial-institutions-worldwide

174   "Mastermind behind EUR 1 billion cyber bank robbery arrested in Spain", Mar. 26, 2018. Europol Press Release. https://www.europol.europa.eu/media-press/newsroom/news/mastermind-behind-eur-1-billion-cyber-bank-robbery-arrested-in-spain

175   "Phishing Tests Are Necessary. But They Don't Need to Be Evil." Ryan White and Jason Bennett Thatcher, Apr. 1, 2021. *Harvard Business Review.* https://hbr.org/2021/04/phishing-tests-are-necessary-but-they-dont-need-to-be-evil

176   "The Godfather of AI' Quits Google and Warns of Danger," Cade Metz, May 1, 2023, *New York Times*. https://www.nytimes.com/2023/05/01/technology/ai-google-chatbot-engineer-quits-hinton.html

177   "Fraudsters Used AI to Mimic CEO's Voice in Unusual Cybercrime Case", Catherine Stupp, Aug. 30, 2019. *The Wall Street Journal*. https://www.wsj.com/articles/fraudsters-use-ai-to-mimic-ceos-voice-in-unusual-cybercrime-case-11567157402

178   Ibid

179   "Internet Crime Report 2021", Federal Bureau of Investigation. https://www.ic3.gov/Media/PDF/AnnualReport/2021_IC3Report.pdf

180   "Fraudsters Cloned Company Director's Voice In $35 Million Bank Heist" Thomas Brewster. Oct 14, 2021. *Forbes*. https://www.forbes.com/sites/thomasbrewster/2021/10/14/huge-bank-fraud-uses-deep-fake-voice-tech-to-steal-millions/?sh=7a25bb0f7559

181   "Voice Phishing Increases Risk of Account Takeover Fraud." Andrew Chan, June 28, 2021. *Neustar, Transunion*. https://www.home.neustar/blog/account-takeover-fraud-fight-back

182   "Mila Kunis thought Ashton Kutcher's Uber investment was a terrible idea", Hannah Frishberg, Apr. 30, 2021. *New York Post*. https://nypost.com/2021/04/30/mila-kunis-thought-ashton-kutchers-uber-investment-was-bad-idea/

183   "Why Uber is a Perfect Part-Time Solution for College Students in LA", *Uber Newsroom*, https://newsroom.uber.com/why-uber-is-a-perfect-part-time-solution-for-college-students-in-la/

184   "(Believe Tech or Not) James Bond Played a Vital Role in How Uber Came to be", Shubham Agarwal, Apr. 16, 2018, *TeckPP.com*, https://techpp.com/2018/04/16/james-bond-uber-believe-tech-or-not/

185   Uber Technologies, Inc, Sep. 30, 2022, United States Securities And Exchange Commission. https://www.sec.gov/ix?doc=/Archives/edgar/data/1543151/000154315122000034/uber-20220930.htm

186   Reddit subject string "Uber driving is an awful use of your time, and I crunched the numbers to prove it." https://www.reddit.com/r/personalfinance/comments/59vutb/uber_driving_is_an_awful_use_of_your_time_and_i/

187   Reddit subject string, "Is rideshare insurance mandatory? Or just regular car insurance?" 2022 https://www.reddit.com/r/lyftdrivers/comments/se3l4c/is_rideshare_insurance_mandatory_or_just_regular/

188   "Insurance Questions Still Remain For Ridesharing Services", Jan 4, 2023. *Coverhound.* https://www.coverhound.com/insurance-learning-center/insurance-questions-still-remain-for-ridesharing-services

189   "Anyone been in an accident?" July, 2016. UberPeople.net, https://www.uberpeople.net/threads/anyone-been-in-an-accident.91439/

190   Ibid

191   "Does Uber notify my insurance company that I'm using my vehicle as transportation?" March 2019. UberPeople.net. https://www.uberpeople.net/threads/does-uber-notify-my-insurance-company-that-im-using-my-vehicle-as-transportation.317875/

192   "I don't recommend calling Lyft in case of accident", Jan. 2016. UberPeople.net. https://www.uberpeople.net/threads/i-dont-recommend-calling-lyft-in-case-of-accident.54400/

193   "FBI Warns of Potential Fraud in Antibody Testing for COVID-19," Jun 26, 2020, FBI Press Release. https://www.fbi.gov/news/press-releases/fbi-warns-of-potential-fraud-in-antibody-testing-for-covid-19

294

194   "COVID-19 Consumer Scams," Federal Communications Commission. https://www.fcc.gov/covid-scams

195   "Look Out for Coronavirus-Related Investment Scams - Investor Alert," Feb. 4, 2020. U.S. Securities and Exchange Commission. https://www.sec.gov/oiea/investor-alerts-and-bulletins/ia_coronavirus

196   "Earn Cash Quarantine Lending Consultancy Services ("Earn Cash"), Jul. 6, 2021. Securities and Exchange Commission. https://www.sec.gov.ph/advisories-2021/earn-cash-quarantine-lending-consultancy-services/#gsc.tab=0

197   "Studying How Cybercriminals Prey on the COVID-19 Pandemic," Apr. 22, 2020. Unit 42, https://unit42.paloaltonetworks.com/how-cybercriminals-prey-on-the-covid-19-pandemic/

198   Twitter Username "Dustyfresh." Twitter, https://twitter.com/dustyfresh/status/1238925029057925122

199   "Three Charged in Prison-Based COVID-19 Unemployment Benefits Scheme," July 21, 2021. U.S. Justice Department Press Release. https://www.justice.gov/usao-edca/pr/three-charged-prison-based-covid-19-unemployment-benefits-scheme

200   "Former South Florida Regional Bank Manager Sentenced for COVID-19 Relief Fraud", Mar. 14, 2023. U.S. Attorney's Office, Southern District of Florida, Press Release. https://www.justice.gov/usao-sdfl/pr/former-south-florida-regional-bank-manager-sentenced-covid-19-relief-fraud

201   "COVID-19 and Stimulus Reports," Federal Trade Commission, https://public.tableau.com/app/profile/federal.trade.commission/viz/COVID-19andStimulusReports/Map

202   "Annual Report of the Departments of Health and Human Services and Justice," For Year 2021, U.S. Department of Justice. https://oig.hhs.gov/publications/docs/hcfac/FY2021-hcfac.pdf

203   "Insurance fraud costs \$309 billion a year — nearly \$1,000 for every American", Dr. Michael Skiba, Nov 13, 2022. *Bristol Herald Courier.* https://heraldcourier.com/business/article_4fb8ab1c-98e2-5f8c-ac1e-6a023105f2b8.html

About the Author

Richard Wickliffe, CPCU, ARM, CLU, FCLS has led teams of fraud investigators for over twenty years at one of the largest insurance carriers in the U.S. He enjoys writing and speaking about creative crimes, fraud, and cybercrimes at venues including CPCU conferences and the FBI's InfraGard conferences. He is the recipient of the FBI's Exceptional Service in the Public Interest Award. Wickliffe is also an accomplished author of crime fiction, having received the Best Popular Fiction award from the Florida Book Awards, with a book optioned by Twentieth Century Fox. From the other wide of this brain, his art and photography have been exhibited in Fort Lauderdale's Art Guild and featured in Smithsonian magazine and Forbes Travel magazine. He resides with his family in South Florida.